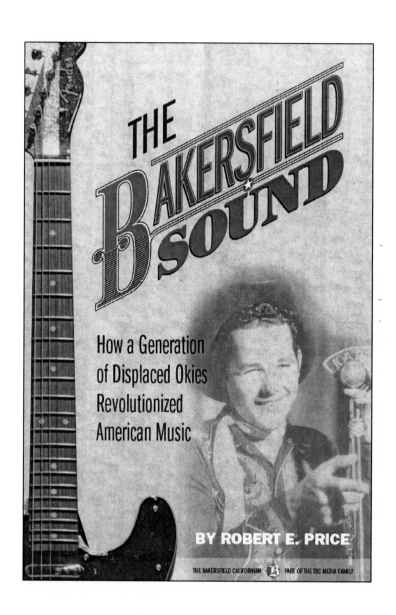

THE BAKERSFIELD SOUND

How a Generation of Displaced Okies Revolutionized American Music

BY ROBERT E. PRICE

THE BAKERSFIELD CALIFORNIAN — PART OF THE TBC MEDIA FAMILY

iUniverse

THE BAKERSFIELD SOUND
HOW A GENERATION OF DISPLACED OKIES REVOLUTIONIZED AMERICAN MUSIC

iUniverse books may be ordered through booksellers or by contacting:

iUniverse
1663 Liberty Drive
Bloomington, IN 47403
www.iuniverse.com
1-800-Authors (1-800-288-4677)

Because of the dynamic nature of the Internet, any web addresses or links contained in this book may have changed since publication and may no longer be valid. The views expressed in this work are solely those of the author and do not necessarily reflect the views of the publisher, and the publisher hereby disclaims any responsibility for them.

Any people depicted in stock imagery provided by Thinkstock are models, and such images are being used for illustrative purposes only. Certain stock imagery © Thinkstock.

ISBN: 978-1-4917-7296-6 (sc)
ISBN: 978-1-4917-7297-3 (e)

Library of Congress Control Number: 2015915099

Print information available on the last page.

iUniverse rev. date: 11/16/2015

CONTENTS

Preface   vii
Introduction   ix

Chapter 1   The Great Convergence   1
Chapter 2   Toward Eden   16

   Snapshot: Otherness   28

Chapter 3   Honky-Tonk Paradise   31

   Snapshot: It's That Kid!   52

Chapter 4   Vegas of the Valley   54
Chapter 5   What's on TV?   63

   Snapshot: The Mosrite   81

Chapter 6   Buck Owens   86
Chapter 7   Merle Haggard   103

   Snapshot: The Man in Black Needs Cash   129

Chapter 8   The Two Defining Songs   132
Chapter 9   The A&R Man   141
Chapter 10 The Mentor, the Muse, and the Protégé   148

   Snapshot: Millennium Eve   167

Chapter 11 The Next Wave   169

Afterword   180
Appendix A   The Founders   182
Appendix B   And a Cast of Thousands   197
Appendix C   The Landmarks   226

Acknowledgments   237
Notes   239
Selected Bibliography   259

PREFACE

In the spring and summer of 1997, I wrote a series of newspaper articles on the twang that made Bakersfield famous. Those articles, most of them published over a four-week period in the *Bakersfield Californian*, clicked in ways I couldn't have imagined. I received letters, postcards, and e-mails from the four corners of the earth—literally. Messages came from Sweden, Brazil, Australia, and Japan. When is the next installment coming out? Where can I buy the book? Do you have Susan Raye's phone number? Do you think she'd remember me from that time I met her in that parking lot in Omaha in 1968?

I followed up that newspaper series with more stories about the Bakersfield Sound—its players, their progeny, and the legacy of that special time and place. Those profiles and essays have appeared in the Country Music Hall of Fame's magazine, the *Journal of Country Music*, and in the Hall of Fame's exhibit supplement, *The Bakersfield Sound: Buck Owens, Merle Haggard, and California Country*. That growing body of work also led to an opportunity to write the companion book for Time-Life Music's *Merle Haggard: The Original Outlaw* boxed compact-disc set. Most of these articles have been published, in some form, in the *Bakersfield Californian*, the media company where I've worked since the axle broke on my trailer in 1988. (Okay, so I borrowed the axle story from Buck Owens. In truth, I moved to Bakersfield on purpose—for a two-year tour.)

Through all those years, people have asked me, "When is the book coming out?" During one stretch of 2013, no fewer than three music documentarians asked that very question between shots. I told them all that other things had gotten in the way and demanded my attention—the regular doses of scandal, murder, and politics that have always made Bakersfield such a great town for newspaper editors. But the time finally came in 2014 when, encouraged by colleagues at the newspaper, I got busy. The result looks at the people, circumstances, aftermath, and heritage of the Bakersfield music phenomenon in ways other works have not—and, in some ways, cannot.

Set some old vinyl on the turntable for ambience, and enjoy.

Robert E. Price
Executive Editor
Bakersfield Californian
June 2015

INTRODUCTION

The young guitar player looks over his shoulder toward the stage door. The band has cycled through its softly urgent instrumental introduction three or four times; the stage lights are low; the crowd is quiet and anxious.

The guitar player glances toward the stage door again, an anticipatory grin on his face. *Are you coming?* he seems to be asking. Still nothing. Two more cycles of the intro ditty.

Then, at last, a figure emerges from the darkness, stage left. A small man, smaller than some might have remembered, moves slowly through the backstage shadows and into the light. And every throat in the building opens.

The audience is so well illuminated that Merle Haggard can see every face almost all the way to the back of the sold-out Fox Theater. The sight apparently moves him because he stops at the very edge of the stage, the footlights silhouetting him in a shimmering aureole. He pauses there in his brown wide-brimmed hat, his wraparound sunglasses perched atop a crook nose, and absorbs the roar. And still he lingers, smiling warmly for a full ten or twelve seconds, accepting this transfusion of respect and affection. Finally, he ambles across the front of the stage to the opposite end and repeats the exchange, nodding slightly, appreciatively, as the ovation soars. Merle Haggard has come home.

It's hard not to consider the possibility that the grayed and shuffling Haggard's one-night reunion with Bakersfield, California, the city of his youth, of his infamy, of his redemption and finest glory, may be his last. At that age, every turn of a man's life, especially a life lived hard, has that flavor.

Haggard understands that. Retirement is not an option. "You people," he told the crowd in Lewiston, Idaho, a few nights before, "are keeping me alive." And he is returning the favor by connecting them to a vital strand of the nation's cultural DNA. Haggard isn't merely breathing life into one of the great American songbooks; his presence personifies the hot, dusty hellhole of oil rigs, cotton fields, and Pentecostal Sundays that was Bakersfield. His physical form evokes the disappointment and persistence, humility, and pride of a generation—and of a city.

It was in this Bakersfield that Joe Limi and Frank Zabaleta opened a bar on the north side of the town's main drag, just south of the Kern River, in 1949. The Blackboard was rough and bawdy, but it lured musicians who didn't know any better than to play what they liked and what they felt. In contrast to the competitive mating behavior that played out most every night around the dance floor, they liked and supported one another through poverty, divorce, and hocked guitars.

This was the world Merle Haggard entered in 1960, paranoid from having spent more than a third of his twenty-three years behind iron bars of assorted severity—self-conscious and marginally employed but more talented than he or anyone else could yet conceive.

Over the next decade Bakersfield would shed its anonymity and present the world with a style and a sound and a face. Not everyone embraced the music and culture that came to represent the Bakersfield Sound, certainly not everyone in Bakersfield, but the genre then called country and western—managed by a Nashville hierarchy preoccupied at the time by commercial imperatives and, consequently, largely bereft of the honesty that had once sustained it—needed that sound, that attitude. And soon, most of America, even the buttoned-up portion, accepted it as part of the landscape.

That sound permanently altered the course of American music, but its evangelists and practitioners—Buck Owens foremost among them—are gone now, or most are. Prodigious songwriter Red Simpson is as mischievous and openhearted as the day Bill Woods first put him on a honky-tonk stage, but he is in his eighth decade. Haggard, his longtime fishing buddy, is just three years behind him.

The 2015 edition of the Strangers—Haggard's backing band and historically one of music's most understatedly tight outfits—includes a guitar prodigy of modest demeanor but outsized talent, one Ben Haggard, twenty-two. He's the one who helped prepare the Bakersfield crowd for that grand entrance, Dad's grand entrance, stealing glances at the stage door as he picked his Telecaster with unconscious articulation.

Sixty years after it first took recognizable shape, the Bakersfield Sound lives on, if somewhat precariously, and modest Ben Haggard is one of its chief ambassadors. Perhaps one day he will be more than that. But the following week in Thackerville, Oklahoma, and New Braunfels, Texas, and a dozen stops beyond, he would be content standing behind and just to the right of the small, behatted man illuminated in the footlights, nodding appreciatively to the people who keep him alive.[1]

• • •

Merle Haggard is one of America's most cherished troubadours of the working class. He is also an innovator who brought attention to one special town, a rural capital at the southern tip of California's vast San Joaquin Valley. At the apex of his career four decades ago, Haggard was part of an assemblage that produced some of the era's most memorable and influential recordings, a combined body of work that was distinctive enough to deserve its own name.

What, exactly, is the Bakersfield Sound? It's been called a raw, stripped-down, trebly concoction, but those adjectives more accurately describe the deliberate earnestness of Buck Owens's music. Merle Haggard's more graceful and nuanced body of work is tougher to categorize, except to say it bears little resemblance to Owens's. Other key players of that era have their own distinctive sounds as well. Haggard's sister Lillian once asked Simpson, "Well, what is it, then?" In reply he whispered, "It's a secret."[2]

The secret is that the Bakersfield Sound isn't a sound at all so much as a time, a place, and a shared dream—a synergy of economic hardship, determination, kinship, and dumb luck. And so it happened in Bakersfield in about 1951.

The secret first took shape, humbly, in a few small blue-collar dives, with young musicians—every one of them, to a man, ecstatic that he could earn money without picking apricots or cotton in the searing valley sun—performing for oil-field workers and Okie field hands. Within fifteen years the Bakersfield Sound was one of the dominant strains of rural music in America and a noteworthy player in broader popular culture.

But the Bakersfield Sound didn't get to that place through the brilliance or encouragement of any one performer, instrument, or nightclub. It got there the same way Dust Bowlers got to California—one state at a time and slowly.

To understand the Bakersfield Sound and its origins, one must appreciate the way music migrates, evolves, and transforms. What we find upon close inspection is that every type of popular American music shares ancestry with virtually every other type of popular American music—folk, blues, hillbilly, rock, R&B, hip-hop, and all their permutations and interminglings. The difference between two supposedly discrete genres can be as subtle as a voice inflection and a hairstyle.

For some reason, though, we've always wanted to categorize and affiliate. America's commercial music institutions—record labels and radio stations—have always thought it important to keep categories of music separate and distinct, even when casual listeners can hear artists crossing those lines. And that crossing happens a lot because music is a living, breathing thing that changes and grows in the same manner as spoken language. Relegating American music to a set of rigid commercial classes is as futile as trying to train the wind, but that hasn't stopped the music industry from trying—and fans of those regimented styles from passionately, even boisterously identifying with their chosen genre and its manufactured accoutrements, be they boots, dreadlocks, or bumper stickers.

Ironically, the zealously insulated product called country music was born of wild diversity. The Nashville industrial mainstream that was and remains protective of its so-called traditional sound claims proprietary ownership of an organism synthesized from far-flung influences. It didn't come out of Ernest Tubb's guitar case, fully formed.

Country has roots in the folk ballads of England, Ireland, Scotland, and Wales, in the call-and-response songs of slaves brought to America from West Africa, in the black gospel music that developed from such songs, in the culture-stirring impacts of the Civil War and Spanish-American War, and in the fields of Mexico and the American Southwest.

Country borrowed instruments from other musical traditions. The fiddle is a violin played with a style and gusto foreign to classical arrangements. The banjo most likely descended from an instrument of African origin, the banjar. The steel guitar came into popularity following the 1915 Panama-Pacific International Exposition in San Francisco, where Hawaiians introduced the world to the slack-key guitar.

The costuming of country music performers was borrowed too. Why, if its origins are in the British Isles, West Africa, Appalachia, and the Dust Bowl, has country music been played by so many singers wearing cowboy hats? Blame the singing cowboy movies of the 1930s and '40s—people such as Tex Ritter and Roy Rogers. When western swing and honky-tonk, the dominant styles of country music in the 1940s, took over from folksy, bluesy Jimmie Rodgers, they adopted the clothing styles of those heroic, Saturday-morning-movie cowboys, rather than the overalls of the hillbilly singers who drew laughs at the *Grand Ole Opry*. So even though the music of Hank Williams and others like him sounded more like Kentucky than Texas, their appearance was the opposite. That's why Buck Owens and the Buckaroos, bejeweled and resplendent on that iconic *Carnegie Hall Concert* album cover, looked like they'd never seen the inside of a packing shed.[3]

Once country music established itself as a defined commercial commodity, however, its gatekeepers locked the doors. Or rather, they tried. Drums, horns, and electrified instruments were discouraged (though not banned) at the *Grand Ole Opry* well into the late 1950s, for example, although a few performers, most memorably Bob Wills, skirted the rules. Country music, Nashville seemed to be saying, was whatever Nashville said it was, and its definition was restrictive.

Into this rigid, industry-dictated mind-set, the Bakersfield Sound was born. Few of Nashville's standards applied here. The tools of rock 'n' roll were accepted immediately: drums, horns, and electric guitars, the Fender Telecaster in particular. So were the era's most popular performers—Little Richard, Chuck Berry, Buddy Holly—along with the personas they brought to the stage. From its inception, the Bakersfield Sound embraced precisely what America's commercial music institutions (the white ones, anyway) had worked so hard to tamp down.[4]

But this parallel West Coast universe didn't come about because Bakersfield players had some sort of unusual courage or insight. The Sound was created out of a cultural stew simmered in the migratory realities of World War II. When southern midwesterners migrated west to the shipyards of the West Coast in the 1940s to help with the war effort, they brought their taste for honky-tonk and similarly unrefined styles, creating an epic musical gumbo. It was from this phenomenon, and all that preceded it, that this close cousin of rockabilly was born.

Like all American music, country music has borrowed, adapted, and evolved, appropriating a type of instrument here and a fashion of dress there, incorporating rhythms and narrative themes from various musical forms, spanning multiple ethnicities and languages. Musicians processed the unfamiliar and synthesized the novel and exotic into a palatable, coherent creation. Dust Bowl migrants were compelled to adapt in every aspect of their new lives in California. It only follows that Okie musicians would do the same on the honky-tonk stages of Bakersfield.

• • •

On an ordinary day, to an ordinary traveler, the view of California's San Joaquin Valley from the front seat of a car descending westward from the Sierra Nevada conveys welcome. From horizon to horizon, the warm greens and browns beckon— provided the smog, trapped by geological formations and meteorological forces beyond any human's realistic control, isn't too dense that day.

For a traveler in the late 1930s, though, carrying family and all essential earthly possessions on a journey of eight hundred grueling miles, mostly over straight, flat desert, it was something more. That alluring valley floor looked like a verdant bed of salvation.

The reality was something quite different from the mythology, of course. The cool rest that followed that long journey was all too brief. Jobs, or vague promises of jobs, waited for some, but for the most desperate and destitute, there was often little to count on but the good graces of farm labor contractors who were often already fully stocked with available workers. Broad vistas of green can be overrated.

Dust Bowl migrants had it tough indeed. They persisted and assimilated—but only as much as they had to, or wanted to, because they were a proud, stubborn lot. In fact, within the context of the Depression and wartime America, they thrived—culturally, at least, if not economically.

The flowering of the Okie culture was something of a defiant act in the face of the established culture in Bakersfield. The locals liked the idea of cheap farm labor until the flood of newcomers overpowered the region's existing social safety net. (Kern County's population grew by 64 percent between 1930 and 1940 and another 69 percent between 1940 and 1950.) The Okies might have been somewhat bearable, however, even in their vast numbers, if not for those drawls—and the music! To many, it was uncultivated, approaching vulgar.[5]

The width and breadth of the migration was so vast, though, that Okie music percolated agreeably within its built-in audience. It took deep root in the sun-parched, blue-collar ambience of Bakersfield, where stifling days gave way to sultry summer evenings, and workingmen of a certain age and disposition almost felt an obligation to come out and play.

It was here that the Bakersfield Sound was born, incubated in the honky-tonks, legitimized on the late-weekday-afternoon television shows, and proselytized to the masses by way of the recording studio. It was here, against all reasonable odds, that a hard-bitten people, steeled by poverty and displacement, created something unique and lasting.

CHAPTER 1

The Great
Convergence

In 1951, America was still reveling in an exhilarating array of postwar possibilities. The country, vast as it was, seemed smaller than it had a generation before. Its imperfect but resolute goodness had triumphed over ruthless, formidable evil. And that seemed to prove, in most Americans' minds, that no obstacle on the scale of our ordinary, individual lives could truly be insurmountable. If victory against such odds were possible, it only followed that personal fulfillment, shared among our fellow victors, was inevitable and limitless.

That vitality had produced such colossal bursts of creativity and innovation that people came to expect that everyday life would gradually change for the better—because it had: examples seemed to appear daily. Tupperware, aerosol paint, hairspray, restroom hand dryers, credit cards—all entered the consumer marketplace within five years of Japan's surrender. Automobiles such as the Nash, the Hudson, the Studebaker, and the Packard, relics of prewar transportation, faded away amid changing wants and expectations. In their place, Americans embraced the sleek 1949 Ford, its distinctive fenders newly integrated into the side of the car body. Chevrolet's automotive revolution was approaching its final stages of development, with the sinewy, cocksure Corvette nearing readiness for its 1953 unveiling. People have never adapted well to change, generally speaking, but the America of the late 1940s and early 1950s was a vortex of anticipation—blind, buoyant anticipation.[1]

Into that time and place came what may have been the most

1

drastic departure ever from the accustomed form and function of the musical instrument known as the guitar.

In 1950, after building a succession of prototypes, Clarence "Leo" Fender, a Los Angeles–area guitar maker, unveiled what he called the Fender Telecaster. The solid-body instrument's name evoked that other great commercial advance in entertainment technology: television, then seeding America's rooftops with thickets of antennae. The guitar's design lines conjured forth pulp-fiction versions of interstellar flight, but its function had decidedly Neanderthal overtones. Those modern curves hardly disguised its essential nature: a crude, factory-built, mass-produced object. The guitar's rough-hewn body, band-sawn from a slab of swamp ash, was attached to a one-piece maple neck that lacked the slightest hint of artistry. No rosewood fingerboard here: the neck was bolted unceremoniously to the body. The tuners were lined up six in a row. Then there was the functional but plain bridge and exposed treble pickup, transferred directly from the steel guitar that had earned Fender his reputation as a maker of worthy electric instruments.

To some musicians, the looks were laughable; compared to the fine Chippendale pieces that Fender's competitor Gibson was producing, this looked like some sort of primitive weapon. There were no loving applications of the luthier's customary craft. With its hard edges and simple manners, the Telecaster looked for all the world like the cheaply manufactured guitar it was. But the Telecaster evoked a certain defiance: this was a new type of guitar built in the service of a new, as-yet-unimagined music.

Since the Tele was built from a single, solid hunk of wood, it could be turned up to eleven without howling or cussing back at you—no feedback; pure, sharp tone all the way up to loud. And that bridge pickup cut like barbed wire. Flip a switch, and the Tele could sound like two tomcats brawling in the alley, like steel glancing off steel, like the glassy din of a transistor radio in search of a station. It located and claimed a hitherto uninhabited slice of the audio spectrum all to itself, that high treble range just north of a hillbilly singer's sinus twang, that pleasure center in the inner ear that craved a spike of sonic brilliance and clarity.[2]

Guitarists across America, but especially in Southern California, were just starting to discover the wonders of this new instrument when Buck Owens moved to Bakersfield and, within a few weeks of his arrival, made his first investment in Leo Fender's most famous creation. It was 1951, and Owens's bandmate, Lewis Talley, had a gently used Telecaster he was willing to part with for thirty dollars. Owens agreed, and American music was never quite the same.

Don Rich performs with Buck Owens sometime before he made the switch from fiddle to guitar—like Owens, his choice would be a Fender Telecaster.
(Photo courtesy of the Buck Owens Private Foundation, Inc.)

The Telecaster gave Owens's music that distinctively raw edge that set the young guitarist and, more significantly, the musical identity of his adopted city apart from everything. The Bakersfield Sound—as that raucous, outlaw strain of 1960s California country music would eventually come to be known—began as a mixture of diverse musical ingredients, but from the very start, the Telecaster stirred it.

Fender Telecaster magazine advertisement, 1952: unrefined and mass-produced, but capable of cutting through a throbbing bass line and, in a pinch, defending the musician from an onstage assault.
(Image courtesy of the Fender Musical Instrument Corp.)

The story of any period of concentrated creativity is a story of people and relationships. That is true of this story as well, and that electrified plank of swamp ash is one of the protagonists. Owens rarely played anything else. Same for Roy Nichols and James Burton, who played lead guitar, individually and together, for Merle Haggard and the Strangers. Ditto for Don Rich, whose contribution to the Buckaroos was not limited to the high-harmony vocals that meshed so flawlessly with Owens's. Rich's seemingly effortless virtuosity on the Telecaster, his creation of a wholly original style wedded to the instrument's particular qualities, guided the sound of country music—and of rock. Entertainer-historian Marty Stuart once proclaimed on one of his many journeys to the mecca of West Coast country, "They should make a Fender Telecaster the size of the Washington Monument and stick it right in the middle of Bakersfield."[3]

Since then, musicians from David Gilmour of Pink Floyd to Keith

4

Richards of the Rolling Stones have embraced the Telecaster. When country stars such as Brad Paisley play the Telecaster, it's not so much an explicit homage to the Bakersfield Sound as it is a marker of its profound and widespread influence, because the Sound has wound its way so thoroughly into the grain and custom of today's music.

To be sure, by the time its historical era had crested, the Bakersfield Sound had become more than just one particular musical instrument's birth story. After all, the origins of the style were broader than country music itself. The stripped-down, bandstand sound associated with Bakersfield, and with Owens in particular, owed as much to rock 'n' roll as to country, and Owens's honky-tonk sound was as much Chuck Berry as Eddy Arnold. Certainly, the Beatles thought so: they issued a standing order that all new Buck Owens albums be sent their way immediately upon availability. When they covered "Act Naturally," it was with Rickenbackers, not Fenders, but that over-the-top treble was there for all to hear.

Even as the Sound was making itself heard as an aesthetic influence in the United Kingdom, its commercial success in the United States had caused a rift in country music's tradition-bound fabric. If today the Bakersfield Sound comprises an accepted, even canonical style and repertoire and remains a dominant influence in contemporary country music, it was not always so.

In the 1960s, a stylistic ocean separated Nashville from "Nashville West," the name critics started using to describe Bakersfield in acknowledgement of the city's chart-topping successes. It was a decade that saw Bakersfield restructure the commercial hierarchies of the country music industry.

In the 1950s and early 1960s, Nashville was Bakersfield's antithesis and simultaneously its fondest aspiration. The two cities behaved like parallel universes that held each other in simultaneous respect and envy, admiration and disdain. The power and centrality of Nashville represented a certain reciprocity to Bakersfield's small-town belligerence—but it was a belligerence that, at its core, still aspired to win begrudging acknowledgement. Bakersfield had long measured itself against the music capital, even while it occasionally thumbed its nose at Music City's pretensions and predictability.

Over time, however, Bakersfield was absorbed into Nashville's monolithic corporate inevitability. Today, Nashville continues to reign supreme, whereas Bakersfield, as an actual country music scene that matters, is a mere remnant of its former self.

Still, once upon a time, a few generations back, the city and its most famous musical style were a single, vibrant living entity.

A Time, a Place, a Vitality

Why do certain places on earth become touchstones of the moment? Sometimes you can't explain why the cast assembled and started working toward greatness, unbeknownst to them at the time.

—Marty Stuart

Why Bakersfield? Why the 1950s and '60s? How did so much talent gravitate to one city so far from the capital of country music, to create music of such lasting quality and influence? Good questions. How did Ernest Hemingway end up in Paris in the 1920s, sipping Pernod with Picasso and Gertrude Stein and crafting the short stories that would profoundly redirect American prose?

The historical event that led directly to the creation of a Bakersfield country music culture, that established the southern Central Valley as the ideal soil, topography, and climate for this new music, was, in popular imagination, the Dust Bowl migration of the Great Depression, an epic tale famously chronicled in the pages of John Steinbeck's *The Grapes of Wrath*.

Beginning in 1933 and continuing over the next few years, the southern plains and southwestern states—a region comprising the states of Oklahoma, Texas, Colorado, Arkansas, and others—experienced massive dust storms that devastated their farms and transformed the region. Severe drought conditions and farming practices that encouraged erosion of the soil left tens of thousands of family farmers bereft; their livelihoods had literally dried up and blown away with the wind. What ensued was one of the largest mass population shifts in the nation's history.

The Oklahoma dirt farmers whose professions—and home lives—had been so cruelly obliterated sought refuge in the West, primarily California. But many found their lives largely unchanged from the pre–Dust Bowl days: picking corn and cotton in Oklahoma for poverty wages and picking fruit in the vast farmlands of the Central Valley for poverty wages were different in only one sense. At least in Oklahoma, where many had been self-employed sharecroppers, a sense of independence, however illusory, had been possible. Otherwise, their culture of servitude on land controlled by others had essentially been reconstituted half a continent away.[4]

Woody Guthrie, the itinerant minstrel from Oklahoma, was one of the first, and certainly the most prominent, to chronicle the migration: his album *Dust Bowl Ballads* was recorded in 1940 for Victor Records in the months after he fled California. In plain-spoken style, with original songs heavily influenced by the Carter Family and Jimmie Rodgers, Guthrie documented the Dust Bowl's surreal effects on the land, the heartbreak and uncertainty of leaving one's roots behind and setting out for California, and the oppression and prejudice that the Okies experienced once they arrived.

Not all the musicians who fueled and fostered the Bakersfield Sound were actually the children of "Okies," as those Dust Bowl refugees were disparagingly called. But many of them were—and every last one of them, poor or not, understood that sort of life and that desperation. Owens, born in Sherman, Texas, in 1929, was the son of sharecroppers whose family's 1937 exodus to California from the Red River region was delayed for more than a decade when their trailer hitch broke in Phoenix. Bill Woods, who led the band at the Blackboard, a legendary Bakersfield honky-tonk, was born in Denison, Texas, in 1924, the son of a Pentecostal minister who worked the desolate oil-field tent camps of east Texas. Merle Haggard, born in 1937 and raised, for part of his youth, in a converted boxcar in Oildale—then an Okie shantytown just north of the Kern River from Bakersfield—was the son of a Santa Fe Railroad worker from Checotah, Oklahoma, who died when Merle was nine. Dozens of Bakersfield musicians like these men first glimpsed their

7

life's calling by the light of a campfire or a front-porch lantern as the sweat from a harsh day in the fields dried on their backs.

They could have thrown their guitars over their shoulders and gone elsewhere to make a living at music—after all, freight trains were free, if you knew how to hop aboard without getting caught or run over. But the fact was, the audiences most likely to appreciate their songs about cotton fields and empty cupboards were right there—in Kern County, at the southern end of California's great San Joaquin Valley. They too were displaced people who hadn't quite found a new home in the world, stuck in between what they once had been and what they dared hope to become.

"Those Bakersfield musicians had a story to tell," Herb Pedersen, singer-songwriter and guitarist for the Desert Rose Band, once explained to me. "That's how they would write the songs. Working, being turned away—that was their experience. They might have made it out here to California, to find work, with little or nothing." And that shared experience—give a listen to the ache in Haggard's "Mama's Hungry Eyes"—clicked with the crowds in the dance halls and honky-tonks of Bakersfield.

"The music was simple but powerful, played by simple-living people who had to leave their farms to come west," singer Tommy Collins, an Oklahoma native who wrote his first hit songs after moving to Bakersfield in 1951, told me. "There's quite a history to the camaraderie that developed between those Dust Bowl people. They weren't apt to go for fancy music."

Not that Bakersfield performers had a monopoly on being poor. Many of the past century's country musicians, from all corners of North America, seem to have risen up from childhoods spent on dirt floors wearing secondhand clothes. But there was a remarkable similarity in the experiences of the people who lived or played in Bakersfield in those days, from Rose Maddox to Dallas Frazier to Red Simpson.

Ferlin Husky, the Missouri native who brought his lively stage persona to Bakersfield's Rainbow Gardens in 1952, understood the way it was. "All those Okies and Arkies and Texans had a lot of hard times and good material for beer-drinkin', tear-jerkin' music. For them," he said, "it was just a natural thing."

The Nashville Sound

> Line up Little Richard and Pat Boone next to each
> other and listen to them both singing "Tutti Frutti."
> It's the same comparison. Nashville was making Pat
> Boone–kinda "Tutti Frutti" records, and Bakersfield
> was making Little Richard.
>
> —Marty Stuart

In some ways, the Nashville of the mid-1950s was not that much
different from today's. Things often tended to sound the same.
Nashville record producers of that era—people such as Don Law
of Columbia Records, Steve Sholes of RCA, and Owen Bradley of
Decca—had been heavily influenced by the big-band sound of the
previous decade, which in some cases they themselves had helped
mold. As a result, the "Nashville Sound," largely a creation of
guitarist-producer Chet Atkins, came to represent a warm, rich
ambience often textured with soft horns, soothing strings, and
lush backing vocals. It wasn't too far from the pop music of the
time, sophisticated charts penned by such arrangers as Nelson
Riddle. "Chet Atkins would eliminate instruments like the fiddle
and steel guitar," said country music historian Cary Ginell. "Atkins
was going after a more uptown, cosmopolitan kind of sound to
combat rock 'n' roll, because rock 'n' roll was taking away the
young listeners."

Steve Earle, the Texas-based singer-songwriter, offered a more
cynical take:

Now country music sounds like archaic rock records. Back
then, though, they sounded like archaic pop records. You've got to
understand, Chet Atkins was not trying to make country records.
He was trying to get as close to making pop records, and sell as
many records, as he possibly could without moving to New York.
Chet Atkins and Owen Bradley and a lot of people you looked
up to were snobs. [Country Music Hall of Fame producer] Billy
Sherrill hated country music ... and he made some of my favorite

9

country records. Nashville was a town that always seemed to be at odds with itself ... It was never comfortable in its own skin.[5]

The phenomenon that was Elvis Presley was largely responsible for Nashville's institutional strategy. The Pelvically Gifted One might have been a country music sensation had he (or his manager, Colonel Tom Parker) so chosen; in fact, Elvis, whose early work was influenced by Hank Snow and Bill Monroe, scored on the country charts before finding his place in history as the first great star of a wholly new pop genre—rock 'n' roll. Nashville reacted to Elvis's resounding arrival on the American music scene by moving away from the rockabilly influences that had always loitered on its fringes. In a rearguard action, the country moguls sought to define the music as an alternative to teen music, as mature music for adults. Twang, especially as produced by an electric guitar, was suddenly frowned upon.

But not in Bakersfield. The vibrant club scene there cultivated a new set of stars and a new hard-driving style, full of Telecaster-driven hillbilly inflection, prominent steel-guitar leads, and bold, in-your-face drums. A new sound was percolating that would explode in the ensuing years. In the early 1950s, poor, young Merle Haggard was idolizing teenage guitar prodigy Roy Nichols at the Pumpkin Center Barn Dance. Meanwhile, Owens was playing the Telecaster alongside Bill Woods at the Blackboard. Billy Mize was at the Lucky Spot. Lewis Talley and Fuzzy Owen were at the Clover Club.[6]

Woods, Mize, and Cliff Crofford recorded what was probably Bakersfield's first foray into popular commercial music when in 1949 they laid down two tracks for Los Angeles–based Modern Records. The effort went nowhere, but it fed something within those three young men: the hunger of possibilities. Within seven years Bakersfield musicians were churning out a steady stream of what could only have been called rock 'n' roll in the style of Bill Haley and the Comets, Buddy Holly, and Eddie Cochran, and they were creating it in Bakersfield clubs and on Bakersfield record labels—a startling array of them, including Mar-Vel, Grande, Fire, Kord, Global, Pike, Rose, Stereotone, Super Sonic, Three Star,

Hillcrest, Bakersfield, and the most famous local microlabel of the era, Tally Records. Operated by cousins Talley and Owen, Tally Records—relieved, for some presumed effect, of the extraneous *e* in *Talley*—was founded as an unambiguously rock 'n' roll label. It never budged much from that sensibility, even after the country music industry started paying attention.

From this earnest, homegrown scene, Nashville and its finicky record producers were far removed indeed. "The Nashville Sound was always more formulaic," explained Paul Wells, director emeritus of the Center for Popular Music, a music archive and research center based at Middle Tennessee State University. "There was always more of a self-consciousness about trying to reach a broader audience, about trying to make new [commercial] inroads. With Buck and Merle, they were just doing what they did. Of course they wanted to reach a broad audience, but they did it on their own terms."

Starting with "You're for Me" in 1962, Owens and Don Rich committed to vinyl a clean, clear sound that hit listeners, as Owens liked to say, "hard as a freight train." Driven along by restless 2/4 meter—no one else in country music was emphasizing drums like the boys in Bakersfield—the Buckaroos produced a sound perfectly suited to both the concrete-floored bandstands of their incubation and the single-speaker AM car radios of their breakthrough. Owens seemed to reproduce better in monophonic than many country contemporaries because in the studio he turned up the treble and cut back on the bass. It was a perfect formula for the low-fi playback devices of the day, those push-button AM car radios and portable transistor radios that were the iPods of their time.

Minimizing the Twang

This driving, urgent, modern sound was what Tommy Collins heard and wanted on his records. When Collins recorded in Hollywood for Capitol in the 1950s, he insisted on hiring that guitar player from Bakersfield who favored a Telecaster—Owens. But when Collins recorded in Nashville for Columbia Records in the 1960s, producer Don Law laid down the law: minimal twang, please. "I don't remember guys like Chet Atkins or Grady Martin using Telecasters," Collins said. "I don't remember anybody in Nashville using them, except when I hired one guy named Fred Carter Jr. But I got the message pretty quick that they were going to do things their way in the studios in Nashville." Carter, who played lead guitar on Bob Dylan's *Nashville Skyline* album, among his many other studio credits, realized he had more in common with Bakersfield than with Nashville. "Nashville was just a better place to be," Carter once told me. "It was clear the teamwork was there and the future was there, while Bakersfield was mostly a club scene ... But Bakersfield was kickin' hard with the rock 'n' roll sound, and that just kinda clicked with me."

Though at the time the "gentlemanly" guitar work of people like Atkins and Martin was widely preferred in Nashville, Carter, who got his professional start playing on the *Louisiana Hayride*, the *Grand Ole Opry*'s bayou brother, was sold on the Telecaster's razor edge: it could cut right through a bass line, through a flourish of drums, through just about anything. Of course, Carter may have initially latched on to the Telecaster for less aesthetic reasons: it was relatively inexpensive and, as he put it, "almost indestructible." "You could play and defend yourself at the same time without hurting the guitar," Carter said. Bakersfield artists saw many of these benefits in the Telecaster too, but convincing Nashville of the guitar's merits in the recording studio was another matter. It wasn't until Owens and others achieved commercial success— and, curiously, rock 'n' rock underwent a significant change—that Music City was finally won over.

Era of the Crooners

At the same time Buck Owens and his Telecaster were finding their way onto the country music charts, around 1960, rock 'n' roll was descending into sappiness. It was as if Nashville's fondest wish had been granted. No longer would mainstream country artists need to stifle the hillbilly enthusiasm that had first won their audiences' affections in favor of what some might have considered orchestrated pretension. Led by Frankie Avalon and a collection of similarly clean-cut crooners, the pop-rock genre had gone soft. Fans who had grown up with Jerry Lee Lewis, Little Richard, and the Everly Brothers found themselves without a place on the dial to turn. Many, lured by the first strains of this new country-rockabilly hybrid coming out of Bakersfield, made the switch.

But the Nashville brain trust did not revert to its pre-Elvis instincts. The same candy-coated Pat Boone style that was gaining a foothold in rock still controlled country music playlists. In fact, it was more ensconced than ever. Most telling was Nashville producers' growing inclination to hire studio musicians from a pool of regulars, people who could record with all sorts of artists. The artists' regular bands would be put on ice until it was time to tour. "You had to use the Nashville A-team," said Buckaroo keyboardist Jim Shaw, "if you wanted to record in a Nashville studio."

Those studio musicians were the best in the country from a technical standpoint, but superior craft does not always result in superior art. Nashville was an approximation of Hollywood's motion picture studio system. It cannibalized its own successes, mimicking best-selling records with others that sounded the same. Those derivative recordings tended to sacrifice creativity and spontaneity for proven results.

But for Bakersfield types who had developed signature sounds outside of the Nashville bubble, employing the countrypolitan style so much in vogue in Tennessee invited certain disaster. Skeets McDonald, Wynn Stewart, Tommy Collins, Buck Owens, Red Simpson—each laid at least one egg in a Nashville recording studio because the industry's template left the final product sounding watered down.

Thereafter, Owens insisted on using his Buckaroos in his recording sessions, and Haggard insisted on his Strangers, with one major exception: Haggard used guitarist James Burton—best known as Elvis Presley's guitarist from 1969 until the singer's death in 1977—on many of his hit records. And because they usually recorded in Hollywood for Capitol Records' Ken Nelson, a man who believed his artists should be able to choose their own teams,

13

Bakersfield musicians were usually able to get their way and their distinct Bakersfield Sound.

Music that germinated in Bakersfield sounded unlike songs created in Nashville for another important reason. In the 1950s and '60s, as today, songwriting was a full-time profession, and Nashville-based commercial songwriters aimed at writing hits. Nashville's signature was apparent even before songs entered the studio; invariably, they had one of a dozen or so authorized themes. A song written from a uniquely painful place, like "Mama's Hungry Eyes," never could have emerged from a Nashville writer's office.

Nashville had "that commercial treadmill, where you develop a feel for what might sell and write to that feeling," said Dallas Frazier, who has seen both sides, having started his career in Bakersfield before becoming a Nashville-based member of the National Songwriters Hall of Fame.

Songwriting has always been an exercise in song plugging, in Bakersfield as in every town. But Nashville, as any publishing-house executive will tell you, had the volume to make songwriting a factory process. The Nashville machine operated by its own inexorable corporate logic. But Bakersfield, fifty-two hours away by Greyhound bus, missed all those business meetings.

It turns out it didn't matter. Owens and Haggard, Bakersfield's two giants of country music, enjoyed an unprecedented run of success during their heyday, rivaling the commercial domination of rock acts such as the Rolling Stones and Elvis. Between 1966 and 1987, Haggard recorded thirty-eight songs that reached number one on the *Billboard* country charts and another thirty-three that reached the top ten. Between 1967 and 1976 alone, Haggard had twenty-three chart toppers.

Owens's success was more concentrated but no less phenomenal: Between 1963 and 1967, according to *Billboard* and *Radio & Records*, he released an unprecedented nineteen consecutive number one songs, and by 1974 another five more had gone all the way to the top. Twenty-six other songs made the top ten between 1963 and 1974, and in 1964 he managed to get number one songs from both sides of the same 45 rpm release: first "Together Again" and then the flip side, "My Heart Skips a Beat."

Over a twenty-eight-year period that ended with Haggard's 1987 hit "Twinkle, Twinkle Lucky Star" and Owens's 1988 rerelease of "Streets of Bakersfield" with Dwight Yoakam, the two Bakersfield recording artists combined for at least 112 top-ten songs, including sixty-three that went to number one.

They had little in common as far as style is concerned: Haggard was the more reserved and traditional of the two, Owens the more exuberant and up-tempo. If Buck had burst onto the scene in 1966 rather than 1961—brace yourself for a blasphemy—perhaps he would have been elbowing the Byrds or Buffalo Springfield for top position on the rock charts.

Whether at its core the Bakersfield Sound was proto–rock 'n' roll, rebel country, fermented western swing, or something else, it's clear something unique was happening there in the 1950s and '60s and on into the 1970s—something that continues to make a difference in country music today.

It shouldn't really be surprising that creative and commercial success could spring out of such a place. Since country music first established itself as a distinct and viable genre, it has always been this way. As Ginell, the country music historian, has noted, the more imaginative country music has been created away from Nashville, whether in Austin, Dallas, Houston, Shreveport, Chicago, or Bakersfield. Nashville has always been managed by a ruling class that puts parameters on the sound, leaving the provinces to create the energy that sustains it all.

Bakersfield, at the pinnacle of its musical greatness, was about as far from Nashville's ruling class as a culture could get. In the Bakersfield of 1951, the only parameter that meant much was the volume knob on a Fender amplifier. Bakersfield pickers kept theirs on ten, and America—at least that portion of it that bought country records—perked up its ears and listened.

CHAPTER 2

Toward Eden

T he Bakersfield Sound would not have existed without the Okie phenomenon, that great mass migration that brought hundreds of thousands of people to California from Texas, Oklahoma, and Arkansas—and along for the ride, their music.

So many songs by Bakersfield performers touched on the Dust Bowl migration, or its multifaceted legacy, that it may seem today as though the creative and commercial phenomenon that opened doors for the likes of Merle Haggard and Buck Owens had its genesis in a single economic cataclysm—the terrible dust storms of the 1930s. The environmental disaster and the musical breakthrough live in the public consciousness today almost as cause and effect.

But the Bakersfield Sound was not the exclusive result of that environmental disaster; other cultural changes played roles too. Though the 1930s Okie diaspora was hugely significant and memorably symbolic, it's only a piece of the story.[1] The phenomenon we think of as this singular migration was really a series of tidal movements, some small, some massive, of southern and southwestern populations into the Golden State. It began with the gold rush of 1849 and achieved significant proportions in the 1920s. It peaked not in the mid-1930s but a few years later, during World War II, when the need for workers in wartime shipyards and aircraft factories attracted workers from all around the country. The Kaiser Shipyards in the Bay Area, for example, drew so many southerners that a hillbilly music culture thrived for several years in and around the East Bay city of Richmond.

James N. Gregory, in his *American Exodus*, a definitive work on the Dust Bowl migration, observes that the mid- to late-1930s westward migration represented not the beginning but the middle, "a phase of an ongoing, long-time relationship between Texas, Oklahoma, Missouri, and Arkansas ... and California." A quarter of a million people had come from those very states in the 1920s, so many of those who headed west in the 1930s already had relatives on the coast who could tell them about jobs and housing and could offer some assistance. Sometimes in the public imagination the historical legend overtakes the facts, and abetted by the popular country and folk music of the 1940s, '50s, and '60s, that's what happened with the Dust Bowl.[2]

The Black Blizzards of 1935

The Dust Bowl was quite real, however—a series of sky-blackening windstorms that cast a shadow over almost half the continent intermittently over a period of years. It devastated lives.

The environmental tragedy began with severe drought. Men worsened the situation by failing to employ dryland farming methods to prevent erosion, which was made worse yet by the infamously blustery winds of the lower Midwest. Great Plains farmers, many of them sharecroppers with little room for error, had plowed through virgin topsoil years before, tearing out the native grasses that helped hold the soil in place and retain its natural moisture. Mechanized farm equipment, gasoline-powered tractors, and combine harvesters in particular encouraged the spread of those unsustainable practices across a wider swath of the country. When all those factors converged, the dust storms escalated from bad to epic.

Robert E. Geiger of the *Associated Press*, who was in Boise City, Oklahoma, to report on the "Black Sunday" black blizzards of April 14, 1935, dispatched his story to Edward Stanley, the *AP*'s news editor in Kansas City. It was Stanley who, in the process of rewriting, came up with the term that came to mean so much to so many: the Dust Bowl.

17

It is indisputable that tens of thousands of economic refugees from Oklahoma, Texas, Arkansas, and elsewhere migrated to the West Coast, particularly Los Angeles and the California Central Valley, between 1935 and roughly 1942. It's indisputable that they brought their culture with them. These southwesterners, primarily rural but also from urban areas, brought conservative social values, a spirit of individualism, stoic notions about honor and duty, contradictory feelings about Saturday-night and Sunday-morning conduct, and a taste for folk music that might be recognizable today as country music. But the migration was only marginally connected to the devastating 1935–38 dust storms of the southern plains. People were, in fact, driven west by factors more economic and social than meteorological.

In fact, the regions most affected by the dust storms of the mid-1930s were southeastern Colorado, western Kansas, portions of New Mexico, and the panhandles of Oklahoma and Texas, although the entire Midwest, as far north as the Dakotas, got a taste of it at one time or another. Many Dust Bowl–era migrants came from those affected places, but the vast majority came from central and eastern Oklahoma, the Red River Valley of Texas, and Arkansas, regions not particularly affected by the dust storms.

The popular image of the Dust Bowl migration is of John Steinbeck's Joad family heading west in search of Central Valley farm-labor jobs, but the reality is that many southwesterners landed in Los Angeles after relatively uneventful journeys. A substantial number of them were middle-class people who landed white-collar jobs. But those who landed in the San Joaquin Valley were by and large agricultural workers.

During the second half of the 1930s, the population of seven California agricultural counties—Yuba, Monterey, Madera, Tulare, Kings, Kern, and San Diego—grew by an average of almost 43 percent, led by Kern, with a staggering 63 percent increase. The San Francisco Bay Area and especially Los Angeles also saw big population increases.[3]

At first most Californians were fine with the influx. Somebody had to pick the cotton. But when economic times took a turn for the worse, welfare rolls skyrocketed, and even locals who had wallowed happily in the glut of cheap labor suddenly began to complain, going so far as to circulate a petition demanding that no more relief be extended to migrants. It was around that time that "Okie," "Arkie," and "Texie" became derogatory terms that carried some of the stigma that whites most often associate with race. In their time, the terms were almost akin to N words, according to Gregory.

The way those terms worked was to almost ethnicize, almost create a notion that an Okie was a different nationality, a different ethnic group, certainly a different social class and an unwelcome person ... Because of the difficult economic circumstances, a group of native-born, Protestant, for the most part Anglo Americans of Scots-Irish heritage, about as white and solid American as you can get, became depicted as an ethnic other.

Okies who hadn't already been carrying a chip on their shoulder when they first got to California started putting them up there about this time, and that bare-knuckled attitude we later began to hear in country music became a little more ingrained.[4]

The Roots of American Music

Country music was already well established in California when the Okies arrived. Singing cowboys such as Ken Maynard, Roy Rogers, Tex Ritter, and Gene Autry—entertainers who came to Hollywood from Texas and the Midwest not as economic refugees but as young men in quest of stardom—had already brought country music's crooning sidekick, western music, to the masses. Stuart Hamblen's *Covered Wagon Jubilee*, with such West Coast stars as Patsy Montana, dominated the Los Angeles radio market from 1934 until the early 1950s. On a smaller scale, a family of transplanted Appalachians, the Crocketts of the San Joaquin Valley town of

Fowler, were well-established regional radio favorites as early as the mid-1920s.[5]

Rural American folk music, including the songs Okies enjoyed most, had deep roots that went all the way back to the British Isles. English, Welsh, Scottish, and Irish music had crossed the Atlantic with American colonists starting in the seventeenth century and had continued to move deeper into the newly settled land of the North American continent for decades, evolving as it went. In the industrial north, where cities were more plentiful and population density was greater, folk music faced economic and cultural pressure to conform to emerging urban popular styles. By the end of the eighteenth century, the northern states were receiving newer material and adopting newer styles, and folk music's rough edges became considerably more smoothed. The more isolated and rural South, meanwhile, preserved the older styles and created new material based on those folk traditions. The economic conditions of the 1930s then captured that musical tradition and propelled it west, all the way to the Pacific Ocean.

Population movements throughout American history have always moved the music, its performers, and its audiences to new places on the map. Wartime migration in particular was a powerful force. The Civil War helped spread and popularize the rural edginess of folk style. So did the postwar environment of the late 1860s. Many displaced southerners moved west to pursue opportunities in mining, ranching, logging, and the railroads. The Spanish-American War and World War I had similar effects on population movement and social interaction. By the mid-1920s, discernible markets for hillbilly music, as it was called, had established themselves in the North and the upper Midwest, as well as the South. The radio barn dance program and the jukebox, which both became popular in the 1920s, helped spread it further.

As it came west, the music itself changed too. During the early twentieth century, the tastes of southern folk started incorporating a strong blues influence, courtesy of the first national star of the genre, the Singing Brakeman, Jimmie Rodgers. By the time the Dust Bowl migration reached its apex in the late 1930s, hillbilly and jazz traditions had mingled, newer blues flavors had developed, western swing had emerged as the next big thing, and the Southwest was creating the freshest, liveliest music in America. That is the music that came to California with the Okies in the 1930s.[6]

"I'm Beginning to Think These Folks Have Something Here"

Construction of the Weedpatch federal labor camp in Arvin began in August 1935 on forty acres leased from Kern County, twelve miles southeast of Bakersfield. It opened four months later with ninety-six tent spaces divided by roads into three blocks and set in a muddy field. Among the organized camp activities, in addition to baseball games, were weekly sings and dances, which took place either on an open-air platform with a covered stage and piano pit or in a warehouse, where a radio played the national and regional stars of the day. Between February and October of 1936, camp director Tom Collins dutifully compiled a list of more than thirty songs that labor camp residents sang or performed, from "She's the Lily of Hillbilly Valley" to "Eleven Cent Cotton and Forty Cent Meat." Woody Guthrie once talked of watching workers gather from miles around at a particular squatters' camp one evening to hear two girls perform. "It cleared your head up, that's what it done, caused you to fall back, and let your draggy bones rest, and your muscles go limber and relax," he declared.[7]

Central Valley businesses noticed. The California radio stations that gave airtime to hillbilly and folk performers were often deluged with appreciative mail, and those that didn't were sometimes subjected to lobbying efforts by Okie listeners. Guthrie, not yet a star, started a hillbilly music show on a Los Angeles radio station and by 1938 was receiving more than a thousand fan letters a month.[8]

Bob Wills, leader of the Texas Playboys, sprinkled his live performances with references to "all of us Okies" and played songs that mentioned specific southwestern locales such as Tulsa and San Antonio. Spade Cooley, a favorite among Southern California defense workers, did the same. Cooley nicknamed his three vocalists Okie, Arkie, and Tex and claimed that each hailed from the corresponding state. He fudged a little.[9]

Spade Cooley and his orchestra, early postwar years.
(Photo courtesy of the Kern County Museum.)

The Farm Security Administration (FSA), which ran the labor camps, recognized the popularity of country music among camp residents. When the Porterville federal labor camp opened in 1940, it was FSA officials who threw the first concert. Faith Petric, a Bay Area folksinger who was active well into her nineties, worked as a young woman in FSA relief offices starting in 1940, and she supplied the music that first night: a stack of Burl Ives records.[10]

The Okies preferred music that reminded them of home, songs that still had their roots in the front porches and campfires of Oklahoma and Texas. The depth of those roots became evident to Petric one night when she saw a song scribbled on the back of an old brown grocery bag titled "The Waco Girl." Petric recognized the lyrics as a version of one of the great nineteenth-century murder ballads, "The Knoxville Girl."[11]

> *I took her by her golden curls and I drug her round*
> *   and around,*
> *Throwing her into the river that flows through*
> *   Knoxville town,*
> *Go down, go down, you Knoxville girl with the*
> *   dark and rolling eyes,*
> *Go down, go down, you Knoxville girl, you can*
> *   never be my bride.*

"The Knoxville Girl" was itself the marker of a long musical migration, having evolved from a 1744, forty-four stanza British broadside called "The Berkshire Tragedy, or the Wittam Miller." As the song moved toward, across, and eventually well beyond the Atlantic, it adopted new settings, reflected in the titles: "The Wexford Girl," presumably set on Ireland's River Slaney; "The Cruel Miller," which appeared as a broadside in Boston; "The Lexington Girl," which might have been set in Massachusetts, Virginia, or Kentucky; "The Knoxville Girl," set in Tennessee; and "The Oxford Girl," set in Mississippi or Texas. Finally, there was "The Waco Girl," set in east Texas—but, curiously, all but unknown to the balladeers of Waco. Music historians trace its roots to Oklahoma, southeastern Oklahoma in particular, and it was that version that the FSA's Fred Ross sang for Charles L. Todd and Robert Sonkin, young amateur folklorists from New York, who recorded it in Arvin in 1940.

To Petric, and indeed to innumerable scholars, this was plain evidence that the Appalachia-to-Southwest path that folk music had taken in the previous century had now taken musical traditions far into the West. And now, here in the Central Valley of California, that tradition was ongoing and very much alive.

Todd, who undertook a project documenting the music of the camps during the summers of 1940 and 1941, wrote an article for the *New York Times* that captured Labor Day festivities in 1941, attended by several thousand, at that same Porterville camp. He wrote that after the sack races and melon-eating marathons, Mrs. Myra Pipkin, who at forty-five claimed to be America's youngest great-grandmother, sang "Happy Was the Miller Boy," "Old Joe Clark," and "Skip to My Lou." And so it went into the evening, one singer after another, concluding with a trio from Shafter performing the migrant anthem "Goin' Down the Road Feelin' Bad." "Say," one unnamed local rancher told Todd, "I'm beginning to think these folks have something here."[12]

On weekend days during the early postwar years, children and teens from the Sunset labor camp, as the Arvin labor camp was also known, would walk a mile east to mingle with migrant workers from the squatters' camps around the town of Weedpatch, which, then as now, was not much more than a single rural intersection in the middle of acres of table-grape vineyards. They would congregate, hundreds of them, at a business called the Collins Auction to hear the performances of two young singers—Bill Woods and Billy Mize, whose parents owned the auction. Some of those young field workers would hear Woods and Mize for many years to come in quite different settings.[13]

Shipyards and Aircraft Factories

The Woods family moved to Arvin in the 1930s, and when the war broke out, son Bill headed north to Richmond and got a job as a boilermaker, first for Kaiser Steel and then for US Steel. After work and on weekends he performed with a western swing band. By 1944, he had his own group.

The war industries had made it all possible. Between 1940 and 1947, some twenty-five million people—21 percent of the total US population—migrated from one state or county to another in search of new opportunities in either the military or the war-related civilian sector. By comparison, only 13 percent moved during 1935–40, and even fewer moved in the half decade before that. During the early war years, 1940–43, rural areas of the United States lost more than five million residents, and all regions of the

24

country lost population except the West. A huge portion of the new wartime labor force, 29 percent, came from four states: Texas, Oklahoma, Arkansas, and Louisiana. And as was demonstrated during that earlier migration, the newcomers brought their culture with them, specifically their country music.[14]

Before the war, the Bay Area was not exactly a hotbed for country music, but in 1942 that changed. Radio announcer Cactus Jack was hugely popular, as were Bob Nolan and the Sons of the Pioneers, who were regulars in East Bay ballrooms. A local singer named Stephen McSwain dressed up in dime-store cowboy duds, renamed himself Dude Martin, and was soon packing in the dance halls of Richmond. Bob Wills and the Texas Playboys permanently moved their base from Texas to California in 1943 but saw no need to change their name. They performed in Oakland four times in 1944, appearing before sellout crowds of nineteen thousand; their box office outstripped such acts as Harry James, Tommy Dorsey, and Benny Goodman. In the late 1940s, they were even the house band at San Francisco's swank Mark Hopkins Hotel, high atop Nob Hill. During that time, they recorded the epochal *Tiffany Transcriptions*, a series of studio sessions that were intended for use in prerecorded (or transcribed) radio programs. Those recordings, distributed to radio stations across the country, would mark the apex of western swing.[15]

Many second-tier Bay Area performers had, or would soon have, significant southern San Joaquin Valley connections. Dave Stogner served a tour of duty in Europe and then went home to east Texas, only to find that virtually his entire family had gone west to work in the shipyards. He followed them to California but found his calling on the country-swing stages of the East Bay. His Richmond-based Arkansawyers was among the most popular bands of the time and place, and years later he hosted country music television shows in Fresno and Bakersfield. Woods, who moved to the East Bay at about the same time, landed a job in Richmond with fiddler Elwin Cross, an opportunity that paved the way to the eventual creation of his own group, the Texas Stars. Within a few years Woods was back in the southern San Joaquin Valley, recruiting performers such as Ferlin Husky and "Cousin" Herb Henson to the barn-dance halls and honky-tonks of Bakersfield. By 1952, he was beginning his legendary tenure at Bakersfield's Blackboard, leading a loud honky-tonk band featuring that Texas-by-way-of-Arizona migrant Buck Owens.[16]

World War II had helped spread the taste for country music far and wide. GIs and defense workers redistributed it not only throughout the United States, but also to Europe and Japan. By the 1960s, the music had begun to stand not for a region but for an entire demographic—the largely lower-middle-class, almost entirely white, blue-collar, over-thirty American. Clubs such as the Blackboard catered to the working class, especially the roughnecks who worked out in the oil fields. These men liked to dance, fight, and drink—not necessarily in that order—and they liked what they liked, whether it qualified strictly as country music or not.

In fact, much more so than elsewhere in the United States, such clubs made no distinctions when it came to musical genres. In 1954, when rock 'n' roll hit hard with the arrival of Elvis Presley, Carl Perkins, and Little Richard, the Blackboard simply went with it—another cultural adaptation that might not have taken place so readily elsewhere. Bakersfield, in the best traditions of southwestern country music and Okie stubbornness, embraced the new sounds. Clubs such as the Blackboard adopted rock 'n' roll and its rockabilly cousin without so much as a figurative blink.

Consider the career of Jimmy Phillips, a Bakersfield Sound–era drummer who was raised at the Arvin federal labor camp. During his years as an active musician, Phillips—who eventually retired to run a barbershop in Tehachapi, California—was the only white member of an otherwise all-black Bakersfield blues band, the Jivin' Kingsmen, in the mid-1950s. He was a member of Jolly Jody and the Go-Daddies, the most popular Bakersfield rock 'n' roll band of the late 1950s and early 1960s. And he appeared regularly, five afternoons a week, on the Bakersfield television show hosted by western swing fiddler Jimmy Thomason in the late 1960s. That's versatility.[17]

The movement of American folk music and rural sensibilities

through two centuries of growth and migration brought important cultural traditions to the West, and World War II essentially finished the job, bringing hundreds of thousands of men and women to the Pacific Coast. Many chose to stay, further homogenizing California culture as they settled in. Still, the Dust Bowl has a well-deserved place in the history of California's cultural development. Timing was critical to the phenomenon. As James Gregory has observed, the unique problems and passions of that decade created the Okie crisis and perhaps "created" Okies. "Had the hostile reception that forced many Southwesterners into the position of social outsiders been absent," Gregory writes, "would there have been an Okie subculture? Certainly not the same one."[18]

As Bakersfield music began to evolve in the 1950s, so did the life of the established Okie. A strong economy and a postwar sense of triumph, patriotism, and optimism helped deliver a higher standard of living than the previous generation had experienced, and the freewheeling, honky-tonk narrative so common in West Coast country music—a reflection of a more confident and strongly defined Okie culture—was something postwar America in general was ready to embrace. The result was one of those rare confluences of people, place, and time, a melding of talent, opportunity, and purpose that built Bakersfield—fleetingly, in retrospect—into a city transformed by music.[19]

Snapshot
Otherness

The assimilated Okies of today's California might have trouble seeing it, but their grandparents' lot in life three generations ago was very much like that of another below-the-radar class of people in California today.[1]

Migrants cross hundreds of difficult miles, including desert, to escape dire circumstances back home for the promise of the Golden State. They're lured, in part, by family members and others of their kind who have already established themselves with some degree of success. They speak, worship, and entertain themselves differently than most of the people who already live here. In fact, they bring an entirely different set of cultural values and preferences to their newly adopted home.

This is the story, more or less, of the Dust Bowl Okies of the 1930s—with one very obvious asterisk. The Okies, so much a part of California culture today, came west as American citizens—largely undesirable, disenfranchised American citizens but citizens nonetheless. Undocumented Mexicans who have reached California by crossing the US border illegally, among other avenues of arrival, can't claim that status. They come, for the most part, because employers in the United States have been willing to hire them.

But Californians, at these two relevant junctures of history, have regarded both migrant groups in pretty much the same way: with disdain. The Okies, though they were south-midwesterners of mostly English-Scotch-Irish descent, were treated like illegal aliens—economic refugees who represented a blight on the public ledger. Growers happy for the cheap, abundant labor were glad enough to see them, but almost no one else was. Now these earlier migrants are fully integrated Californians, and another group of migrants has taken their place at the bottom of the socioeconomic order.

By the second decade of the twenty-first century, California had about three million undocumented immigrants, most of them Mexican nationals. That is about the same percentage of the state's population that Okies represented in the 1930s—about 12 percent. Native Californians—and there's irony in that fuzzy term—don't like to see immigration coming at them in uncontrollable torrents, as has been the case with both of these migrations. Their reasons are understandable: huge, concentrated migrations can drain public resources. Certainly, a large percentage of undocumented Mexicans perform farm labor that few will touch, as did the Okies and other ethnic groups before them, but collectively they've also taxed the government's safety net. Hospitals are packed, schools crowded, and social services overburdened—same as before with the Okies.

The simple otherness of Mexican immigrants disturbs some people too—same as before with the Okies. Mexican immigrants speak Spanish; the Okie migrants typically spoke with grammatically tangled twangs that, to the ear of many established Californians, sounded only marginally reminiscent of English. Mexican immigrants practice Catholicism; the Okies brought evangelical Christian fundamentalism to the West. Both were departures from the staid, upright Protestantism of white, pre–Dust Bowl Californians. Mexican immigrants favor Latin rhythms or Tejano; the Okies preferred Bob Wills and Gene Autry. Many of these things were foreign to Californians of the cultural status quo—even though many "established" white Californians were descendants of people who had come west in other migrations, not so long before, from the lower plains.

To the rest of California, these Okies were ethnic "others" who, despite their skin tone, occupied an ethnoracial borderland on the "fringe of whiteness," according to historian Neil Foley, and their presence prompted an unusually forceful response. Many were turned away at the California border for lack of "papers" that might prove they had jobs or families waiting for them in Los Angeles or the San Joaquin Valley. Most notoriously, the Los Angeles Police Department, just a tad outside its jurisdiction, set up indisputably unconstitutional "bum blockades" near California border towns such as Needles to turn away Okies who had that look of indigence. Illegal Mexican immigration inspired the Minutemen civilian border patrol, construction of seven hundred miles of fence line along the US-Mexican border, and a series of immigration reform debates that, during the early 2000s, thrust the Republicans' House leadership into a corner, pinched between anti-immigration conservatives and a growing Latino voting bloc.

A cynic might say that as soon as the Okies started edging closer to middle-class status, acquiring refrigerators, television sets, and mortgage payments, they switched from the pro-labor stance of the Dust Bowl's first wave to more conservative values. In truth, Tom Joad hardly turned into a Reagan Democrat at the first sign of prosperity. Okie migrants had had union activism somewhat thrust upon them in the first place, and left to their own purest, natural inclinations, they would have been apolitical at best. Second- and third-generation Okies evolved, by and large, into hard-shelled conservatives not particularly sympathetic to the economic plight of the Mexican laborers whom they had displaced in the fields in the 1930s—and whom, by the mid-1950s, they had surpassed in the American-dream food chain.

But Okies' differentness was as undeniable as that of the Mexicans with whom they shared that social and economic relegation. Their twang, their chicken-fried cuisine, their praise-the-Lord religiosity, and their music endured, and that culture was still firmly in place when the Bakersfield Sound era reached its apex in the mid- to late 1960s. Today, even if the music has largely merged with the Nashville mainstream, the Okieness of that collective migrant clan has held steady through advancing years. Unlike other parts of the state, such as the Bay Area, where Okies have assimilated seamlessly into the local culture, Okieness—forged in part by animosity and rejection—is still a powerful presence in Bakersfield.

CHAPTER 3

Honky-Tonk Paradise

S ix musicians, howlingly gaudy in matching sequined shirts, white cowboy hats, and Roy Rogers scarves, are pickin' and twangin' to a good ol' hillbilly standard. Sister Rose, all sparkles and fringes, is howling into the microphone: "Ya fought all the way, Johnny Reb. Johnny Reb, ya fought all the way ..."

Suddenly, life erupts into an imitation of art, and a chaotic tumult of elbows and fists rolls across the dance floor, carving a swath of destruction through the saloon like Lee's army at Fredericksburg. Dancers scatter, and unattended longneck bottles foam and rattle onto the worn wooden dance floor. Two men, then three, then six, maul their way toward a side door.

And the Maddox Brothers and Rose play on without hesitation, just as fast and loud as before. When you perform at Bakersfield's most popular honky-tonk, as Rose Maddox once explained, that's rule number one: don't stop when a fight breaks out—just put your head down and play, man, play. That's how it was at the Blackboard, the biggest, loudest, roughest bar in Bakersfield for the better part of a quarter century.

The windowless cavern of a saloon that represented the freewheeling cradle of the Bakersfield Sound, the most legendary of the city's half-dozen country music incubation stations, wasn't always a safe place to be. The Blackboard wasn't the sort of joint that required management to enclose the night's entertainment behind protective chicken wire, but neither was it devoid of menace.

Its heyday, 1952 to 1963, generally coincided with Buck Owens's

31

tenure as the lead guitar player for Bill Woods's Orange Blossom Playboys and assorted other local bands, including his own. But the club stayed open well into the 1970s. Long after Owens found national fame, the Blackboard hosted first-rate pickers—and punchers.

Nashville had the slick studios and the celebrity mansions, but Bakersfield had raw-edged Telecaster guitars, bare-knuckled codes of conduct, and for some, the vague but definite sense that something special was happening here, at places such as the Blackboard.

Joe Maphis felt it. He wrote his 1952 hit "Dim Lights, Thick Smoke (and Loud, Loud Music)" while driving to his home in the San Fernando Valley following his first performance on the Blackboard stage. He and his singing wife Rose Lee had never seen anything like it back in southern Virginia, where they had been stars at the Old Dominion Barn Dance—not the thick fog of cigarette smoke, not the cavern-like darkness, and especially not the dancing. Folks back in Virginia sat politely and watched.[1] They had never heard anything like it either. On the night in question, the band, Buck Owens and his Schoolhouse Playboys, had played at a volume the Maphises had never imagined possible. "So [afterward] they got back in the car," Dwight Yoakam, who years later heard the story from Rose Lee, once explained. "Joe Maphis just shook his head. He said, 'Hon, I believe that was the loudest thing I've ever heard in my life.' She said, 'I know, they were great—but I can't hear.'"[2]

Honky-Tonk Angels

The Oxford American dictionary provides two definitions of "honky-tonk": (1) a cheap or disreputable bar, club, or dance hall, typically where country music is played; and (2) a style of country and western music of the 1950s associated with honky-tonks. Oxford left out a third sense of the term: "honky-tonk" also describes the very human behaviors taking place inside said honky-tonks, to a soundtrack of said music. In combination, honky-tonk life, in all its messy glory, is essentially this: boy meets girl, boy loses girl—accompanied by fiddle, Telecaster, and all too often, several highballs.

The iconic photo of Blackboard owners Frank Zabaleta and Joe Limi, about 1952.
(Robert E. Price collection.)

The term's origins are unknown, but theories abound. One is that "honky-tonk" mimics the sound of keystrokes emanating from a battered, ill-tuned piano in a raucous brothel—onomatopoeia, in the language of literary devices. Another is that the term comes from the firm of William Tonk & Bros., founded in 1880, whose upright pianos, first manufactured in 1889, were branded with the name Ernest A. Tonk.[3]

The term is thought to have first appeared in broader popular culture in Hank Thompson's 1952 hit "Wild Side of Life," which contained the famous line "I didn't know God made honky-tonk angels." The song's narrator ruminates on the cruel nature of this unfaithful new kind of woman—the honky-tonk woman. So long before the Rolling Stones were glimmer twins in each other's eyes, "honky-tonk women" had already been tagged as fallen women, sexual predators, femme fatales, vamps in sequins and snaps.

Thompson's interpretation was challenged, however, when Kitty

Wells answered a mere month later with "It Wasn't God Who Made Honky-Tonk Angels." The song, a huge hit that was initially banned at the *Grand Ole Opry*, suggested that the culture's good-time girls had simply been driven to their behavior by equally fickle and wayward men who had "caused many a good girl to go wrong." The takeaway, regardless of one's position, was the image of an adult, working-class playground where dramas of seduction, lust, betrayal, and heartbreak might play themselves out on just about any midsummer night.[4]

Although the term had been in use since at least the 1890s, honky-tonks were strictly a postwar phenomenon. They seemed to rise along with that sense of entitlement that adult white men enjoyed in the postwar years. These were the men who had stormed the Normandy beaches, liberated Europe, and seen the lights of Paris—or had at least helped build the ships and planes that got those men in a position to do so. What small pleasure should ever be denied them?

The advent of the honky-tonk also coincided with the decline of the dance hall, the demise of big band, and the rise of the four- and five-man combo as the new musical currency. Family entertainment? That was *Lassie* and *Father Knows Best*. Adult entertainment? That was a honky-tonk.

At a typical barn dance, the menfolk would have to go out to the buckboard to pull on a jug. It was the same for the dance halls that replaced the barn dance; if you wanted a nip, you'd head out to the parking lot. No women allowed: they were back inside with the kids, sipping soda pop. But the honky-tonk—this was an unabashedly grown-up preserve where not only men but also women could imbibe with impunity and revel in moral autonomy. Stirred with loud music and low lights, it became the volatile cocktail of a singular time, place, and culture.[5]

Joe and Frank's Place

The Blackboard began as a café where truckers, oil-field workers, and other blue-collar types would meet for their breakfast and morning coffee. While shoveling down corned beef hash or biscuits and gravy, they'd read messages scrawled in chalk on the "blackboard" walls—notices about job openings mostly, but occasionally also the can't-miss ponies scheduled to run that day and anything and nothing in particular.

So in 1949, when two local men bought the business at 3601 Chester Avenue, Tommy's Place, as it was then known, already had a faithful, built-in clientele. Thirty-eight-year-old Joe Limi was a short, stocky man who had come to the United States from Italy at the age of nine. Before the war, he had driven a truck for his family's liquor distributorship; that's how he met his future business partner. Frank Zabaleta, thirty-six when he went in with Limi, was a tall, good-natured California-born Basquo who happened to work at a liquor store on Limi's route.

Their bar wasn't much to speak of at first, "just one little area about the size of two living rooms put together," said Fuzzy Owen, who, even as an inexperienced musician of twenty, knew a small-potatoes gig when he saw one. Nevertheless, he accepted the job, and beginning in 1949, his three-piece band took up a cramped corner of the tiny, rickety tavern.

Two years later, though, the building seemed almost ready to come crumbling down under the collective weight of a billion termite eggs. "You could just about grab a handful of door, it crumbled so bad," Limi's younger brother, Adolph Limi, remembered. So Limi and Zabaleta knocked the place down and started over, building it bigger and better. This time alcohol and mischief, not pie and coffee, were the main attractions. Eventually, the bar swallowed up the small restaurant, and thereafter the Blackboard's menu didn't extend much beyond pickled eggs and peanuts.

Hanging around outside the Blackboard: Oscar Whittington, Billy Mize, Herb Henson, Bill Woods.
(Photo courtesy of the Kern County Museum.)

"You couldn't miss a night," said Rosa Dykes, who always feared she'd lose out on something good by staying home. Every night after work, she and her fellow telephone-switchboard operators would push their way through the Blackboard's palm-stained double doors and hit the dance floor. And it's a good thing they did—if on one particular night in 1952, Rosa had simply gone home, she'd have missed out on meeting one Hershel Dykes, her future husband.[6] Before long it was the hottest nightspot in town. Over time, performers such as Tommy Collins, Fuzzy Owen, Lewis Talley, Billy Mize, Bonnie Owens, Jean Shepard, Wanda Jackson, Roy Nichols, and Red Simpson took their places onstage.[7]

Patrons danced by the light of intermittent cigarette cherries and an overhead orb that glowed red with a message of reassuring consistency: Schlitz. From the perspective of a present-day devotee of classic country music, the procession of stars—some still years away from their greatest successes—almost defies belief, but it was happening here at least twice a week. Many among Bakersfield's working class, having sweltered in the packing sheds and oil fields for eight hours or more, lived for these evenings, when temperatures turned sultry and cold beer was the best possible salve for sunburn.[8]

Booze and Brawls

The bare-knuckled bravado of certain patrons came to represent an essential part of the Blackboard's redneck glamour and an undeniable aspect of its legacy. At one point in the Blackboard's disreputable history, it was not uncommon for a man to stand on a chair and offer to fight anyone in the place, and there'd instantly be a show of hands of those willing to oblige him. Off the two combatants would go, outside into the parking lot, and fifteen minutes later they'd be back at the bar for another beer—no hard feelings.

Legend suggests that the bar had three fights a night, but those who spent a considerable amount of time there say it was not nearly that wild—perhaps just one fight a week, perhaps even fewer. Frequency of fisticuffs notwithstanding, the self-preservation-minded Blackboard patron developed good peripheral vision, if only to dodge the occasional flying beer bottle.

Dancers spin around the Blackboard's dance floor as Buck Owens and Oscar Whittington share vocals with the Orange Blossom Playboys. Bill Woods on steel guitar, drummer unknown.
(Photo courtesy of the Kern County Museum.)

"We had one fight this Saturday night … where the whole place was going at it," remembers Greg Limi, Joe's nephew. "The sheriff was there, the highway patrol, you name it. They were dragging people out by their feet and stuffing them into patrol cars, four at a time.

"We went to break up this one fight—these two women were fighting—and a guy stepped in and tapped us on the shoulders. He says, 'Nah, let 'em fight. The gal on the bottom is my wife, and she deserves it.' So we let 'em go at it for another couple of minutes."

A later version of the Orange Blossom Playboys: Buck Owens, Johnny Cuviello, unknown, Bill Woods, unknown, unknown, pictured on the stage of the Blackboard saloon.
(Photo courtesy of the Kern County Museum.)

"It wasn't so bad," said Al Cordero, the off-duty sheriff's deputy who for eleven years worked the door as a bouncer—a gun on one hip, a nightstick on the other, and a toothpick balanced artfully on his lower lip. "Once in a while you'd get a fight. There was one murder, where they shot a guy. Took a couple shots at me too."

Most any reason for a fight would suffice, and sometimes no reason was required at all. For some patrons, driving one's knuckles into a fella's front teeth was practically a form of recreation.

"There were these same five guys who always caused trouble," said Adolph Limi, who, as a backup bartender, poured forty-cent drafts off and on until about 1953. "They'd just walk up to a table, and if a guy didn't look right, they'd knock him down, right there, while he sat at the table. 'Course they were permanently eighty-sixed. But people would let them back in through the escape doors."

Oscar Whittington and Kenny Hays harmonize on the Blackboard stage.
(Photo courtesy of the Kern County Museum.)

Sometimes if the brawlers weren't too punch-drunk, they would all collapse amicably at the same table and whistle for a barmaid. "It wasn't like it is today," said cocktail waitress Wanda Markham, the wife of Blackboard trumpeter and saxophonist Don Markham.

"Back then, you had a fistfight, and then one bought the other a drink. These days they start shooting."[9]

It was like that at most Bakersfield clubs, including the Blackboard's chief rivals, the Clover Club, the Lucky Spot, and later on, Tex's Barrel House. And it didn't matter whether the band was Bill Woods and the Orange Blossom Playboys, Bob Smith and the Bluebonnet Playboys, Jolly Jody and his Go-Daddies, or a young Merle Haggard, just two or three years out of San Quentin. Fightin' and drinkin' were just as integral a part of the whole honky-tonk package as the music.

Beyond the beer and over the noise of the brawling, a new sound was taking shape, a new attitude evolving. This was the germination period for the Bakersfield Sound—born in the 1930s from the Bob Wills–Jimmie Rodgers school of country and western and brought to full flower in the 1950s and '60s by the likes of Haggard, Owens, and Freddie Hart.

The earliest strains emanated from the dance halls—places such as the Beardsley Ballroom in Oildale and the Rainbow Gardens and Rhythm Ranch, both south of town toward the Weedpatch federal labor camp, and the Pumpkin Center Barn Dance, a repurposed Quonset hut that represented the cultural core of the farming burg of Pumpkin Center. But the Blackboard was the first serious, adults-only saloon where the music was as hot as the beer was cold, and dim lights and thick smoke provided a cover for the furtive indiscretions of consenting adults.

Wednesdays and Thursdays were guest-star nights. George Jones would play one night; Glen Campbell, a decade before he got to Phoenix, would play another. The Blackboard, in fact, became the must-stop spot in Bakersfield for performers such as Bob Wills, Ferlin Husky, Roger Miller, Patsy Cline, Little Jimmie Dickens, Connie Smith, Tex Ritter, Dallas Frazier, Lefty Frizzell, Tommy Duncan, and nearly until the time he went to prison for stomping his wife to death, Cooley.

The Everly Brothers perform at Rainbow Gardens in about 1958 with, from left, Lawrence Williams (seated at the piano), Billy Mize, Jelly Sanders, and Buck Owens, far right. Other performers are unidentified. Note the audience members in the far right foreground: at this show, at least, probably owing to the Everly Brothers' broad fan base, the Rainbow Gardens sometimes had racially integrated crowds.
(Photo courtesy of the Kern County Museum.)

Young Buck Owens got a job at the Blackboard in 1952, playing with Bill Woods's band and making twelve dollars and fifty cents a night, enough money to make a dent in his bills for the first time in his life. How young was young Owens? "After a few days watching that guy walk around with his guitar," Cordero said, "I decided to check his ID. He only needed a couple of months to be of age. I figured that was close enough."

It was at the Blackboard in 1956 that singer Wynn Stewart introduced Owens to Harlan Howard, the man with whom Owens would cowrite such songs as "Excuse Me (I Think I've Got a

Heartache)" and "Foolin' Around." Long before those hits came along and made Owens's life considerably less subsistent, however, he was working that tiny stage almost nightly, sweating over his Telecaster the way he had once sweated in the citrus orchards of his youth. Meanwhile, as Howard recalled, bandleader Bill Woods would puff on his pipe and flirt with girls.

The Blackboard was the kind of place that had mirrors at the back of the bar, a jukebox, a wooden dance floor, and a long shuffleboard table that Owens visited most every break. He usually faced off against Markham, the band's horn player.[10] It also had a bevy of gum-popping cocktail waitresses. Some had been recruited by Zabaleta himself, who would stop in at such places as Little Sweden's Drive-In, at Union and Kentucky, and pitch jobs to the fountain girls. "He'd always come in and order a French dip and a peanut butter milkshake," remembers former Blackboard waitress Jeannie Robbins. "And he'd ask me, 'When are you going to come to work for me?'"

The best known of the Blackboard's hired help was undoubtedly Bonnie Owens, the singing cocktail waitress. Buck's former wife (and Merle's future bride) worked on and off at two Bakersfield night spots for the better part of a decade, even after she became the regular "girl singer" on *Cousin Herb's Trading Post* TV show and a recording star in her own right. The money was better working the tables than singing onstage; every time she set down her tray and picked up a microphone, Bonnie deprived herself of a few dollars. She was primarily a relief waitress; if someone was too sick to come to work at the Clover Club or the "Board," where her sister Betty Campbell worked, and if her touring schedule as a singer permitted it, Bonnie would put on her waitressing shoes.

It was a good place to find inspiration, especially if a songwriter's subject was the vagaries of the human heart, which often manifest themselves in that setting. "Bonnie would write songs right there on the job," Robbins said. "If her section was slow, she would stop and grab a cocktail napkin and write down a few lines right there. Then, later on some different night, she'd get up on the bandstand and sing it." Forty years later, Bonnie still remembered the words to one such song, "No Tomorrow": "'For me there will be no tomorrow. The sun in my life went down today' ... That's the very first line I wrote in Bakersfield, and it started there at the Blackboard," Bonnie once explained. "I'd think of a line. I'd hear something, a little piece of a song, and I'd say, 'Well, I haven't heard that before,' and I'd write it down."[11]

The Edison Highway Strip

Four miles southeast of the Blackboard were destinations two and three on the honky-tonk highway—Bob's Lucky Spot and the Clover Club, saloons that cultivated their own galaxy of local stars. Bar stool to bar stool, they were a mere five-minute stumble apart from each other.

Johnny Barnett was the benevolent bandleader at the Lucky Spot, the saloon where Merle Haggard once sang and made the connections that eventually elevated him from club performer to international star. Like Haggard's, Barnett's upbringing was something of a hard-luck tale, just minus all the jail time. Born in Oklahoma, Barnett was orphaned at the age of seven and raised by an uncle and an older brother. Barnett moved to Plainview, Texas, at the age of twenty and found himself a wife. In 1940, tired of washing dishes at a hamburger joint for a dollar a day, he packed up his young family and went west to the promise of California. He found work picking apricots at twice his old wage—two dollars a day—and worked for a time in the Southern California shipyards. By 1944, he was in Tehachapi, working nights playing music in a local bar.

In 1950, Barnett went to the Lucky Spot—near the corner of Edison Highway and Mount Vernon Avenue, a quarter mile from the Clover Club—to work for club owner Bob Warner. Eunice, Barnett's second wife, landed a job as a waitress. In short order Barnett was fronting a regular band, the Happy-Go-Lucky Boys, with bassist Cliff Crofford, guitarist Gene Moles, and drummer Jimmy Wright. Over the years, Billy Mize, Jelly Sanders, and Fuzzy Owen were among those who spun through the band's revolving door. The boys earned twenty-five dollars a pop in side money performing on Bakersfield TV shows hosted by Jimmy Thomason, Henson, and Mize. It was decent money, and the show was great advertising.

By 1961 or '62, tiring of his seven-night grind, Barnett got permission to hire a relief singer two nights a week. The new man, a startlingly crisp baritone who'd been singing four nights a week at the High Pockets club, was Haggard, just a year out of San Quentin State Prison. "They would just throw together a band," Fuzzy Owen said. "It was a different band every night, but it was pretty good. Sometimes I was in the band, sometimes Merle, once in a while both of us together." As talented as he was, Haggard lacked a little when it came to professionalism. He had a tendency to forget the words to the songs, and Owen razzed him mercilessly about it. Finally, Haggard had had enough; he put his mind to the task and learned the lyrics he needed to know. "Merle was really nervous when I first heard him sing," Owen said. "He was paranoid, just got out of the joint. But he was good. Even his mistakes sounded good."

Barnett cut just one record during his career, a pair of singles recorded in 1962 by Bakersfield's Tally Records. The A side was a Haggard tune, "Second Fiddle" (not the same song recorded by Buck Owens), but the B side, "Too Old to Hurt," has the better story. Bakersfield singer-songwriter Red Simpson was playing with Barnett's band one night, and during a break he stepped over to the jukebox to chat with his sister. She'd just broken up with a longtime boyfriend. "Red asked her how she was doing," Barnett recalled in a 2001 interview. "She said, 'I'm too old to hurt and too wise to cry,' which seemed like a pretty good line for a song. … and Red took it from there."

Cast members from *Cousin Herb's Trading Post* knew their way around the Lucky Spot quite well, but the Clover Club, a former card room, was really their home base. It was here that they parlayed their small-town, small-screen fame into some semblance of actual income. Bonnie Owens, who worked all three of the major clubs, was particularly associated with the Clover Club.

Thurman Billings, the owner, recruited waitresses the same way Zabaleta found cocktail girls for the Blackboard: he plucked them from hamburger joints. One day Billings and his wife approached

Bonnie at the burgers-and-malts place where she worked, at Union and Truxtun Avenues, and asked if she would like to make better money. They knew Bonnie already, having seen her sneak her way onto the Clover Club stage more than once to sing alongside Fuzzy Owen, her boyfriend at the time, and his cousin, Lewis Talley. Billings knew she had also sung a little at the Blackboard, with Bill Woods's permission. "Anytime you want to sing," Billings told Bonnie, "you get up and sing."

Lewis Talley, cofounder of Tally Records, outstanding in his field and resplendent in a white stage tuxedo.
(Photo courtesy of the Kern County Museum.)

And so she did, setting down her cocktail tray once or twice a night to perform next to Fuzzy, Lewis, and other performers: sometimes fiddler Jelly Sanders, sometimes guitarist Billy Mize or Roy Nichols.

The Clover Club was also important to Red Simpson—it was the first top-tier Bakersfield club to give him a job onstage. He was working at the Wagon Wheel in Lamont, not far from the old Weedpatch camp, when Fuzzy saw him and arranged to bring him in as a piano player.

In 1963, Barnett quit the Lucky Spot and moved to the Mojave Desert town of Ridgecrest to take a milk delivery route. After a year, he moved to the eastern range of the Sierra Nevadas, first the town of Lone Pine and then Bishop, where he started playing music again two nights a week—and stayed for the next twelve years. In the mid-1970s, he returned to Bakersfield and worked for a janitorial service. His days as a performer were over.

Country music didn't have a pension plan for its practitioners in the 1940s, '50s, and '60s—still doesn't, for the most part—so Barnett was forced to keep working into his eighties, stocking shelves at County Fair Market in Lamont to supplement his Social Security check. Only the older grocery store customers, if anyone, remembered Barnett from his previous life. The Lucky Spot itself, at 2303 Edison Highway, was torn down sometime in the early 2000s. Today the old honky-honk is just an asphalt lot and, fifty feet back from the road, Lucky Spot Auto Body and Paint. Alas, the Clover Club is gone as well—and so is the building that once housed it. Now the spot that would be 2611 Edison Highway is just a long stretch of desolate salvage yard.[12]

Buzzkill Strikes the Scene

Drinking drivers had little to fear from the law in those days, at least in comparison to the tough laws and strict enforcement common today. Patrons of the Blackboard, located a half mile south of the Kern River approach into Oildale, would zip over to the southeast end of town to Bob's Lucky Spot, on Edison Highway, where Billy

Mize might be performing, or just a few blocks down the street to the Barrelhouse, on the Garces Circle, where for a time Haggard was on the bill. Bakersfield was a musical cornucopia to be savored, but the only way to fully enjoy its manifold bounty was to drain one's bottle, pay one's tab, and move on down the road. "Buzzed driving" was not in the common vernacular, but it was part of the experience.

During its peak years of popularity, the Blackboard hosted an open-mike jam session every Sunday afternoon from three to seven, and it was usually packed. "Then they'd close for two hours," said Hershel Dykes, "and we'd all go over to the Lucky Spot or the Clover Club and party for two hours till the Blackboard opened again at nine."[13]

More likely, though, they'd just head next door to Sammy's Smoke Shop, which had pool tables and cheap beer, at least until the place was turned into a parking lot. "It was just a beer joint, but I could tell you a lot of things about it," said the smoke shop's owner, Sammy Hambaroff, who preferred to keep all the good stories to himself. Among its other attractions, the smoke shop was a short walk from the local cathouse, an ill-kept secret that for years remained a last-chance option for many male bar-goers. It helped that the Bakersfield Police Department and its two corrupt chiefs of that era, Horace Grayson (1946–66) and especially Jack Towle (1966–73), not only tolerated brothels but also allowed their top assistant to accept protection money from the city's most prominent madam—this, according to a 1970 Kern County Grand Jury report that, undoubtedly to the relief of many, was never made public.[14]

Starting in 1980, political pressure by advocacy groups such as Mothers Against Drunk Driving prompted legislatures across the country to ramp up under-the-influence laws. The sobriety checkpoint was born, and the demise of honky-tonk culture, already underway due to changing musical tastes and socioeconomic evolution, gained momentum. Customers, increasingly wary of the enforcement gauntlets between clubs, started staying home, and working musicians felt the financial pain. So the scene suffered from both ends.

The Blackboard closed quietly sometime in the late 1970s or early '80s. No one seems to remember exactly when, and official records are incomplete. Frank Zabaleta died in June 1976 at age sixty-two, Joe Limi in September 1994 at age eighty-three. In later years the building was home to a pizza restaurant, an indoor shooting range, and a sports pub that—no small irony here—featured boxing memorabilia. On September 7, 2001, to the surprise and dismay of many, a bulldozer took out the first chunk of the old saloon; by September 11—a date memorable in Bakersfield and across the world for other reasons—the building's demolition was complete. The Kern County Superintendent of Schools office, which at the time managed the Kern County Museum and had begun acquiring lots adjacent to the museum's campus, including the site of the old saloon, had given the order. Bakersfield's premier honky-tonk had been reduced to a vacant, grassy field, slated for some future museum attraction.

Hanging out in a hallway before a show with Bob Wills, far left: Billy Mize, Jean Shepard, Johnny Cuviello, Bill Woods, circa 1962.
(Photo courtesy of the Kern County Museum.)

But in the memories of country pickers and bar-hoppers of a certain age, that incongruent patch of green will forever be the spot where the Blackboard once stood. No one who lived through that time—not the musicians, staff, or patrons—will easily forget the place where ordinary folk came to dance, drink, fight, flirt, and perhaps, outside of their hard, workaday lives, find some small province of freedom and belonging. The Blackboard was not just about honky-tonk country music but was a special time, place, and sound.

"Those were the days, man," Hambaroff said. "Darn it, I wish they could bring those days back."[15]

They're Tearing Down the Honky-Tonks

The Rainbow Gardens, an all-ages dance hall on Union Avenue, is now the Basque Club. The Pumpkin Center Barn Dance, where the house band was Cousin Ebb and the Squirrel Shooters, is now a dilapidated retail store on a once-remote stretch of Taft Highway soon to be overrun by burgeoning Bakersfield. The Beardsley Ballroom, an Oildale landmark that hosted the likes of Bob Wills, is long gone, having burned down in a suspicious fire. Trout's, once regarded as second tier among the most passionate honky-tonkers of the day, gradually absorbed the reputation of others as they went out of business and today qualifies as the last surviving saloon from Bakersfield's golden age.

Perhaps the only other repurposed structure that's left to remind old-timers of the boozy good old days is Tex's Barrel House—or, as it's known now, the Deja Vu strip club.

The Barrel House was located a mile south of the Blackboard on the Garces Circle. At one time it was important to the local music scene, largely because of its close proximity to that more famous saloon, but also because the once-raucous country juke joint brought in good local acts on a regular basis in the 1950s and '60s. The oil-town connotations of its name probably helped too. Then as now, Bakersfield was populated with Texas transplants who worked in the oil patch; a barrel house is a building at a refinery where barrels are filled with various grades of oil for shipment.[16]

The club in later years, as happens so often, became a shadow of its former self. In the early 1980s, Bryce Martin, then the music writer for the *Bakersfield Californian*, visited what remained of the place and later characterized it like this: it was an "unremarkable and poorly lit pod of indifference [that] held mostly elderly and low-income patrons content with shuffling along in a flat-footed version of the Cotton-Eyed Joe. And the usual bar drunks you find anywhere." It was just as well that this depressing scene was replaced by pole dancers and overpriced liquor.[17]

This brings up an important point about all these Bakersfield Sound–era honky-tonks: some people may consider them revered icons of past glory and musical acclaim, but when it comes right down to it, they were just bars where people drank—in many cases too much and for far too long into the night.

That black hole where Merle Haggard's besotted narrator is betrayed by the bottle that let her "memory come around"? That's every bar, everywhere in the universe. It just so happens that Haggard's saloon of inspiration was probably a composite of the dank, smoky honky-tonks of Bakersfield, California.

Snapshot
It's That Kid!

In 1955, almost nobody who lived more than three hundred miles from the Mississippi River had heard of Elvis Presley. The young singer, having recorded a few songs at Sun Records in Memphis, had just signed on as a performer with the *Louisiana Hayride*, a *Grand Ole Opry*–style television show based in Shreveport, but his fame hadn't spread much beyond that region of the Deep South.

Between hayrides, Presley and his band made touring loops across the Louisiana border into east Texas. On one such swing, Elvis, then nineteen, stopped in to perform on newly opened WACO-TV in Waco, where country fiddler Jimmy Thomason had just debuted his live *Home Folks Show* for the local Saturday-night viewing audience. Thomason and his wife, Louise, had launched *The Louise and Jimmy Thomason Show* on brand-new KAFY-TV (now KBAK) in Bakersfield a year and a half before. But in June 1954, Thomason left the television show for an ill-fated run at the California State Senate, and by the following year they were back in Waco, where they had worked a few years before.[1]

The Thomasons were happy to give the young singer a place on their show, but as soon as Elvis broke into "That's All Right (Mama)," they realized Elvis was more than a country boy with rhythm. "When he started singing, two of the engineers got up and started running back and forth, like they wanted to climb the walls," Louise Thomason said. "They just panicked. They thought he'd throw the station off the air. They'd never seen anything like it." But Elvis's act was so well received that he came back for three or four subsequent performances on WACO-TV.

After one such Saturday-night show, Elvis and the Thomasons walked out the door of the station into the parking lot, where a misty rain was falling. There sat Elvis's pink Cadillac, covered with wet paint. "His name was painted on the side door, and it must have been painted in watercolors or something, because the letters were streaking down the side," Louise said. "Elvis just stood there and looked at it." The King-to-be could withstand the adoration of thousands of screaming fans at any given time, but his Cadillac's paint job apparently couldn't weather a little rain. His young career managed to survive that indignity.

The Thomasons had signed a six-month contract with WACO, having intended to return to Bakersfield at the end of their stint. When Jimmy informed Elvis of this, the nascent rock 'n' roll god suggested he hitch a ride. "He told Jimmy, 'Well, I sure would like to be going back with you,'" Louise Thomason said. "The fact that he was getting into the rhythm and blues, which was not very big at that time, may have made him think that way. He thought California would understand his music better. He thought he would be accepted better."

Jimmy Thomason brushed it off as idle conversation—in fact, it may have been just that—and the fiddler later told his wife he didn't know what he might have done with Elvis. "I was just all for it," Louise said. "But Jimmy told me, 'Louise, he's seen too many rhythm and blues shows.'"

About a year after returning to Bakersfield, where they had launched the second incarnation of their local television show, the Thomasons were seated one night around the living room sofa watching the Dorsey Brothers' television show, starring Tommy and Jimmy Dorsey. Suddenly, a familiar name was introduced. "My God, Louise!" Thomason gasped. "It's that kid!"

As surprised as they were, though, Louise and Jimmy Thomason never second-guessed their decision to dissuade Elvis from coming west. "It would have been a wrong move for us to take him on as a manager, or whatever," Louise said. "There wouldn't have been trouble getting him a job at the Blackboard or any of those places, but as far as getting a direction for his career ... If he had relied on us, it wouldn't have worked."

That kid did all right for himself without their help, but the mind reels at the thought of Elvis sharing the Blackboard stage with Buck Owens—a closet rockabilly singer himself, as it turned out.

Astrophysicist Stephen W. Hawking has a theory about time, fate, and history that may help explain the many Elvis sightings reported so dutifully over a twenty-year period in those mostly defunct grocery-store checkout line tabloids. If time splinters into an infinite network of parallel realities, like streams branching off from a great river, there must be a reality somewhere in the great time-space continuum in which the King took Bakersfield by storm, and Little Debbie snack cakes stock is worth about the same as Microsoft.

CHAPTER 4
Vegas of the Valley

Bakersfield wasn't a honky-tonk hotbed merely because talented and innovative performers started gathering there in the 1950s. It was a cultural mecca because music consumers—the audiences—created a self-perpetuating critical mass. A big part of it was Bakersfield's location on old Highway 99, California's most traveled north-south highway for the better part of the twentieth century, but the town's proximity to Los Angeles and the diversity of its population were also factors.

Midcentury Bakersfield was a mix of established white Protestant families; poor and working-class black families, many of whom had migrated from the South a generation before; Latinos, both native and itinerant; and the recently arrived Dust Bowl transplants from the Southwest. Each of those groups had its own music and its own places to enjoy it.

The beer joints and honky-tonks where the Okies gathered weren't what most visitors thought of when they drove into town. That distinction went to the bars and clubs that lined Highway 99 (Union Avenue, to locals), which were favored by the whites of old, established Bakersfield—nightspots whose flash and neon gave the strip an almost Vegas-like feel.

Picture a convertible full of young, flat-topped men giddy with testosterone and life, smoking and hooting as they cruise down a wide, neon boulevard. Multiply that by thirty. Now picture a line of vehicles behind them all, endless to the horizon: haggard truckers behind family vacationers behind just-got-paid cotton pickers behind middle-aged couples in hats and ties and pearls and fur stoles, all rolling into Bakersfield.

On a Saturday night in the early 1950s, with the windows down, Union Avenue was one lively place. And the music that poured out of the nightclubs, lined up two hundred feet apart in some places, came in many flavors. Along 99, between Ming and California Avenues, country and western music was but one choice. The strip offered the Hacienda, Maison Jaussaud, the Bakersfield Inn, El Adobe, Saddle & Sirloin, the Crystal Inn, and dozens of alternatives in between, each beckoning with its own garish, megawatt-lit signage. This was the Champs-Elysées of the Central Valley, where the euphoria of postwar self-realization, bottlenecked by an immature state highway system, created a singular time and place. This was BAKERSFIELD—said so right there in huge blue capital letters arching thirty feet over Union Avenue.

That glory, that irrepressibility, might be hard to envision today against the ghosts and ruin of one of the most decrepit stretches of highway in the valley. If you want a prostitute, if you want a bag of crack, go to one of those side streets just off Union. But once upon a time, it was something to see. The Broadway of Bakersfield, as it was sometimes called, was a mecca of energy and opulence.

Union Avenue didn't become a glittering oasis in one broad, visionary stroke. Its transformation from country road to well-traveled highway began in the 1920s, when Detroit started building cars that were strong enough to get people from one major city to another with some degree of comfort and certainty. Motoring became a recreation—for many, not just the means but the end as well.

By the end of the decade, traffic along 99 was heavy enough to convince brothers Oscar and C. L. Tomerlin to build the Bakersfield Inn, a lavish hotel designed in the style of a Spanish villa. Completed in 1930, the building at 1101 Union Avenue was widely credited (inaccurately) with establishing the word "motel"—a contraction of "motor hotel"—to describe this new kind of amenity.

Other motels and restaurants followed in steady succession throughout the 1930s and '40s, until postwar affluence, can-do spirit, and good old-fashioned commercial momentum conspired to justify the construction of Union Avenue's most striking and memorable feature. The Bakersfield sign—a 130-foot-long, thirty-ton footbridge—was built in 1949 to link the two halves of the Bakersfield Inn, which had grown from its original 26 rooms on the west side of Union Avenue to 325 rooms on both sides. But quite apart from its function, the sign became an icon unto itself. On a clear day, a motorist could read the sign's six-foot-high blue porcelain letters from more than a mile away.

By 1952, a single three-mile stretch of Union Avenue had twenty-three motels, twenty-nine restaurants, and forty-four gas stations or automotive repair shops, along with dozens of other businesses.

Union Avenue's long, glorious run as a cultural and economic phenomenon lasted just over a decade. The beginning of the end came in July 1963, when the new freeway—the present Highway 99, drawn two miles west of Union Avenue—was completed, routing travelers around Bakersfield's old urban core. Union Avenue was transformed into a side road.

In 1965, a confederation of property owners from Union Avenue and Golden State Highway, their prospects dashed by this progress, financed the construction of two huge forty-nine-foot-tall signs along the new freeway that beckoned motorists with the cheery rhyme "sun, fun, stay, play."

The first sign, erected in 1966, advised drivers to "Exit Union Ave. 1.8 miles." A second sign, erected at the opposite approach into the city, followed in 1968. Motorists, by and large, were not persuaded to go anywhere but where the highway was taking them, and eventually, the "sun, fun, stay, play" signs, like Union Avenue itself, fell into ruin, and in 1983, they were removed. By that time, Union Avenue had been transformed into a boulevard of blight. Its most readily identifiable icon, the Bakersfield arch, came down in 1999. Other Union Avenue landmarks followed in short order.

Good Bones

If you look hard today, though, you can still glimpse that long-lost exuberance: a stately architectural profile here, a bold structural line there. You can find remnants of past glory—ruins from the time, a half century ago, when Union Avenue was a teeming thoroughfare, when summertime traffic sometimes lined up bumper-to-bumper all the way back to the rural crossroads of Greenfield.

This was the 1950s, a wholly different transportation era. An automobile trip from one end of the state to the other was a two- or three-day undertaking, in part because of the predominance of dangerous two-lane highways that linked towns and because automobiles were somewhat less sturdy than today's. Highways then had cross-traffic, perilously placed roadside trees, and, in places such as the Grapevine—the aptly named steep descent from the Los Angeles–Kern County border to the valley floor— treacherous curves.

In those pre-interstate days, it made sense to break up long, physically demanding journeys into manageable pieces, and an overnight stay along glittery, neon-lined Union Avenue was a much-anticipated diversion for many travelers. "You'd see people stopped along the side of the road having picnics," recalled Gary Jaussaud, whose parents operated one of Union's more prestigious establishments. "People thought they needed to stop and refresh themselves, and a lot of people traveling from Los Angeles to San Francisco, or vice versa, stopped here."

Those people mixed easily and often with the locals for whom Union Avenue was the after-hours center of their cultural universe. "We'd go out just about every night in those days," said Ben Sacco, who recalls driving around in a brand-new 1949 Ford. "There was only one country club at the time—Stockdale Country Club—and that was strictly for the elite, so the younger guys went to the clubs. It was that or the movies. We preferred the clubs." Groups of single young men—and to a lesser extent, single young women—might have dinner at El Adobe and then catch the early show at the Saddle & Sirloin, where legendary saxophone star Joe D. Gulli held court for years. Then they'd head south to Maison Jaussaud for the ten o'clock floor show and drop in at the Crystal Inn for dancing to big-band music until two in the morning. "Dancing in those days was the thing to do," Sacco said. "No rock 'n' roll. That son of a gun, Elvis Presley—he ruined it all."

Think things weren't lively in Bakersfield in the mid-1950s? A page of advertisements from the *Bakersfield Californian* offers up no fewer than fifteen shows, including Bob Wills, Tommy Dorsey, and Spade Cooley. *(Image courtesy of the* Bakersfield Californian.*)*

A night out on Union Avenue might include a stop at the plush Hacienda, a sister hotel to the Haciendas in Fresno, Indio, and Las Vegas. Here, a club-hopper might catch country music fiddler Jelly Sanders, whose style was refined enough to appeal to a broad audience. Or a night out might include a stop at the Bakersfield Inn, where the head chef, Nacho, served up delectable ribs, chops, and steaks in the Havana Room and where bandleader Bunky Valdez packed in the crowds after nine.

The countrified, working-class crowd had its own favorite places along Union Avenue, mostly south of Ming Avenue. There was the Highland Inn, just north of Panama Lane, and Pinky's, just south of Panama Lane. There was the Bill Woods Roundup, just south of Wilson Road, and the Rainbow Gardens at 2301 South Union. Farther north, country fans could visit Wild Bill's, at Union and Eighteenth Street, or in later years the Funny Farm. "Those places had a lot of hillbillies, and they tended to be a little rowdier," remembered guitarist Gene Moles. "But they were fun."

Union Avenue wasn't just a popular stop for out-of-town travelers and the local nightclub set. It was a glitzy hub that brought in the rich and famous from the world over. Maison Jaussaud (the French approximation of House of the Jaussauds) was the ritziest Bakersfield restaurant of its time—and possibly all time. Built in 1949 by Dermide Jaussaud (known affectionately to friends and patrons as "He Babe"), his wife Louise, Dermide's brother Martin Jaussaud, and Martin's wife Lillian (nicknamed "She Babe"), the chalet with the distinctive stone facade was at the center of the action from its opening in 1950 until its sale in the mid-1980s. It enjoyed a glittering heyday. "One night, sometime in the mid-1950s, the shah of Iran and his wife came in for dinner. They arrived in a car caravan, with an entourage of about forty people," Gary Jaussaud remembered. "Bob Hope came for dinner a lot, and so did Dick Clark. Charlton Heston too. If you were passing through Bakersfield and you were a person of their stature, that's where you had to go."

Maison Jaussaud never could have survived on the money and goodwill of the rich and famous, of course. It needed the support of common travelers and especially the local community—and it got that support, though not without some anxious moments early on. "Nobody knew if people would take to a fancy restaurant with a French maître d' and all," Jaussaud said. "But they did."

Jaussaud had male waiters (with the exception of one waitress), silver service, tableside food preparation, and an all-French kitchen staff—in short, a product that was utterly foreign to a midsize California farm town. But the restaurant eventually developed that sort of following; customers from the far reaches of Kern County sometimes literally arrived in buses, decked out in furs and suits. Preferred customers, some of whom ate at Jaussaud nightly, had their own tables. Certain young bachelors became fixtures. "These guys were well-mannered and dignified, but you knew what they were doing there: looking for chicks," Jaussaud said. "They were like the Rat Pack."

Bakersfield's proximity to Las Vegas and Los Angeles made it a natural stop-off point for a long succession of top-name acts, although most of them were either unproven up-and-comers such as Johnny Carson and Dorothy Dandridge or over-the-hill veterans whose names still packed in crowds, such as the Marx Brothers and the Three Stooges. Jane Russell appeared at Jaussaud; so did Carol Channing and the Ink Spots. Every two weeks, for a quarter century, there was a different headliner, almost always a star of reasonable stature. And the Jaussaud clientele counted on it. "Anybody that was anybody went to Jaussaud's," said Jimmie Icardo, one of the better-known regulars who later bought a piece of the business.

Union Avenue's pinnacle of popularity was during the era immediately before home electronics created different habits and different expectations. "Television spoiled people," Jaussaud said. "You went out to see people and be seen. People dressed up in nice clothes. People were so easily entertained back then."

Jaussaud gradually faded from the city's cultural map as Vegas-bound acts increasingly gave way to rock bands and a younger, rowdier crowd that mixed uncomfortably with the restaurant's otherwise faithful upscale dinner patrons. Jaussaud, unlike its competitors, had been largely unaffected by the new freeway. In fact, many welcomed the rerouting because it made travel along Union Avenue faster and safer. But as the years wore on, the customer base grew older and less willing to brave the crowds and the noise. "And their kids," Jaussaud said, "were bored by the thought of it." The era of dancing and fine dining was coming to an end. "After a while it got to where people went to dinner to get full, and then they went home," Jaussaud said. "The whole market dynamic changed. It was a slow, painful process."[1]

Lakeview

Not much more than a mile away from the heart of Union Avenue—a straight shot east on East Fourth Street—is Lakeview Avenue. During the 1950s and '60s, it was the center of the black community's nightlife; today, the empty lots and boarded-up buildings make it difficult to envision the bustling nightclub scene that was. But back then, Lakeview boasted several clubs and bars—among them Mom's Place, Pastimes, the Blue Note, and the Dellwood Club, with its slot machines.

The list of big-name performers who stomped the stages of Lakeview's clubs, a major stop on what was then called the "chitlin' circuit," is long and illustrious. Ike and Tina Turner, B. B. King, and James Brown all, at one time or another, headlined a local bill.

The scene had its roots in the 1920s, when several black families migrated to what was known as the Sunset Mayflower District, lured to the area to help harvest cotton and other crops. Some sought to escape the South's sharecropper economy, Jim Crow laws, and other enduring remnants of plantation slavery. But living conditions in the Mayflower District weren't any better: dirt-floor shacks and lean-tos were common. Merle Haggard might have recognized the abandoned railway boxcars that some families appropriated.

Despite the hardships, the area's population took off in the 1930s, and an ensuing economic upswing helped establish better housing and created a healthy atmosphere for neighborhood business. Lakeview Avenue, which bisected the area between East California Avenue and East Brundage Lane, became the commercial focal point. Black-owned grocery stores, service stations, and laundromats started to pop up, and a small commercial district began to thrive.

In 1952, John S. "Tudy" McDaniels, a city fireman, borrowed $15,000 and opened the biggest and most popular nightclub on Lakeview Avenue. A combination liquor store, nightclub, and diner, the Cotton Club drew well-known black performers such as pop crooner Nat King Cole, doo-wop duo Bob & Earl, and bluesman Johnny "Guitar" Watson. Local bands filled out the schedule during the week.

Black residents in the district and from all around Bakersfield, many of them itinerant cotton pickers who were paid by the day, flocked to the area on weekend nights. On a typical Saturday night, McDaniels's Cotton Club packed in seventy-five to a hundred attendees, at five dollars and fifty cents a head—even more when the featured act was a bona fide star. Tina Turner's performances were especially memorable. "Boy, she shook the roof down," McDaniels recounted in a 2001 interview. "She sure could put on a show. My wife would be working the door, and I would come by and check every station to make sure everything was fine, and she would be throwing money on the floor, putting it in the garbage can. She said, 'We sure are making a lot of money tonight!'"

But the Cotton Club began to suffer the same problem that the Blackboard, way across town, had to deal with regularly. Fistfights, muggings, and even murders became common, and as crime in the Mayflower District began to increase, business dropped off. By the early 1970s, Lakeview Avenue's clubs started to disappear. The Dellwood Club was destroyed by fire. Others were shut down by the city for code violations such as poor electrical wiring. Some closed because their owners were simply too old to carry on.

McDaniels, for his part, saw the writing on the wall, and he locked the doors of the Cotton Club for the very last time in 1972. Perhaps he was prescient. Something fundamental in the way people entertained themselves was changing.[2]

Lakeview wasn't the only place where the long era of public music was winding down: Union Avenue, along with places like it across America, was by then changing as well. Honky-tonks still thrived, but their day was coming too.

CHAPTER 5

What's on TV?

O ne day in the late 1940s—no one is quite sure of the date—an itinerant laborer from East St. Louis, Illinois, jumped off a Union Pacific boxcar and planted his feet on the fertile soil of California's Great Central Valley. Or so the legend goes.

We've heard Cousin Herb Henson's story before: A stranger, gifted with charisma, talent, and pluck, shows up one day unannounced. The townsfolk, whether they realize it or not, have in some way been less than whole. The stranger fills their psychic void, and then, his work done, he disappears as inconspicuously as he arrived. This archetype, that of the wandering, unorthodox savior, is usually punctuated with some sort of bittersweet coda that further strengthens the myth. Think the Pied Piper, Shane, Batman.

Henson might have been one of thousands of hobos who rode the rails, decades ago, in search of a new start, a drifter whose random act of arrival became a historically decisive one for his adopted city. Or he may have known exactly what he wanted from the day he set off on the defining journey of his life. In any case, the central California city that welcomed then-anonymous Herbert Lester Henson in 1946 was very different from the one that bade him good-night in 1963.

Henson cultivated, mentored, and promoted an entire generation of Bakersfield-area musicians with a long-running weekday television program that, along with a half-dozen rival hosts, brought a long succession of the famous and not-quite-famous into central California homes. He was a musician himself, but the regional fame Henson would eventually achieve had less to do with his skill on the piano and more to do with his greatest gift—affability. You'd have to be a sourpuss not to like stocky, amiable Cousin Herb.

The *Cousin Herb's Trading Post* gang hosts the Farmer Boys, Capitol Records artists from Farmersville, circa 1956: Bobby Adamson, second from left, and Woody Murray, fourth from left. Also pictured, from left: Bill Woods, displaying a double-neck guitar of unknown provenance, Jelly Sanders, unknown, Herb Henson, unknown, Joyce Years, Fuzzy Owen.
(Photo courtesy of the Kern County Museum.)

Like so many other country musicians living in California in the 1940s, Henson spent time working in the cotton fields of the San Joaquin Valley. But Henson was too personable to labor long in the patch, and he soon landed a job playing piano at the Wagon Wheel saloon six nights a week in Modesto, 202 miles north of Bakersfield. It was in Modesto that he met Chester Smith, a young radio personality and singer (and later, a regional television-station proprietor of some renown) who encouraged him to consider radio. The opportunity arose when Henson made the acquaintance of one Bill Woods of Bakersfield. Move south, Woods told Henson, and we'll see what transpires. Henson, ready for a change, took Woods up on his offer and promptly charmed himself into a job at KMPH.

The essential *Cousin Herb's Trading Post* lineup: Lewis Talley, Fuzzy Owen, Bonnie Owens, Roy Nichols, Al Brumley, and Herb Henson.
(Photo courtesy of the Kern County Museum.)

Fame put him on hold for a while, though, so in the interim Henson took a job making door-to-door laundry pickups for Ted Saulsbury Cleaners. But even then he yearned to perform. Sometimes, while making a house call, he'd spot a piano in a customer's living room, and one thing would lead to another: inevitably, Henson would end up plinkety-plinking out some gospel standard, and he would eventually leave with more laundry than the customer had ever intended to send out. "Herb just had a fine gift of gab; a natural-born pitchman he was," Woods once said of Henson. "I've never heard anybody who could sell like him."

Soon enough, Henson started making a name for himself as a comedian-musician in Bakersfield dance halls and honky-tonks. He was an immediate hit with the public, though not universally loved by some musicians. "'Cousin' Herb took Jack Trent's job playing the piano at the Clover Club," recalled Red Simpson. "Ol' Jack wasn't too happy about it either. He tuned all the keys wrong on them, just to mess with him. That first night, 'Cousin' Herb couldn't even play. Had to come back the next night." History records no subsequent acts of saloon sabotage, however, and Henson was soon the best-known nightclub piano player in town.

That status got him through the office door of KERO-TV's general manager in 1953. Another station in town, KAFY-TV (later known as KBAK-TV), had just launched a live weekday music program, and Henson wanted to offer his services as competition. Jimmy Thomason, a Waco–born fiddler, who with his wife cohosted *The Louise and Jimmy Thomason Show*, had staked a claim on daily, late-afternoon viewership at KAFY just a few weeks before, and KERO, as Henson undoubtedly suggested in his impassioned pitch, couldn't let that foray go unchallenged.

Cousin Herb Henson welcomes special guests to his show—Johnny Cash and the Tennessee Two, with Marshall Grant, far left, and Luther Perkins, third from left, circa 1957.
(Photo courtesy of the Kern County Museum.)

By the time the meeting was over, Henson had his own television program, *Cousin Herb's Trading Post*. The two hosts went head-to-head, differing just enough to appeal to distinct segments of the viewing audience. Thomason was a master of western swing; Henson's style was more honky-tonk, with a certain gospel sensibility. Henson had a kind of neighborliness too; as his folksy nickname seemed to suggest, he was practically a relation, which meant he was welcome in your living room.

Before There Was Oprah

When television first came to the San Joaquin Valley in 1953, the three major broadcast networks provided only limited programming. Local stations everywhere found themselves with gaping holes between affable Dave Garroway in the early morning, newsman Douglas Edwards at five in the afternoon, and a golden-era prime-time lineup that included the likes of *Make Room for Daddy* and *Your Show of Shows*. The stations filled those programming voids with *Romper Room*, the long-running preschoolers' show that was franchised into local markets beginning in 1953; the slapstick syndicated kids' show *Lunch with Soupy Sales*; and a parade of cooking shows, talk shows, and after-school, clown-hosted cartoon shows. In most cases, this meant finding local personalities and cultivating local talent. In Bakersfield, and in cities throughout the South and Southwest, that naturally included country music.

Henson and his rivals—not only Thomason but also Billy Mize, a steel guitarist with matinee-idol looks; his cohort Cliff Crofford, who teamed with Mize to bring *The Chuck Wagon Gang* to Bakersfield audiences; and Dave Stogner, another Texas fiddler who brought front-porch charm from Fresno south to Bakersfield—almost immediately became household names.

Together, they permitted their audiences to put aside their worries for forty-five blessed minutes, five days a week. Every weekday afternoon, just before the local news, Cold War rumblings, McCarthy hearings, segregation debates, and Sputnik sightings were banished from living rooms across the southern San Joaquin

Valley. Some old friends had stopped by to play a little music, and all was right with the world.

Joe and Rose Lee Maphis, far right, back up Tom Brumley and the *Cousin Herb's Trading Post* band—from left, Herb Henson, Billy Mize, and Bonnie Owens—during a live telecast on Channel 10.
(Photo courtesy of the Kern County Museum.)

Along the way, those Bakersfield television hosts launched several careers and procured audiences for the country music variety programs in the years to follow—two of them, notably, involving Bakersfield's most famous country music performer, Buck Owens. *Buck Owens' Ranch Show* and *Hee Haw* were polished and professional productions, but it was on live local television that Buck perfected his stage patter and learned how to smile. *Trading Post* and other programs like it also whetted cultural appetites that made possible everything from *The Glen Campbell Goodtime Hour* to *The Beverly Hillbillies*.

Jimmy Thomason

The culture that assembled at the intersection of Texas, Oklahoma, and Louisiana produced a sweet, lively musical patois that reflected the region's mishmash of ethnicities, economics, and worldview. In Louisiana, at least, it also produced a unique breed of politician. After the discovery of oil and gas in 1912, politicians in the poverty-riddled state found themselves on top of a tax-revenue gold mine, and they spent from the state treasury with virtual impunity. Most infamous were populist governors Huey Long and, somewhat less notoriously, his brother Earl Long.

But sandwiched around the second and third of Earl Long's three terms was the antithesis of this corruption, perceived or otherwise: Jimmie Davis. The "singing governor," whose "You Are My Sunshine" had already become one of the biggest hits in country music history to that point, specialized in sacred music. Davis sang his way into office, performing during campaign stops and even after he soared into office: his 1945 hit, "There's a New Moon over My Shoulder," was recorded and released while he was the state's sitting governor.

From this bubbling kettle of music and politics came Jimmy Thomason, who joined Davis early in the 1944 gubernatorial campaign. Members of Davis's Sunshine Band weren't simply sidemen but campaign aides as well, and Thomason became a central part of the apparatus. As soon as Davis, a Southern Democrat, defeated Lewis L. Morgan, who'd had the backing of Earl Long, Thomason was appointed secretary of the state Board of Tax Appeals.

Politics seems to have been almost as much a part of Thomason's life as music because Davis was not the first singing governor he was drawn to. Back in 1936, Thomason had portrayed Caesar the Fiddle Teaser on W. Lee "Pappy" O'Daniel's Austin, Texas, radio show. A seminal figure in the history of western swing, O'Daniel, a Mississippi transplant, had been the announcer for the Light Crust Doughboys, Bob Wills and Milton Brown's original western swing band. O'Daniel's garrulous, outsized personality—he was spoofed in the film *O Brother, Where Art Thou?*—gained him many fans, and in 1938 they urged him to run for the governorship. With a

Bible-thumping campaign themed around the Ten Commandments and the Golden Rule, O'Daniel attracted massive crowds and won the election in a rout. He served as Texas governor until 1941, when he was kicked upstairs to Congress. Thomason's attraction to Davis and the trappings of governing and campaigning, therefore, should not have been a surprise.

The cast of *The Jimmy Thomason Show*: Thomason, Gene Moles, unidentified, Tom Brumley, Hughie Smith.
(Photo courtesy of the Kern County Museum.)

Davis left office in 1948 (for the first time; he was elected again twelve years later) and bought a nightclub in Palm Springs called the Stables, and the Thomasons joined him there. Davis had a nationally televised variety show for CBS, broadcast live Wednesday nights from the Stables, and the Thomasons were regular performers—Jimmy on fiddle and vocals, Louise as a featured vocalist. But the Davises grew tired of the California desert after two years—it was more Davis's wife, Alvern, actually—and they went home to Louisiana in 1950.

The Thomasons eventually relocated to Bakersfield, where Louise's parents had moved in 1941, and Jimmy got a job as an announcer on Bakersfield's KAFY radio. Within three years, he had the first country music television show around. Henson debuted soon after.

An All-Star Lineup

The battle for the affections of San Joaquin Valley viewers between Henson and Thomason was decided not so much by ratings or advertising revenue as by Thomason's ever-shifting ambitions. Henson won the television ratings war by default when Thomason decided to follow the music-and-politics path of his two mentors, quitting his show in Bakersfield after several months to run in the June 1954 primary against state senator Jess R. Dorsey. Louise Thomason carried on as host for about two months to fulfill the terms of their contract. It was a mistake. At the polls, Dorsey won 64 percent of the vote, and the Thomasons, out of jobs, moved back to Waco.

That is not to say that Henson's KERO-TV show wouldn't have won anyway. Al Brumley Jr., who served as producer of *Trading Post* for five years, explained its special appeal. "You were family to those people [in the viewing audience]," he observed. "We were on five days a week. People just didn't miss it. None of those other shows compared to his." It helped that KERO boasted a powerful broadcast signal that boosted the program to the north, well past Fresno, and to the west, all the way over to the craggy coastline at San Luis Obispo.

Henson's opening-night cast of Mize, Woods, Johnny Cuviello, and Carlton Ellis was eventually fortified with several performers from local honky-tonks—musicians such as Owens, Lewis

Talley, Fuzzy Owen, Bonnie Owens, and Roy Nichols. The list of guest stars over the years reads like a who's who of country legends: Ernest Tubb, Tex Ritter, Tennessee Ernie Ford, Merle Travis, Johnny Cash, Gene Autry, Bob Wills, Lefty Frizzell, Spade Cooley, and toward the end, a young Barbara Mandrell. Unlikely performers such as Rudy Vallee, Lawrence Welk, and the Lennon Sisters also showed up from time to time.

In 1961, a viewer named Bill Rea called Brumley's office to say he had a "brother-in-law who sings," and Brumley agreed to audition him. The stranger walked into Brumley's office and picked up the Martin guitar he kept in a corner. Brumley later said he knew almost from the first note that this guy, a year out of San Quentin, was a keeper. Merle Haggard was added to the show's lineup two nights a week. Favorable fan mail arrived in stacks, and soon Haggard was performing five nights a week on *Trading Post*.

Henson was smart enough to know when to share the spotlight and with whom to share it. The other performers gave the show its color and variety; Henson was the anchor, the foundation, and he thoroughly convinced members of the viewing audience that they were all part of it. "Herb was the greatest emcee I ever heard in my life, and I've been around a lot of them," said Brumley, the son of gospel songwriting great Al Brumley Sr. and brother of Tom, the Buckaroos steel guitar player. "Herb could put people in the palm of his hand. He was smart, because he surrounded himself with good talent. He didn't try to hog the show."

Henson's TV commercials were every bit as entertaining as his nightly program. "You never knew what he was gonna say," Brumley said. "They'd put copy in front of him, but he didn't always pay attention to it. He'd just ad-lib if it suited him. He was a natural because he was himself. One day he was doing a live commercial for an army-navy store, and there were a bunch of rakes and hoes in the background, and right when he was talking one of those rakes fell on his head. He says, 'Uh-oh, I've been raked.' People remembered that. He could get away with just about anything."

Many of Henson's regular guests used the exposure as a springboard to greater fame. Some started young. There was Mandrell, of course, who joined the show as an occasional guest in 1959, at age ten. Her *Trading Post* exposure helped her land a job on *Town Hall Party*, based in Los Angeles, and she debuted on Red Foley's ABC-TV show, *Five Star Jubilee*, as a young teen. Everyone in her band played Bakersfield-built Mosrite guitars, although Barbara, encouraged by her music-store owner father, Irby Mandrell, preferred the pedal steel and saxophone. Years later, in 1980, NBC gave Mandrell her own Saturday-night variety show, *Barbara Mandrell & the Mandrell Sisters*, which made her a household name.

Ronnie Sessions joined *Trading Post* in 1958, at age nine, a year after taking his first guitar lesson from Andy Moseley of Mosrite guitar fame. He stayed on for three years, and the experience served him well: Sessions went on to make guest appearances on *The Jelly Sanders Show*, *The Tommy Dee Show*, and *The Billy Mize Show*. He reached the country charts in 1968 with Hoyt Axton's "Never Been to Spain" and worked for another twenty years in the music business.

Then there was Dallas Frazier, who debuted with Henson as a big-eyed fourteen-year-old. When he joined the *Trading Post* in 1953, Frazier had just signed with Capitol Records and recorded two minor hits: "Ain't You Had No Bringin' Up at All" and "Love Life at 14." "Don't ask what I knew about love then, because it wasn't much," he said. But Frazier, who went on to become a hall-of-fame songwriter, was learning plenty about live television. His voice was polished, but his stage demeanor gave him away as the babe he truly was: older Bakersfield viewers might remember Frazier as the bandanna-wearing kid who sang with one end of his neckerchief in each hand. As he warbled through a tune, Frazier kept time by yanking on the bandanna in a shoeshine motion against the back of his neck. Some might have considered it a nervous tic, but Frazier says he picked up the habit from Ferlin Husky, his first Bakersfield mentor, on whom it somehow looked dashing. At age fifteen, Frazier joined Cliffie Stone's *Hometown Jamboree*, a popular Los Angeles–based TV show that featured stars such as Tennessee Ernie Ford and Tommy Sands, and his star was on the rise.

Dallas Frazier, a protégé of Ferlin Husky and a contemporary of Tommy Collins, was a regular performer on Herb Henson's television show as a preteen. *(Photo courtesy of the Kern County Museum.)*

Henson himself recorded for the Shasta, Decca, and Capitol labels. His version of the Arlie Duff composition "Y'all Come" became his signature song, and he often closed his show with a modified version called "Hurry Back." Henson also performed regularly in concert and, as a host-headliner, routinely drew ten thousand fans to outdoor shows—most notably at Hart Park, just east of Bakersfield. "Country was hot then," Woods once said. "You could play a tambourine and draw a crowd."

No one drew crowds in Bakersfield better than Henson, whose local prominence rose to another level in 1960, when Valley Radio Corp. bought KIKK radio, switched its format to country music, and hired him as president and general manager. The station's call letters were changed to KUZZ, to play on Henson's celebrity, and Cousin Herb, whose TV show maintained his status in living rooms throughout the Central Valley, became "Kuzzin Herb."

On September 12, 1963, two dozen country music stars gathered at the eleven-month-old Bakersfield Civic Auditorium (now the Rabobank Theater) to celebrate the tenth anniversary of *Trading Post*. Glen Campbell, Buck Owens, Tommy Collins, and Roy Clark were among the guest stars. It was to be Cousin Herb's last hurrah.

At this point, Henson's life had become a paradox. His public face projected sheer optimism. He was as popular as ever now that he'd become Kuzzin Herb, and he was looking at big things ahead on TV too, having quietly made arrangements to switch from KERO to competing KBAK. And now he'd be hosting his ten-year anniversary concert, surrounded by some of the industry's biggest West Coast stars.

But privately, a shadow had crept over his life, and he had begun to suspect that his days were short. In October 1963, the month following the big anniversary show, he suffered a heart attack. He told his wife, Katherine, how painful it was to think that another man might raise their four sons. Then, about six weeks after the big show, Henson woke up in the middle of the night and roused his wife from her sleep. As young and pretty as she was, he told her, she should marry again after he died.

Henson's son Rick will never forget the events of November 26, 1963. He recalls that his celebrity father, finished with that evening's *Cousin Herb's Trading Post* broadcast, had come home for the day. Katherine was off playing with the KUZZ bowling team, so Cousin Herb went for a walk over to his sister's house, a regular activity prescribed by his doctors. A few minutes later, there was a knock at the door of the Henson home. Someone needed to use the telephone: Cousin Herb was lying in the street. The four boys—Rick, Dusty, Mike, and Rusty—were taken to their aunt and uncle's house. Their aunt tried to keep the boys' minds elsewhere, but that proved difficult. Every five minutes, it seemed, a TV announcer was telling viewers that Cousin Herb had died. News broadcasts had been full of grief and speculation for four days now, ever since the assassination of President Kennedy. And now this—the music man of Bakersfield, dead at thirty-eight. "It was like losing the president all over again," Brumley said.

Three years later, Buck Owens bought KUZZ. He saw no reason to change the call letters.

Filling the Void

Several entertainers stepped up to fill the void. Some, of course, had been there all along. Foremost were the Thomasons, who'd launched WACO-TV's own live-music program, *The Home Folks Show*, back in Waco before returning to Bakersfield in 1956. None of the others had credentials that approached those of Thomason, whose remarkably varied career, beginning with a stint back in Waco as a nimble-fingered string changer for Milton Brown and His Musical Brownies, was nearing its end. The others who populated Bakersfield TV were still in early- to midcareer.

Billy Mize had filled the Thomasons' slot during their self-imposed two-year exile with his own program, *The Chuck Wagon Gang*. His partner was Crofford, who later wrote songs for Walter Brennan and composed mid-1970s film soundtracks, including those for *Smokey and the Bandit* and *Every Which Way but Loose*. After the Thomasons returned, Mize rejoined the *Trading Post* gang, and he became the show's host in October 1963 when Cousin Herb was forced to scale back following his first heart attack. After Henson's death the show moved to KBAK, and Mize continued as the show's host for its final years. The Thomasons essentially switched places with Mize, landing on KERO-TV.

They all had one friend in common: Bill Woods, the longtime Bakersfield bandleader. The Woods connection was a factor even for one latecomer to the Bakersfield music-television scene, Dave Stogner, who arrived a year and a half after Henson's death. Two decades before he came to Bakersfield, Stogner had been a pipe fitter for a naval shipyard in Richmond, California. Because so many people had moved from the Midwest to work in defense jobs, country music had become big in the Bay Area, and Stogner, who had assumed that the war would put a crimp in his still-fledgling music career, had found work as an entertainer. He joined Elwin Cross and the Arizona Wranglers, a five-banjo, single-fiddle onslaught of Okified western swing; it was through the Wranglers that Stogner met and became friends with Woods, a bandmate then just a few months out of high school. They played together with the Wranglers for a year before quitting and forming their own band, the Arkansawyers, a sight to behold in their matching striped overalls.[1]

Eventually, Stogner moved back to Fresno, where he had been a regular on several radio programs, and Woods, after keeping the Arkansawyers together for a few more months, returned to Bakersfield. They launched their respective careers in the emerging medium of television at about the same time, 150 miles apart—Woods in September 1953 with Henson, Stogner in October 1953 with *The Dave Stogner Show* on Fresno's Channel 47, KJEO-TV. Twelve years later, with Woods's support and encouragement, Stogner brought his show to Bakersfield's KLYD (later KGET), bringing along that theme song so familiar to Fresno viewers:

Hello, friends and neighbors.
How do you do?
We're gonna play and sing
and we hope we bring
some happiness to you.

DAVE STOGNER AND HIS WESTERN SWING BAND

KLYD's Kountry Korner—5:00 P.M. Monday through Friday

The cast of *The Dave Stogner Show* on Channel 17, KLYD: Kay Adams, Red
Simpson, unknown, Dave Stogner, Daryl Stogner, unknown, Norm Hamlet,
circa 1966.
(Photo courtesy of the Kern County Museum.)

For the first six months, Stogner hosted a videotaped music
show that originated in Nashville, introducing prerecorded singers.
It evolved into an all-live, one-hour show with local heroes such
as Mize, Buck Owens, and Jan Howard, as well as Nashville-
based guests such as Dottie West and Roger Miller. The show also
featured a Stogner-crafted studio lineup of Norman Hamlet on
steel guitar, Red Simpson on piano and guitar, Sonny O'Brien on
drums, and, starting in 1965, Dave's teenage son Daryl on bass.
Dennis Payne sat in every once in a while, as did Ray Salter, Kay
Adams, and Stogner's old friend Woods.

Sensing a change in America's musical tastes, Stogner left
Bakersfield in 1967. "Dad had the feeling that something was
happening in country music," Daryl Stogner said. "You could see
the pendulum swinging, and he was ready to step away." Hamlet

went on to take a job playing steel guitar for Haggard's band, the Strangers, and Simpson signed with Capitol Records. Stogner, who recorded songs for the Decca and Mosrite labels, went into semiretirement. He died in 1989 at age sixty-nine.[2]

Thomason, whose show ran for more than eight years in its third and final KERO incarnation, was forced to quit in 1974 because of impending heart surgery. In 1975, he began teaching a course on the history of country music at what was then called California State College-Bakersfield (now California State University-Bakersfield), a pursuit that lasted several years. He died in 1994 at age seventy-six.

Mize's final run at more enduring fame came in 1972, when he taped two pilots of *The Billy Mize Music Hall*, which he hoped to sell into national syndication. Despite guest appearances by Merle Haggard on one show and Marty Robbins on the other—and a new-look Billy, with medallion, leisure suit, and sideburns—the show wasn't picked up.

There were other Bakersfield TV hosts along the way. The best of the rest was Jelly Sanders, a fiddle player who'd come west from Oklahoma in 1938 at age seventeen. He became a familiar sight on Bakersfield bandstands and television sets in the early 1950s and got his shot at the limelight for about six months in the early 1960s, filling in at KBAK during one of Mize's longer expeditions into Los Angeles. When Mize came back, Sanders returned to his role as sideman.[3]

National Notoriety

By the mid-1960s, television had begun to reflect the changing nature of American society. Vietnam and the Beatles conspired to alter the nation's mood and its entertainment tastes. Country music's popularity began to wane, and the broadcast schedule seemed to have fewer slots for locally originated programming. By the end of the decade, if viewers wanted country music variety shows, they had to turn to Glen Campbell or Johnny Cash. But many also turned to Buck Owens.[4]

Owens's first national TV appearances were in 1963 and 1964—guest spots on ABC's *Jimmy Dean Show* and NBC's *Kraft Music Hall*. In 1966, at the height of his hit-making powers, Owens forged a deal with two wealthy country music patrons, Oklahoma City furniture store owners Don and Bud Mathis, to create a new syndicated show. Dubbed *Buck Owens' Ranch Show*, the half-hour program, first broadcast on March 15, 1966, was taped on a soundstage at Oklahoma City's WKY-TV. It lasted for eight seasons.

Three years later, Owens landed what for many Americans was the defining role of his career. *Hee Haw*, first telecast on June 15, 1969, placed Owens in the living rooms of people who might never have owned a country record. He left the show in 1986 (it went on without him until the early 1990s) and turned his attention to the other great pursuit of his professional life: the radio business. By this time, Owens had built a media empire of some renown, with KUZZ still the flagship.

It's somehow fitting that Owens's vast broadcast holdings remained so closely associated with the single radio station that bore the name of Bakersfield's original broadcast pioneer, that lovable pitchman who is remembered fondly to this day.

Cousin Herb's widow, Katherine Henson Dopler, settled quietly back in Oklahoma after his death. For forty years, people continued to ask her about her late husband. "It amazes me that people in Oklahoma know him," said Dopler, who died in 2009. "A lot of people, I guess, have moved back here from California over the years, like we have. They tell me, 'Yeah, we watched him every night.'"[5]

Snapshot
The Mosrite

There could have been a little bit of Glen Campbell in Semie Moseley. Maybe just a dash of Elvis too. At six feet four inches tall and two hundred pounds, with thick, dark hair, a movie-star smile, near-virtuoso proficiency on the guitar, and a warm, appealing baritone voice, he might have been a hit maker himself. But Moseley was infatuated—no, obsessed—with guitars, so much so that while still a teen he started building them himself. And build guitars he did—perhaps fifty thousand, most of them manufactured at the Mosrite guitar factory, located in a warehouse just across the tracks from the Bakersfield Convention Center.[1]

The Mosrite guitar is highly regarded today among musicians and collectors—and justifiably so. Gene Moles, a Bakersfield session guitarist who worked as an assembly-line inspector for Mosrite, remembered Moseley's creation as a thing of beauty. "It was a well-designed instrument," said Moles. "It felt good to a guitar player when he grabbed it. It had a narrow neck and a low profile, so you didn't have to push down as hard on the strings to play it. And it had what we called 'speed frets,' where you could slide up and down the neck without getting held up on speed bumps" of high-profile frets.

At the peak of production in 1968, Semie, his brother Andy, and their crew of 107 employees were cranking out a thousand Mosrite guitars a month—acoustics, standard electrics, double necks, triple necks, basses, Dobros, and even mandolins. Glenn Campbell played one. So did Barbara Mandrell, Little Jimmy Dickens, Tommy Duncan, and Ronnie Sessions. Joe "King of the Strings" Maphis famously played a gaudy, 1954-vintage custom-built double-neck Mosrite with his name inlaid on the fingerboard. Don Rich, the Buckaroo mainstay who built his reputation on the Fender Telecaster, bought the first Mosrite to ever come off the assembly line—serial number 001. The Lemon Pipers, one-hit rock-chart wonders with 1968's number one "Green Tambourine," borrowed the Who's adolescent-rage shtick and smashed their Mosrites onstage at the end of their concerts. On his "Spanish Castle Magic," Jimi Hendrix used a

Mosrite Fuzzrite that is now in the Rock and Roll Hall of Fame. And later on, punk rockers such as the Ramones and B-52s adopted the guitar for such hits as "I Wanna Be Sedated" and "Rock Lobster," respectively.

Semie Moseley shows off a double-neck Mosrite guitar.
(Robert E. Price collection.)

But the client who turned Mosrite (pronounced "mows-right") into a household name, at least among guitar enthusiasts, was Nokie Edwards, lead guitarist for the kings of 1960s surf rock, the

Ventures. Edwards fell in love with the guitar, and by 1962, the entire Seattle-based band was playing Mosrites on songs such as "Walk, Don't Run" and the theme from *Hawaii Five-0*. The band, having signed a special distribution agreement with Mosrite, even featured the guitar on an album cover. The Ventures were Godzilla-huge in Japan, and orders for the Ventures-model Mosrite (suggested retail price: $462, steep for the mid-1960s) poured in. The brand had passionate adherents in the Far East, in the South Pacific, and beyond. Then the company's fortunes turned, and Mosrite forever became a footnote in the history of guitar craft.

Semie Moseley was born in Durant, Oklahoma, in 1935, two years after his brother Andy. The family followed a migratory path similar to that of many Bakersfield Okies, landing first in Chandler, Arizona, in 1938 and then in Bakersfield two years later. Semie's mother worked at a dry-cleaning business; his father with the Southern Pacific Railroad.

The brothers experimented with guitars from their early teen years, refinishing instruments and building new necks. In 1954, at the age of nineteen, Semie built a triple-neck guitar in his garage: the longest neck was that of a standard guitar, the second-longest neck was an octave higher, and the shortest neck was that of an eight-string mandolin. Later that year he presented a double-neck to Maphis, then a Los Angeles–area TV performer.

In 1956, floated by an investment from Ray Boatright, a Los Angeles–area minister, the brothers opened up shop as Mosrite of California. At the time, Semie was still working as a luthier for LA-based Rickenbacker guitars, but when he proudly told coworkers he was making his own product, he was told his services were no longer required. Now it was sink or swim.

At first, it was all custom, handmade guitars, built in garages, in tin storage sheds, or wherever the Moseleys could find a space to put equipment. In 1959, Andy moved to Nashville for a year to pitch the Mosrite name. He sold a few guitars to *Grand Ole Opry* performers and to road musicians. And this focus on custom guitars was enough to keep the factory going.

Then in 1961, Gene Moles happened to meet Nokie Edwards in a tavern in Tacoma, Washington. Moles was in the Pacific Northwest to play in Dusty Rhodes's band. He was late to work one night at the Britannica, having been engaged in moving his family north from Bakersfield, and he discovered Edwards on the bandstand. Apparently, Edwards had been conscripted to fill in on guitar.

Moles and Edwards hit it off immediately and in time grew so close that they'd get together and write songs; "Scratch" and "Night Run" were two of their early efforts together. Two years later, Edwards and his wife stopped by the Moles home south of Bakersfield on their way to a Ventures recording session in Los Angeles. It was during that visit that Edwards fell in love with Moles's Mosrite—serial number 002. He asked Moles to introduce him to Moseley. Moles obliged, and Edwards promptly struck a deal with Moseley to buy what would later become known as the Ventures model. That handshake launched the company into the big time and created for the instrument an instant mystique.

Sales of the Bakersfield-built guitar gained steadily over the next five years, and Semie soon became a rich man. With his company having achieved a certain stability, he turned toward his other great interest: the church. Staunchly religious, having been raised in a Pentecostal household, he increased the pace and scope of his touring, bringing gospel music to churches of all denominations across the country. At one point he auditioned for a job as a movie stand-in for Elvis Presley, and he was hired. But by the time the studio asked him to formally sign on, he had learned enough about the role and the movie industry in general to sour on it all. Citing religious reasons, he begged out.

Business opportunities came and went. Sears, Roebuck and Company anted up millions of dollars in a buyout offer, but Moseley turned it down. He purchased the Dobro Manufacturing Co., and according to Moles, the company "had Dobros coming out of [its] ears." Still, Moseley expanded the Mosrite line: the Ventures model; the Celebrity 1, 2, and 3 acoustic models; a larger, thick gospel-acoustic model (Semie gave away dozens to churches across the country); the Serenade acoustic; and the electric Californian, which had a Mosrite neck and a Dobro body.

He and Andy also branched off into the recording business with Mosrite Records. Irby Mandrell, an Oceanside, California, music-store owner who sold Mosrites, saw to it that his talented teen daughter, Barbara, was signed to the label. "Semie was responsible for Barbara's first recording session, 'Don't Hold Your Breath,' written by Billy Mize, although Freddie Hart gets credit in Barbara's book," said Brian Lonbeck of Bakersfield, who played lead guitar—a

Mosrite, of course—in Mandrell's band for a decade. When she was involved in a serious car accident in 1984, Semie built her a cane that was also a guitar. Or perhaps it was vice versa.

By now things were rolling, and Andy focused his attention on the record label while Semie stayed with his first love, the guitar company.

Then, in a period of a few months, it all collapsed. In 1968, Mosrite's distribution arrangement with the Ventures came to an end after five years, and a new, much-ballyhooed deal with the Thomas Organ Company, maker of the Vox guitar, proved disastrous. Mosrite's partner was unable, or unwilling, to market the guitar, and Mosrite couldn't survive the hit. Was the ill-fated deal a premeditated act of corporate bad faith designed to strangle Mosrite sales? There was no way to prove it. "We had no witnesses or anything," said Andy Moseley, who went on to start a Nashville recording studio, Sound Control Studio, that his son Mark now runs. "That's what we came to believe. But I'm not sure that's the way it was."

Mosrite filed for bankruptcy on Valentine's Day in 1969. Emerging from the bankruptcy later that year, the Moseleys tried to deal directly with stores, and they sold 280 guitars in 1969 before they came to the shop one day and found locks on their doors. Two years later, Semie was able to retain the Mosrite name for himself, and in 1970, he started making guitars again in the Bakersfield-area farming burg of Pumpkin Center. He moved his factory three times in the next twenty years: to Oklahoma City in the mid-1970s; to Jonas Ridge, North Carolina, in 1981; and to Booneville, Arkansas, in 1991. Six months after moving to Arkansas, he became ill with bone cancer. Just six weeks later, in August 1992, he died.

Mosrites are highly sought-after collectors' items today. The first three 1963 production-line guitars, originally sold to Rich, Moles, and Edwards, were at one point worth an estimated $30,000 each in Japan. And Bakersfield-era Ventures models are worth $3,000 to $4,000 in new condition. There's still a certain demand for them. Online blogs and chat rooms devoted to the guitar still thrive. "They really represented some of the finest craftsmanship in guitar-making anywhere," said Artie Niesen, owner of Bakersfield's Front Porch Music and a collector who owns more than one hundred Mosrites. "They were great guitars." They still are, nearly five decades after the sun set on the Mosrite empire.

CHAPTER 6

Buck Owens

B uck Owens never did get rid of that off-white, secondhand Fender Telecaster he bought off a bandmate. Though his trusty axe, heavy as a sledgehammer and not much more attractive, continued to ring as earnestly as the day he purchased it, the years were not altogether kind.

One night at the Blackboard in 1955, Owens propped his guitar unsteadily against an amp, and it crashed to the floor with an awful, discordant thud. When Owens picked it up, he saw that a portion of the ivory nut at the top of the neck had chipped away, springing loose a string. There was more music to be played that night, and he was suddenly without his guitar.

Fiddle player Jelly Sanders stepped in and surveyed the damage. He turned to Owens. "You got a comb?"

"And I said, 'Yeah'—'cause in those days you carried a comb," Owens recalled. "And we took out a little piece [of comb tooth] and stuck it back in there and wet it with brandy so it would stick." And so it did, better than he could have imagined.

Twenty-five years later, after Buck Owens had become Buck Owens, he showed the barroom repair job to a guitar technician, who eagerly volunteered his services: he could fix that broken nut and make the guitar as good as the day Owens bought it. Owens politely declined. You don't fool with tradition, he reasoned, whether it's a song or a singer or a guitar. That comb tooth stayed right where it was.[1]

It was classic Buck—stubborn, pragmatic, and not terribly worried about what people might think. The record-buying public, and eventually even Nashville, would learn to love him for it. They loved the hits, anyway. The man—well, that was something else. Owens's eight-by-ten glossy might have turned up on a few Nashville dartboards over the years.

Almost always, the irritation stemmed from Owens's tendency to find enough "country" in a noncountry song to make it country. That was the case with Chuck Berry's rock 'n' roll standard, "Memphis," which appeared on Owens's *Tiger by the Tail* album in March 1965, the very same month Owens placed an advertisement in Nashville's *Music City News* proclaiming, "I Shall Make No Record That Is Not a Country Record."

That might have seemed a contradiction to some, but Owens meant everything he said. He had his own definition of "country," and it did not necessarily jibe with that of every fence-building, genre-wary country music disc jockey in America. Though Owens today is remembered as the epitome of unadorned honky-tonk music, back in the day he tweaked many a programmer's ear by expanding popular music's traditional and commercial boundaries. For the most part programmers went along with him.

Like Bob Wills before him, Owens had big ears. He heard the music from across the tracks, across the cotton fields, across the rigid social boundaries that kept America apart from itself. Had he been born under a different star, Owens might have been a master of the blues, but he happened to be born white and raised on the Texas-Oklahoma border in the middle of the Great Depression. If he was going to play any kind of music at all, it was destined to be country music—not that he didn't gnaw on the fence a little.

First, there were those "Corky Jones" recordings—two rockabilly sides, including "Hot Dog," cut in 1956 for Pep Records. "Corky Jones" was the pseudonym Owens chose to obscure the songs' true authorship.

Why? Back then, country and rock 'n' roll occupied opposing, hostile camps; the twain simply did not meet. Country music was increasingly for grown-ups, whereas rock 'n' roll was popularly associated with juvenile delinquency and teen rebellion. Owens's country music career, still embryonic, might not have withstood a blackballing by the rockophobic country-radio establishment.

He wasn't known for his saxophone playing, but Buck Owens was giving it a try in this undated photo.
(Photo courtesy of the Buck Owens Private Foundation, Inc.)

But rockabilly—or some combination of country with rhythm and blues—was old hat to Owens. In 1956, the year Elvis recorded

"Blue Suede Shoes," Owens, along with bandmates Bill Woods, Henry Sharp, Oscar Whittington, and Jelly Sanders, had already been playing their loud, driving, danceable version of country music for a half decade.

So it shouldn't have been a shock to Nashville purists or anyone else when, starting in 1965, Owens and his Buckaroos started cranking out rock and rock-pop songs such as "Memphis," "Johnny B. Goode," and even Simon & Garfunkel's "Bridge over Troubled Water." Nevertheless, it was.

Owens brought in a rock drummer for 1964's "My Heart Skips a Beat," and a fan wrote to tell him he was going to stop buying Buckaroos records unless Owens started cutting back on the beat. For 1968's "Who's Gonna Mow Your Grass," Buck used a fuzz-tone guitar-distortion device, popular among rock bands of the era—think "Satisfaction" by the Rolling Stones or "Incense and Peppermints" by the Strawberry Alarm Clock—and in the process instigated a similar revolt by the not-so-silent minority.

"People would get upset if it wasn't what they thought country was," Owens once said. "And there's no latitude for deciding that. I've had different influences from time to time in my life ... but as I look back, my biggest influences might have been Bob Wills and Little Richard. What do you make of that combination? But that's where I was coming from."

Owens's rockabilly proclivities were made manifest on some of the work he did as a session guitarist for Capitol Records, notably his work for the Farmer Boys. During the 1950s, Owens led a double life, recording by day in Hollywood with a cadre of top session musicians (including future luminaries such as Glen Campbell) at Capitol's studios at the corner of Hollywood and Vine and then making the winding trek over the Grapevine to play the Bakersfield honky-tonks by night. He became one of the record label's most sought-after studio guitar players, so much so he inspired a little jealousy and consternation among some of those he recorded with.

Dwight Yoakam retells, from Owens's perspective, one of Owens's favorite stories about that time. His phone had been ringing all day, and Owens figured he knew who it was, and he didn't want to answer.

> *It got to be about ten o'clock at night, and here's this "bang bang bang bang" on my front door. I'm about to go to bed. What in the world? Who's up at the house? Who's at the front door? Walked over to the front door, opened it. It's Tommy Collins. He lived on the other side of town ... He just waltzed past me and go, "Buck, I know you been down there playing other people's records at Capitol. Buck, you gotta tell me this—please, if you're going down there playing on other people's records, tell me you're not playing any of them licks you're playing on my records."*

"He was that worried about Buck's signature thing on his records," Yoakam said. "And if you listen to those Tommy Collins records [from 1954–56], some of that harsh Telecaster, Fender twang, that Bakersfield guitar edge, that razor blade thing, it's Buck."[2]

Owens did more than just record country music—he laid down the guitar on comedian Allan Sherman's albums and supplied ukulele on other sessions. His years at Capitol made him a seasoned master of studio craft. In the high-pressure major-label studio environment where time equals money, Buck also learned to work efficiently. In their heyday, Buck and his Buckaroos could cut three songs in one three-hour session. Because the Buckaroos were also Buck's road band, they could solidify the new material on the bandstand before coming in to cut it. Buck boasted that he could finish a whole album in one week's time. This, naturally, made for a more profitable back end once the record hit the streets.

But in the late 1950s, those heady days of stardom were still on the horizon. Though he had finally signed with Capitol and recorded a couple of singles, Buck's records had yet to make a dent on the airwaves. He began to grow restless in Bakersfield and in

1958 pulled up stakes and moved to Tacoma, Washington, where he had an opportunity to run a tiny, low-watt radio station.[3]

Buck Owens and Tommy Collins chat in a Capitol Records recording studio, circa 1957. Jelly Sanders on fiddle, unidentified on guitar.
(Photo courtesy of the Buck Owens Private Foundation, Inc.)

Young Mr. Ulrich

The station featured live music—starring Owens, of course—but also local talent. One of the Tacoma-area musicians who found their way to the station was a teenager named Don Ulrich, who went by the stage name Don Rich.

Born in 1941 in Olympia, Washington, Rich was a guitarist, fiddler, singer, and songwriter. He got his professional start at age fifteen playing lead guitar in the band of a regional star, Ted

Mitchell. He was still only nineteen when he met Owens, and the two started playing together at dances and on a Tacoma-area television program. At that point, Don primarily played fiddle.

The duo split when Rich, honoring a promise to his mother, enrolled in college, but their separation didn't last long. In December 1960, Rich quit school and asked Owens to hire him back into the band. (Owens liked to joke that, in a please-take-me-back letter, his friend spelled it "c-o-l-e-g-e"; in another version of the story, Rich asked for a "j-o-b-b.") Owens, who had returned to California six months earlier after "Under Your Spell Again," one of his early recordings for Capitol, started getting serious airplay around the country, gladly agreed to it.[4]

The Buckaroos' best-known lineup: Doyle Holly, Willie Cantu, Tom Brumley, Don Rich, Buck Owens.
(Photo courtesy of the Buck Owens Private Foundation, Inc.)

By 1961, they were dual protagonists in a newly restructured band now dubbed (after a suggestion by temporary bassist Merle Haggard) the Buckaroos. Their first recording session as a team produced a batch of hits, including "You're for Me" and "Kickin'

92

Our Hearts Around." A signature Owens-Rich collaboration also ensued: "(Excuse Me) I Think I Have a Heartache."

Owens was the unchallenged leader of the band—the star—but Rich's presence couldn't be ignored. His high-tenor harmonies, which shadowed every nuance of Owens's lead vocals, lent a certain air of refinement to the music that made the Buckaroos' sound instantly recognizable. With Rich onboard, the Buckaroos' sound was all about finesse in the service of the beat, about being on point, about nimbleness and agility. The music had a pure joy about it, a pleasure in its own virtuosity. Youthful, grinning Rich brought more than a coltish playfulness to the proceedings; he brought an uncanny smoothness and fluidity as well.

The Buckaroos pose outside New York's Carnegie Hall in March 1966. The photo was used for the *Carnegie Hall Concert* album cover. From left, Willie Cantu, Tom Brumley, Buck Owens, Don Rich, Doyle Holly.
(Photo courtesy of the Buck Owens Private Foundation, Inc.)

Rich's most lasting contribution, however, was as an instrumentalist—not as a fiddle player, but as a master of the Fender Telecaster. And he was not just any instrumentalist: once he seized the Buckaroos' lead guitar chair, Rich quickly emerged as an innovator whose style merited scrutiny.

Owens didn't truly know what sort of musician he had in Rich until March 1961, when Rich made the full-time switch. By late 1962, "what he did was, he learned to play my playing style, and then he took it up a notch or two," Buck said in his posthumous 2013 autobiography, *Buck 'Em.* "I spent a while teaching him how to play certain things, and before long he completely surpassed me. Eventually he was playing licks I couldn't even play."[5]

And so it was Rich, not Owens, who emerged as a guitar innovator whose style would influence generations of pickers. Rich recognized the Telecaster's unique qualities, its ability to bridge the distance between the raw, barbed-wire high notes that rang in your teeth and the pithy low tones that rattled your sternum. His playing style employed the familiar steps of the blues scale—the minor pentatonic—and mixed, in rapid succession, twangy, bent notes up the neck and those low open strings. Here were mini-dramas of conflict and resolution that momentarily raised tensions and released them, that suspended the listener in space and then placed him securely back on the rooted earth. This internal dialogue served as a counterpoint to Owens's singing in a way that gave the music a restless, bounding athleticism.

There was a certain badness to Rich's characteristic and insistent use of the minor third and dominant seventh—blue notes—which rubbed against the grain of Owens's rhythm guitar, which strummed the customary major chords, and against the duo's arching harmony vocals, also very much in the major. This internal tension—a musical squaring of the circle—gave the music its great tensile strength and pop.

It was inevitable that such genius would inspire followers of equally recognized virtuosity. "Don Rich of the Buckaroos is a personal hero of mine," Billy Gibbons of ZZ Top said in a 2012 interview. "Nobody could play a Telecaster like him. We loved

Buck a whole lot—he's originally a Texan, you know. You guys should consider carving Bakersfield's answer to Mount Rushmore with all those greats taking over a mountain."[6]

"Why Don't He Just Do What He Does?"

When Owens's success did come, it came relentlessly. Starting in 1963, the number one songs began piling up like junk mail after a two-week vacation. Owens was making three albums a year and appearing regularly on television with the likes of Dick Clark and Ed Sullivan. As his success mounted, Owens increasingly was given carte blanche with regard to his style and song selection in the studio.

"Each time I would release one of those things, the label would shudder: 'Oh my God, all these weird things he's doin' ... Why don't he just do what he does?'" Owens recalled. "But doin' what you do makes you stagnant ... I was always afraid, but never afraid enough not to try it."

His confidence peaked in 1967 when he released "Johnny B. Goode" as a single. It went to the top of the country charts but earned him some enemies. "Man, there were guys burning me in effigy," Owens said.

> Guy from a radio station, WPLO in Atlanta, sent me pictures of a bonfire—this is the truth—with the explanation, "This is a bonfire we held last week, and we burned every Buck Owens record in the radio station." They were really upset with me. But how could they say that song wasn't country? 'Way down in Louisiana, down by New Orleans ...' Go on, listen to his lyrics. If that ain't country, tell me what that is. My opinion was, and always has been, if Chuck Berry had been a white man, he'd a'been a country singer.

Owens might not have been on the ramparts of social change

during those heady days of the civil rights struggle, but by recording a song by a black performer, he was sending his listeners a subtle message.

Owens's electrified twang and his tendency to push at the boundaries of the genre weren't the only things that set him apart. There was something about the way he went at things in general, such as building his own mini-empire in California instead of buying a Nashville mansion like everybody else who was anybody. "My problem with Nashville was simple," Owens said. "I don't like the way they do talent, and I don't like the way they cut records."[7]

Expanding His Reach

The record-buying public certainly liked him though, as was evidenced by Owens's first significant foray into television since the days of Herb Henson. His widely syndicated *Buck Owens' Ranch Show*, the half-hour program he taped in Oklahoma City starting in 1966, lasted for eight seasons. It might have lasted longer if even greater success hadn't overtaken him.

Oklahoma City furniture store owners Don and Bud Mathis owned and sponsored that first season, but Owens then bought them out. He saw no reason to change the production arrangement at Oklahoma City's WKY, however: four times a year, he traveled back to Oklahoma with the Buckaroos, met up with his guest stars, and in marathon taping sessions, shot thirteen "as-live" shows over three challenging days. Owens's son Mike Owens became the show's announcer and ultimately its director, and another son, Buddy Owens, a.k.a. Buddy Alan, occasionally performed on it. Guest stars included Merle Haggard, Hank Williams Jr., Waylon Jennings, Charley Pride, Conway Twitty, Wanda Jackson, Jimmy Dean, Roy Clark, and Tommy Collins.

Owens eventually developed a system: starting in 1969, he and the band would record the instrumental tracks at Buck Owens Studios in Oildale and then sing live in Oklahoma City, with the boys "air-strumming" in the background. At its peak, the *Ranch Show* was in one hundred markets around the country, fifty-two weeks a year. It ran until 1973—some 295 original shows plus dozens of additional programs repackaged with new and previously broadcast performances, totaling 380 shows in all.

In Bakersfield on a late-1960s Saturday afternoon, a country music couch potato could watch, in succession, *Buck Owens' Ranch Show, The Wilburn Brothers Show, The Porter Wagoner Show* (featuring Dolly Parton), and wrap it up that evening with *Hee Haw.*

Hee Haw eventually proved to be the undoing of the *Ranch Show.* When Buck Owens renegotiated a new deal with Yongestreet Productions, which then owned *Hee Haw*, the producers made him shut down the *Ranch.* They had noticed what everyone in the band had long known all too well: Owens was playing the same thing on both shows—literally. "It had become painfully obvious," said Jim Shaw, Owens's keyboardist. "Very often we'd do the same song on the *Ranch Show* and then *Hee Haw.* We'd use the exact same instrumental tracks, and Buck would just sing them fresh at the taping. They got aggravated. They said, 'Hey, you're competing against yourself.'"

Hee Haw, first telecast on June 15, 1969, was more than enough television exposure for Owens anyway. As much as he did for the pure, electrified side of country music, Owens probably did just as much, through *Hee Haw*, to bring country music culture into the forefront of American mass consciousness. What Owens actually thought of the show depended on what day you asked him.

The *Hee Haw* Conundrum

Did the show—a hillbillified version of *Laugh-In* that he coemceed for a decade alongside Roy Clark—bring country music into homes that hadn't and might otherwise never have properly appreciated it? Did it create new fans? Or did it just force the show's stars to make southern-fried caricatures of themselves and undermine country music's claim to cultural seriousness? Buck admitted giving interviewers contradictory answers on his feelings about the show. Perhaps Owens's judgment on the matter was colored a bit by all that money he made—$400,000 per year for twenty days of work per year over seventeen years, money that solidified his Bakersfield empire.

Hee Haw was a cultural phenomenon that penetrated to some far corners of the nation. Owens was always heartened when he heard new artists cite *Hee Haw* as a defining memory from their youth. Future generations have the Internet, a resource that makes it possible to discover a different televised Buck Owens. There, in the vast archival universe contained on the web, exist lost performances of Buck and the Buckaroos that effectively bury the camp and silliness of *Hee Haw* and bring the band brilliantly back to life in live performances that reshuffle the deck of history.

Reba McEntire joins a mugging Buck Owens on *Hee Haw*. McEntire guest-starred on the show six times over a decade's time.
(Photo courtesy of GPSI.)

Imagine an antithesis to *Hee Haw*—a television experience that would allow Buck Owens and the Buckaroos to simply do what they did best: play their music, live and unfiltered, in real time.

Guest stars such as Wynn Stewart, Tommy Collins, and Merle Haggard might drop by, and the Buckaroos, in all their Nudie Cohen–suited splendor, would stretch out in instrumental forays. And except for some agreeably bland studio patter, the show would be wall-to-wall music—and in color.

What you would have is *Buck Owens' Ranch Show*, which continues to exist in the eternal present that is the Internet, where it is available on demand. Reconsidered as a pair, the *Ranch Show*—its commonly used shorthand name—and *Hee Haw* reveal Buck at his pinnacle of power and influence and in the depths of ultimately regrettable self-parody.[8]

Ray Charles and Buck Owens appeared together twice on *Hee Haw*. They sang "Cryin' Time" on September 29, 1970, and "Together Again" on December 1, 1970. *(Photo courtesy of GPSI.)*

Yin to His Yang

Rich struck out on his own only a few times—and not very far when he did. He and the Buckaroos made a number of albums without Owens, including *The Buckaroos Play the Hits* and *The Buck Owens Songbook*, an all-instrumental sing-along collection that might be considered one of the first country karaoke albums. Rich released his own LP, *Fiddlin' Man*, in 1971, though by this time he was far better known for his virtuosity on the guitar. He had become a national celebrity, thanks to *Hee Haw*. But as Buck wrote in his 2013 autobiography, "Don was never interested in stepping out entirely on his own and becoming a star. All he really wanted to do was make music with me and the Buckaroos."[9]

Rich was a playful man, slow to anger and quick to diffuse a potentially bad situation, but as he approached his midthirties, his life took a dark turn. In early 1974, during a performance in New Zealand, Owens noted that Rich had forgotten the words to a song he'd sung many times before—a lapse Owens had never previously witnessed in his right-hand man. It was at about that time Owens wondered whether his valuable sideman had developed a drinking problem. Owens flew in Don's wife, all the way to New Zealand, and the three of them sat down for an intervention of sorts. Rich cut back, but not all that much.[10]

In the tragic, penultimate chapter of Rich's life, Owens grew increasingly worried about his friend's fondness for motorcycles. He had seen too many riders die, and he begged Rich to sell his Harley-Davidson. "Chief, I'll make you a deal," Rich finally said, as Owens recounts in *Buck 'Em*. "I promise that I'll only ride it on dirt." Owens didn't know enough about motorcycles to know that Harleys were strictly road bikes. On July 17, 1974, Rich, a month shy of his thirty-third birthday, struck a highway center divider on his way to the Central Coast. Owens, forty-five years old at the time, lost his partner, brother, and best friend.[11]

"I was in such bad shape that I was convinced he'd just show up one day like nothing had happened," Owens wrote in *Buck 'Em*.

*I kept waiting, but he didn't come back. Years later,
Jim Shaw [Buckaroo keyboardist and longtime
confidant] told me he thought I'd had a nervous
breakdown when Don died. To tell you the truth,
it was a lot worse than that ... I honestly thought
I wasn't going to be able to survive and there were
days when I really didn't care if I survived or not ...
On the day Don died, something permanently
changed inside me.*[12]

Indeed, Buck Owens was never quite the same.

The Crystal Palace

After he left *Hee Haw* in 1986, Owens focused on his other great
love, the radio business. He had purchased KUZZ radio (then at
800 AM) in 1966 and a year later bought 107.9 FM, which he
turned into KBBY, a rock station. The FM station went country in
1969, reverted back to rock in 1977, and finally became KUZZ's
primary dial location in 1988. Owens's broadcast empire at various
times included Bakersfield TV station KDOB (later KUZZ-TV)
and Phoenix radio powerhouse KNIX.

In 1999, his family company sold its two Phoenix radio stations
to Jacor Communications for $142 million. Owens Broadcasting,
owned by Buck and family members Michael, Buddy, and Mel
Owens, sold country station KNIX (102.5 FM) to Cincinnati-based
Jacor for $84 million. And Owens MAC Radio, a partnership
between Owens Broadcasting and MAC America Communications,
sold adult contemporary station KESZ (99.9 FM) to Jacor for
$58 million. Eventually, Buck cut back his radio holdings to just
KUZZ-AM, KUZZ-FM, and their sister station, KCWR.

That left the restless former star with time and unspent energy.
Owens wasn't doing much recording other than his surprising hit
with Dwight Yoakam, a remake of "Streets of Bakersfield," and
"Act Naturally" with Ringo Starr. He continued to be a force in
the city's civic and business life, but something was missing.

In 1996, that something came to fruition when the Crystal Palace, Owens's restaurant-museum-showplace, opened to considerable hoopla. A $6.7 million investment, it proved worthy of all the money and effort put into it. With its huge collection of photos and country music memorabilia, it put Bakersfield right back on the map as a musical pilgrimage stop.[13]

And Buck was indescribably proud of it. "My money," he told Nicholas Dawidoff a year after its opening. "Money I made. I could have built it a lot of places. Here's where it all happened. Here's where it belongs."[14]

Many top names packed the club those first dozen years, but its most important headliner was Owens himself, who after many years behind a desk gave himself back the opportunity to do what he did best.

Owens took those Crystal Palace shows seriously. That was certainly the case the evening of March 25, 2006. Owens arrived at the club early and had a chicken-fried steak dinner, his favorite meal. Afterward he told band members that he wasn't feeling well and was going to skip that night's performance. But on his way out, a group of fans stopped him and introduced themselves. They had traveled all the way from Oregon to hear him perform. Owens spun around and returned to the stage. As he told the audience that night, he just couldn't bear to have anyone driving back to Oregon disappointed, so he hoisted his trusty Telecaster over his shoulder one more time. Later that night, a few hours after the performance, he suffered a fatal heart attack. Buck Owens, the reigning prince of Buckersfield, was dead at age seventy-six.[15]

For all his skills as a businessman, for all his renowned independence and stubbornness, for all his importance to country music history, the thing Owens always liked to do best was pick and sing. And that's what he did every Friday and Saturday night up until the day he died. Owens's ten-year run as the Crystal Palace's headliner made for a fitting exit for a performer whose career had started in those dimly lit honky-tonks not far away.

CHAPTER 7

Merle Haggard

The courtroom transcript contains only spoken words, not stage directions. Still, as you read the document, it's hard not to imagine the scene.[1]

Kern County Municipal Court, January 1958: Bakersfield defense attorney Ralph McKnight has asked the judge to grant his client probation and spare him a prison sentence. But he can offer little to recommend that sort of judicial benevolence beyond the unwavering maternal love of one woman, seated behind him in the gallery. "This mother has tried very hard," McKnight says, nodding toward her deferentially.

The Honorable Norman F. Main looks down at the lengthy rap sheet, glances across the courtroom at anxious Flossie Haggard, and then studies the wiry young punk sitting sullenly at the defense table. "If he had tried half as hard as his mother did ..."

And down deep, twenty-year-old Merle Haggard knows that the judge speaks the simple, undeniable truth—a truth that will echo in his ears, almost word for word, for many years to come. "Mama tried to raise me better, but her pleading I denied ..."

"Mama Tried," which reached number one in 1968, was typical of the songs that launched Haggard into the pantheon of great country songwriters. But in the half century since that courtroom scene, Haggard's music has more often celebrated the sons and daughters who tried—the hand-to-mouth, paycheck-to-paycheck, rent-to-own people who drove the trucks, picked the cotton, punched the time clocks, and yes, sometimes committed the crimes, both petty and grievous, as they struggled against a system that seemed weighted against them. His music honored not just the working class but the tier below as well, the hungry class. Haggard has sung about back doors, swinging doors, and cell doors, but he has never strayed far from the defining themes of his life's work: blue-collar pride and personal dignity—basic Okieness.

Haggard has always expressed those things with a graceful, lilting baritone and a poetic genius that belies his well-deserved reputation as a wild, hard-partying rebel. His harrowing Huck Finn–meets–Harry Houdini youth, spent hopping freight trains, singing for beer, stealing cars, surviving automobile wrecks, botching burglaries, and escaping from jails, was more than ample fodder for the story lines that make up his prolific body of work. Punk, prodigy, potato packer, ditch digger, cotton picker, convict, patriot, iconoclast—Haggard has been all those things and more.

It is a vision of life so deeply felt and authentic that it transcends any number of artificial political or cultural constructs. The Grateful Dead, those acid-tripping hippies from San Francisco, covered "Mama Tried" on their 1971 album recorded live at the Fillmore East, a recording known among Deadheads as *Skull and Roses*. It is interesting that the Dead would pay tribute to Haggard at the very peak of his 1970s redneck fluorescence. It was one of those delicious cultural contradictions that come down the pike all too rarely. That Haggard's music spoke across the cultural divide to the stoned counterculture was surely a testament to its homespun integrity, to its true connection to the earth. Maybe it meant that Haggard, who it turned out was known to smoke a little weed himself, was something of a crypto-hippie too. That point is debatable. What's not is that Haggard's music occupies its own special place above the banal games of politics. Like all great artists, he is a principle unto himself, operating stubbornly above the fray.

A teenage Merle Haggard, at home in Oildale, already had the look of a tough.
(Photo courtesy of the Kern County Museum.)

The Roots of His Raising

Haggard never lived in Oklahoma but was born and raised in
Oildale, an unincorporated hamlet just across the Kern River from
Bakersfield that might just as well be part of the Sooner state.
Oildale differs from poorer rural corners of Oklahoma only in
terms of climate and longitude. Culturally, it might be considered
the westernmost settlement of Oklahoma. Migrants from the
southwest plains had been bringing their plainspoken ways to
California a decade before the first Dust Bowl storms of the mid-
1930s. The Haggards were part of that first wave of Okies.

James Haggard, Merle's father, was a hardworking man and
a devoted husband. As a young man, he played the fiddle in local
saloons, but his wife Flossie, a faithful member of the Church of
Christ, insisted he stop once they were married. But music never
left their lives. The family sang quartet music from the popular
Stamps-Brumley songbooks and gathered around the family radio
most evenings to listen to the eclectic collection of stars that came
into their home.

Before settling in California in the late 1920s, the Haggards
and their two small children, Lillian and Lowell, were migrants,
moving from town to town around the vast nation, a fresh crisis
seemingly attending their every move. Hard luck seemed to track
them. In 1929, James suffered serious burns to his hands in an
industrial accident in Pennsylvania, and while he rehabilitated
in Chicago, Flossie's health deteriorated. James's physician
recommended they move to California for her sake, and as soon
as James was well enough, they did, moving in with the family of
Flossie's sister in rural Arvin, thirty miles south of Bakersfield.
Their arrival coincided with the stock market crash, a Wall Street
cataclysm that would trigger the worst economic depression in
modern history.

It was not economics but the valley's searing heat that proved
most daunting to the Haggards, and after two months James took
his family back east again—this time to Checotah, Oklahoma—
to try their hand at farming. Their leased plot was sold out from
under them, but they quickly found a second farm and prospered

well enough to afford a 1931 Ford Model A and—glory of glories—a dog.

Things changed one dark and stormy night in early 1934, when a neighbor knocked at the Haggards' front door. The visitor explained that his wife was sick, and he needed to get her to the doctor. Could he borrow the family's Ford? James told him the Ford would never make it across the muddy dirt roads, but James could take the man and his wife in the horse and wagon. The man declined the offer and left. One night three months later, the Haggards awoke to find their barn in flames. It was arson, the family always suspected, payback for refusing the use of their car that night during the torrential downpour. Lillian remembered the devastation: "The animals all got out, but the car didn't." The fire also destroyed all their feed and seed grains. Discouraged, James and Flossie decided to quit the farm and move to town, where James and a partner opened a two-pump Mobil gas station.

But James Haggard seemed to be snake-bitten. Within a few months he was felled by appendicitis. Downcast, he looked at his circumstances and felt California beckoning once again. Flossie was in agreement, and so, fortified by her sister's enthusiasm (and a forty-dollar "loan" Lillian said the family didn't really need) and the promise of some farm work, they set out on July 15, 1935. The Haggard family, assembled in a battered 1926 Chevy, all their worldly possessions in tow, headed down Route 66 to the Golden State.

A Child Grieves

Merle Ronald Haggard was born almost two years later. By then, James Haggard had landed a forty-dollar-per-week job as a carpenter with the Santa Fe Railroad, allowing him to support his family better than most Depression-era fathers. He had also acquired a refrigerated box car that had been moved off the rails and onto a lot a hundred yards south of a heavily used main track line. This he fashioned into the basic frame of a sturdy, 1,200-square-foot home.

Merle demonstrated a love for music almost from the start.

He recalls pointing to the radio and asking for "stewed ham"—toddler talk, his mother eventually realized, for country singer Stuart Hamblen, whose four o'clock afternoon broadcast out of Los Angeles was a family favorite.

The idyll of childhood was whisked away one night in June 1946, when Merle, then nine, came home from a Wednesday-night prayer meeting to find his father paralyzed from a stroke. James Haggard died the next day. Flossie Haggard was forced to take a $35-a-week job as a bookkeeper for a meatpacking company, and suddenly it was just mother and son, the older siblings Lowell and Lillian having already set out on their own.

Merle blamed himself for his father's death. "That was just what his nine-year-old mind believed," recalled Lillian, who was twenty-five at the time. "He couldn't figure out why his father had died." Some months earlier, Merle had fallen ill with coccidioidomycosis, a potentially fatal soilborne fungus commonly known in the US Southwest as valley fever. Little was known about the disease, which doctors in those days treated like tuberculosis. True to form, the family doctor ordered Merle to remain in bed, a directive that made sense for tuberculosis but not necessarily for little-understood valley fever. After a restive, fitful recovery that lasted a few weeks, Merle was given a clean bill of health, to everyone's relief. And then James Haggard suddenly died. "He somehow connected the two things," Lillian said. "This was before we had the sort of psychiatry that might have helped a boy with that sort of burden."

Having a single, working mom didn't help things either. When Merle wasn't being shuttled from one relative to another, he was alone and restless. He hopped his first freight at eleven and was returned home by the police, but he continued to ride the rails and cut classes at school. Brother Lowell struck upon a useful distraction: he gave Merle, now twelve, his first guitar, a used Sears, Roebuck model somebody had left as payment at the gas station where Lowell worked, and the boy taught himself how to play by listening to records. By now Merle was a huge fan of Bob Wills, whose addictive hybrid of big-band swing, cowboy ballads, and distilled jazz and blues had seduced so many of Merle's age and disposition. Merle's passion for music increased manifestly in October 1950 when Lefty Frizzell seized the airwaves with "I Love You a Thousand Ways."

"Oh, God, he was unbelievable," Haggard said later of Frizzell. "He was different. He had his own tone … He had done this little stint in jail, so he knew more about being away than a lot of people did. He was really good at writing about separation—that was his main subject matter—and he wrote about it with sincerity and [in] the only vocabulary he knew." Merle, still an adolescent, learned to imitate Frizzell's distinctive guitar "curls" and his lilting vocal melismas—groupings of notes sung to a single syllable of text, a style Frizzell's contemporaries dubbed "Frizyllables."[2]

By this time, Merle was attending Standard School in Oildale. One morning, a few weeks before eighth-grade graduation, the school's chorus teacher was late for class, so Merle, always full of mischief, called the class to order and, with a grand sweep of his arms, began directing them through one of their songs, mimicking the teacher's distinctive style of conducting. The teacher, naturally, walked right in on this raucous scene. Such cheekiness might have drawn a laugh from a good-natured teacher or detention from an ill-natured teacher, but this particular teacher recommended expulsion. The principal agreed. Merle was forced to move in with his aunt in the tiny farming burg of Lamont, fifteen miles south of Bakersfield, and finish the year at Mountain View School.[3]

The bitter taste of injustice was still sour in his mouth when Haggard started at Bakersfield High School the next fall. His head was even more full of music by this time, and he neglected to attend many of his classes that first week. "He couldn't focus on school," remembered Lillian, who had landed a job as the school registrar. "He kept cutting class. He had a pass for the railroad because our dad had worked for the Santa Fe, but he preferred hopping freights because it was more fun."

Merle's counselor, Fred Robinson, could see what was happening too, and he and Lillian were determined to step in before things got out of hand. "Fred came over and said, 'What do you think about having him hauled off to spend the weekend in juvy?'" recalled

Lillian. "'Think that might straighten him up?' I agreed it might, and that's what we did. But Merle didn't think it was fair—the punishment didn't fit the crime. So he got out of there the first day, just walked out. And that was the start of it." Lillian felt so bad about it that she didn't get around to telling her younger brother about her role in his first incarceration for years. "I felt guilty for having said yes to this. He was never really an evil person. He was just a troubled kid."

One Jail Cell after Another

From that point on, Merle was incorrigible. He'd run away from home, come back whenever he felt like it (or was hauled back), and then run away again. He'd take any job he could find—pitching hay, sacking up potatoes, working as a roughneck in the oil fields. Flossie, desperate to straighten her son out, put him in one juvenile detention center after another, but few could hold him. Merle seemed like a boy who couldn't grow up fast enough.

At fourteen, he and his friend Bob Teague ran away to Texas, where Merle accomplished two noteworthy goals: he purchased his first pair of cowboy boots in a secondhand store and lost his virginity in an Amarillo whorehouse. "I think the cowboy boots affected me more," Merle said years later. "I mean, the gal just affirmed what I already knew, but the cowboy boots made a new man out of me."[4]

Four months later, the friends set out for California again but were arrested for suspicion of robbery before they could get across the line. This was a rare instance where Merle was actually innocent of the charges, but even after the actual thieves were apprehended and the boys got home, Merle paid for his truancy with a stint in juvenile hall.[5]

He skipped out again though, and he and Teague took off for Modesto, two hundred miles to the north. Teenage Merle did manual labor, worked as a short-order cook, drove a truck, and committed a burglary here and there. The highlight of their brief stay in Modesto was Merle's first job as a performer: he and Teague were hired at a bar named the Fun Center, where they sang the songs of Lefty Frizzell and Jimmie Rodgers—the only tunes they knew at the time. The two were paid five dollars a night, plus all the beer they could drink. They were, as the locals liked to say, Okie-rich.

When he got home, Haggard was arrested for truancy once again and was sent to the Fred C. Nelles School for Boys in Whittier. He ran away, was rearrested, and was sent to the high-security Preston School of Industry. He was released after fifteen months and then was arrested yet again for helping a kid he'd met at Preston beat up a slow-witted, harmless boy in an attempted robbery—an act for which Merle would always feel ashamed. So it was back to Preston once again. When he got home, Merle was somewhat more inclined to behave.

In late 1953, he and Teague bought tickets to hear Lefty Frizzell perform at the all-ages Rainbow Gardens dance hall. Haggard was in awe of Frizzell. "He was dressed in white—heroes usually are," he recalled. Before the show, Merle caught sight of Roy Nichols, the teen guitar phenom who played in Frizzell's band, and he called out to him, asking what it was like to work for a star. "Not worth a shit," answered Nichols, who was about to quit and take a job with the Maddox Brothers and Rose.

Some of Merle's friends were able to get backstage to meet Frizzell before the show, and they told the star about their friend who played and sang just like him. Frizzell told them to bring him back, so they fetched Merle, who summoned up the nerve to sing a couple of songs for his idol. Frizzell was so impressed that he refused to take the stage until Merle went first, backed by Frizzell's own band. Merle sang two or three songs, and the audience—by chance, the young Bonnie Owens among them—loved him. Teague was convinced that some initially thought Merle *was* Lefty.

Haggard's career as a working-class hoodlum/troubadour continued until, at sixteen, he took off with a local girl and set up housekeeping in Eugene, Oregon. That lasted three months, and when it ended, he hopped a freight and returned to Bakersfield. At seventeen, Haggard married a local waitress, Leona Hobbs, and almost immediately they produced a child. Merle supported the family with manual labor and the occasional petty crime. At age eighteen he moved up to car theft, drawing nineteen months in the Ventura County jail after one particular escapade, followed by a ninety-day sentence for pillaging a scrap-metal yard. Through it all, Merle continued to live a double life, performing in clubs even as he descended deeper into the life of a career criminal.

He lied about his age and was able to sneak into places such as the Blackboard, the Clover Club, and the Lucky Spot. The bands would occasionally let him sit in, and he gradually started becoming well known around town, in a positive way. He put in a guest appearance on KBAK-TV's *Chuck Wagon Gang*, starring Billy Mize and Cliff Crofford, and afterward, Mize took him aside and told him he could go far if he behaved himself. But as hard as the music pulled him, the dark side was pulling harder.

His fateful spiral gained terminal speed one night in late 1957, just before Christmas. Haggard and a couple of hooligan friends got drunk on cheap wine and decided to compensate for the shortage of good available jobs by pulling a heist. Leona, unaware of their plans, bundled up the baby and accompanied them to Fred & Gene's Café, a small diner co-owned by a friend's cousin. The drunken trio, believing it was the wee hours of the morning, attempted to pry open the back door of the restaurant. They were off by four hours or so—in fact, the café was still open and serving customers. The owner came around back to investigate all the racket, and the surprised conspirators, tripping over one another in their comedic haste to escape, jumped in the car and peeled out.

Haggard was identified and arrested the next day, but he escaped from the county jail simply by walking out with a group of other arrestees headed for court. He was picked up a few hours later having a Christmas Eve cocktail at his brother Lowell's house. The deputy, Tommy Gallon, allowed him to finish his drink before hauling him off. Judge Main, however, allowed Haggard no such courtesies: he sentenced him to fifteen years in the state penitentiary at San Quentin.

"If he had tried half as hard as his mother did …"

The Bakersfield Californian
22 Thursday, Dec. 26, 1957

Burglar Suspect Captured After Brief Freedom

A jail inmate who escaped by falling out with fellow prisoners en route to municipal court enjoyed 30 hours of freedom before he was apprehended Christmas Eve and returned to jail with an additional charge of escape added to his record.

Merle Haggard, 20, 110 Beardsley Ave., was taken into custody by Deputies Tommy Gallon and Robert Mooney at the home of the escapee's brother on Panama Lane at 4:30 p.m. Tuesday.

Haggard, who was jailed on suspicion of burglary Dec. 19, apparently joined the detail of prisoners on their way to court at 10 a.m. Monday, replacing a man who was being interviewed by a parole officer. The prisoner joined the group 'as it was leaving the jail to enter the prison transportation van, and officers said Haggard apparently made his escape at that time. The prisoner count at court arrival was correct, the transportation officer said.

Haggard, his 17-year-old wife, and a third suspect, were taken into custody during the early morning hours of Dec. 19. The officers said they found a check protector, purportedly taken from the H. Russell Taylor Fire Prevention service, 1811 Golden State Hwy. The machine was found hidden under the blanket covering the Haggard's 8-month-old daughter, with her parents at the time of the arrest.

Local Woman Says Father

It merited no better than page 22 in this clip from late 1957, but the apprehension of one Merle Haggard, age twenty, had lasting ramifications.
(Image courtesy of the Bakersfield Californian.)

Turning Twenty-One in Prison

During his dual career as a country music singer and petty criminal, Haggard had always seen himself as a rising star. So had most of the people who'd had the pleasure of hearing him sing. But San Quentin, his home as of March 26, 1958, saw him differently— as California A-45200. Haggard was not a model prisoner, at least not at first. He steamed up some home brew right under the guards' noses, got caught, and was put in solitary. He not only turned twenty-one in prison, as he sang in "Mama Tried"; he also spent his birthday in a nine-by-twelve cell with only a pair of pajama bottoms, a Bible (which doubled as a pillow), a blanket, and a cement floor. He spent seven life-changing days there, separated from death row by only a vented plumbing alley. Among his neighbors across the way was convicted rapist Caryl Chessman, the notorious "Red Light Bandit" of Los Angeles with whom Haggard conversed on and off through the thick walls and long hours.

From this stint in solitary, Haggard emerged a changed man. He asked for a more challenging job in the prison textile mill, studied for his high school equivalency degree, and was allowed to join the prison band. But parole was not forthcoming. "I'd been in the joint for eighteen months before I got my first parole hearing. I got the result the same way I got my San Quentin sentencing: Someone put a note between the bars of my cell. Why didn't anyone have the courage to tell me to my face what I already knew—that my first parole request had been denied."[6]

His second appearance before the parole board was a success, and his sentence was reduced to five years, the last two years and three months on parole. That meant Haggard had just ninety days to go until he could walk.[7]

He wept when he read those words. "Going to prison has one of a few effects," Haggard said years later. "It can make you worse, or it can make you understand and appreciate freedom. I learned to appreciate freedom when I didn't have any."[8]

On November 3, 1960, at the conclusion of the longest three months of his life, prison officials gave Haggard fifteen dollars and a bus ticket home. He'd spent seven of his twenty-three years inside of one institution or another, locked up. But never again.[9]

Haggard returned home to a wife and two children—the younger child having been conceived with another man while Haggard was away in prison. Haggard got himself a job digging ditches for his brother Lowell's electrical company while he tried to line up a job in a club, hoping he wouldn't have to explain where he'd been for almost three years.

Soon enough, he landed a fill-in job at the Lucky Spot, playing with fiddler Jelly Sanders and others on the Tuesday and Wednesday nights when Johnny Barnett's house band was off. It was there that he met Charles "Fuzzy" Owen and Lewis Talley, cousins from Arkansas who worked at the Lucky Spot as fill-in musicians and fancied themselves recording executives-in-training.

The First Break

In 1962, somewhat emboldened by his modest successes, Haggard auditioned for *Cousin Herb's Trading Post* and made the cut, joining the show's lineup two afternoons a week. Favorable fan mail started pouring in, and soon Haggard was performing five days a week on *Trading Post*. It was at about that time that Fuzzy Owen convinced Haggard to record for Tally Records, now operating out of a tiny, old Quonset hut in Oildale. Using a borrowed tape machine and a rinky-dink, three-channel console that barely qualified as a mixing board, Fuzzy recorded Haggard singing two songs: a Haggard original composition titled "Skid Row" and Fuzzy's own tune "Singing My Heart Out." The two traveled to Phoenix to polish up the tapes and then pressed two hundred or so copies to distribute to radio stations. The songs didn't do much, but they were enough to get the attention of Capitol Records' Ken Nelson, which had been the plan all along. "When I put out records with Merle, it was with the intention of selling to a major label," said Owen, who by then had become Haggard's manager. "The idea was to build him up so he'd be worth something." The hook had been set and the bait taken.

While Capitol had Haggard on hold, deciding what to do with him, the singer was, predictably enough, growing restless. So when his old pal Dean Holloway showed up one day, Haggard was easily talked into taking a quick trip to Las Vegas. They hit the strip and decided to stop in at the Nashville Nevada Club, where country star Wynn Stewart was part-owner and full-time headliner. And who should be there playing lead guitar but Roy Nichols. Stewart had been out of town, having gone to Nashville to shop for a bass player to replace the departing Bobby Austin, and Nichols invited Haggard up onstage to sing a few. At that moment, none other than Stewart himself walked into the room. Haggard's performance must have made an impression on Stewart. Sometime later, Steward told Haggard that if he was willing to learn to play the bass guitar, he had himself a job, for $225 a week, which was more money than Haggard had ever seen in his life.

For six months, from late 1962 until early 1963, Haggard played bass and sang in the band. But Haggard and Las Vegas were not cut out for each other. Haggard gambled away more than he earned, and he went home to Bakersfield with his tail between his legs—though not before persuading Stewart to permit him to record one of his originals, "Sing a Sad Song." Haggard put the song to vinyl in 1963, and it was released on the Tally label in early 1964, climbing to number nineteen on the country charts. Finally, Haggard had the hit record he'd been hoping for.

All His Friends Are Strangers

That year Haggard started putting together his own band. He had Fuzzy and Lewis, of course, and he brought in Fuzzy's girlfriend Bonnie Owens, a regular on *Trading Post* who had been slinging shots and Schlitz at local clubs most evenings.

In mid-1964, the newly formed band was playing an engagement at a club in Orangevale, just northeast of Sacramento, when an acquaintance of Bonnie's, songwriter Liz Anderson, came in with her husband and their teen daughter. The family invited Merle and the band over to their house after the show for breakfast, hoping

Merle would take an interest in some of the songs Liz had written. Haggard was less than thrilled, but he agreed to go. "They dragged me to her house at 4:00 a.m.," Haggard said years later.

> *I didn't want to listen to her songs; I just knew they weren't any good. I'm sitting over there eating bacon and eggs on a footstool, [and] she's at a pump organ—a little bitty girl—and she starts singing these fucking great songs, like "All My Friends Are Gonna Be Strangers" and "Just between the Two of Us." I couldn't believe it. I said, "I'll record all of those. I think 'Strangers' is a hit, and if 'Just between the Two of Us' isn't a hit, I'll kiss everybody's ass in Sacramento."[10]*

Haggard didn't have to kiss any asses, and he was right about Strangers too—in fact he liked the song so well that he started kicking it around as a possible band name. A local deejay, Red Butler, volunteered to help him decide between two possibilities, the other being the Sam Hill Band. Listeners voted, and history suggests they chose wisely.[11]

"Just between the Two of Us," a duet with Bonnie, was their first and only big hit together. The song spent twenty-six weeks on the charts before being overtaken by "Strangers," which proved to be Haggard's breakthrough song. "We'd sent records to disc jockeys all over the country, and we'd include hand-written notes in each one," Bonnie said years later. "When we started doing it, we'd put Merle's record in with mine. It wasn't long until I was putting my record in with Merle's." By January 1965, Merle Haggard and the Strangers had hit the top ten with "All My Friends Are Gonna Be Strangers." The two songs finally won over Ken Nelson, and in April 1965, with Fuzzy's blessing and encouragement, Haggard signed with the label.[12]

More hits started to come, starting with Haggard's own "Swinging Doors." Haggard had an inkling he had something special on his hands because weeks before he was to go into the studio to cut the record, Buck Owens called wanting to know if he could record it instead. If anyone knew how to spot a hit, Haggard reasoned, it was Buck, who'd suddenly developed the Midas touch. Therefore, "Swinging Doors" must have been gold. They were both right.

Haggard's marriage to Leona Hobbs had crumbled the year before, and the children—now there were four—were living with Merle's mother. At about this time, Bonnie, who'd been having some trouble getting along with Fuzzy, was touring Alaska. Haggard realized he missed her. He flew up to Seattle and called her up: could he visit and maybe look for some club work? Bonnie was wary, but she agreed to it. Two weeks later, on June 28, 1965, the two were married in Tijuana.

Hi There —

Just A Little Thank You For Making "Swingin' Doors" Such A Big Success For Me, And To Say That I Hope "The Bottle" Doesn't Let You Down!

Thanks Lots
Merle Haggard

Merle Haggard sent thank-you cards to the country's disc jockeys, many of whom did indeed play his 1966 hit "The Bottle Let Me Down." The song was Haggard's second major self-penned hit, after "Swinging Doors." *(Robert E. Price collection.)*

By this time, Bakersfield had become something of a country music mecca. It had hosted a renowned club scene for more than a decade, and now Buck Owens's success had lifted the town to another level. But Merle was probably more strongly influenced by Tommy Collins and Wynn Stewart than Owens. Haggard admired Stewart's style onstage, particularly his phrasing, and he admired Collins's songwriting.

Haggard, who had always been his own man, had a powerful gift for songwriting as well, a distinctive touch that was all his own. "It's amazing to me the things that come out of Merle's mouth when he's writing," Bonnie said years later. "I never heard him talk like that. He'd say later, 'Bonnie, I don't ever remember saying those words. It's like God put them through me.' I knew he said them. I was there. I'd write them down. 'Today I Started Loving You Again' was one of them. 'If We Make It through December' was another. I'd say, 'Are you sure that's what you want?' And he'd say, 'Yeah, read it to me.' I would. Then he'd say, 'I do not remember saying that line.' He was just amazed."

His gift was never more evident than one night in Dallas in 1967. It was two in the morning, and Haggard was hungry. He asked Bonnie to go down the street and get him a hamburger. When she got back to their motel room just a few minutes later, he'd scribbled the words to "Today I Started Loving You Again" on a brown paper bag. He sang it to her as she cried.

Haggard's gift was clear to the generation of songwriters that followed as well. "Merle was the guiding light to my adult writing," said Dwight Yoakam, whose kinship to Buck Owens is his better-known link to Bakersfield. "Merle was an adult writer. Buck was a dance bandleader. Buck kept the dance floor full. But Merle made you sit down [and feel]. If you want to have a heartache, sit down and listen to 'Holding Things Together' ... I probably learned more about songwriting from that one song than from anything I've ever heard ... I learned about how you chronicle heartache."[13]

This early edition of the Strangers had few equals: Haggard had Roy Nichols and James Burton on lead guitar, Glen Campbell on rhythm guitar and harmony vocals, Ralph Mooney on steel, and Glen Hardin on piano.

The Strangers: Eddie Burris—with whom Haggard cowrote "Okie from Muskogee"—Fuzzy Owen, Jerry Ward, George French, Roy Nichols. Front: Merle Haggard and Bonnie Owens.
(Capitol Records publicity shot/public domain.)

Though the country music establishment claims it, Haggard's music has always had a laid-back, exotic, almost jazzy sensibility to it. Some of this might have owed to Bob Wills's Texas Playboys, but it was also largely due to Nichols's snaky, elusive guitar licks, which were replete with unexpected note choices, and his bluesy, swooning turns of phrase. As a Telecaster artist par excellence, Nichols was the yin to Don Rich's yang. The Owens sound was frequently hurried, urgent, restless in its gait. Buck's songs sounded like turbo-charged versions of Ray Price shuffles, spurred on by Rich's brilliant picking.

By contrast, the Haggard sound was more often than not a loping, almost leisurely two-beat, adorned by Nichols's saucy commentaries, which seemed to unfold without any sense of hurry.

Whereas the freight-train sound of the Buckaroos seemed anxious to get to the next station down the line, the Strangers savored the moments they lived in. Part of that sense of joy came from the way Nichols's fingers seemed to bend time itself, turning the music back on itself in swirling eddies of twang.

The Freedom of Jazz

A shy, soft-spoken man, Nichols said little and sang even less and was never comfortable with praise. It was Haggard, he always said, who deserved the credit for pushing him to higher creative levels and giving him the space to soar. Nichols had been inspired by the French-Belgian guitar virtuoso Django Reinhardt, but Haggard's jazz influences were deep as well.

Haggard loved the idea that he could fuse the two musical genres and in fact has long referred to his music as "country jazz." He has always given generous exposure to his sidemen, and after Nichols's retirement, the guitar chair in the Strangers was held by a succession of hot pickers, including the dazzling Clint Strong and, most recently, Haggard's own prodigy son, Ben Haggard. "I realized that jazz meant that you could play anything," Haggard, the only country musician to have appeared on the cover of the jazz bible *Down Beat*, once said. "It meant that you were a full-fledged musician, that you could play with Louis Armstrong or Johnny Cash."[14]

As a vocalist, Haggard betrays a tension between denying and acknowledging sentiment. His is the voice of a people not given to emotional display—think of the deadpan masks in the Depression-era photos of Walker Evans and Dorothea Lange. In younger years, Haggard's voice was a marvelously flexible instrument, given to flights of soaring, almost acrobatic expression. Later, it began to limit itself to what it does best, keeping to a quiet, almost conversational middle range, holding its tremulous whiskey-soaked bottom notes in reserve. The voice of this latter-day Haggard is perhaps even better suited to the poignant material that made the young Haggard famous.

Just as the sound of the Telecaster colonized the soundscape of country music, Haggard's vocal timbre and phrasing became the archetype of the contemporary male country singer's voice, a model for countless Nashville hat acts—the ideal balance of hard palate and nasal brightness with a slight quaver of vibrato. It was a voice that could be either warm and supple or steely and tense, as the situation demanded.

By the end of the 1960s, the hits were coming regularly for Haggard. The honors began stacking up as well. Haggard was voted the top male vocalist by the Academy of Country Music Awards, and he and Bonnie were named the top vocal group for the second year in a row.[15]

Haggard also put aside his concerns about his criminal past, taking Johnny Cash's advice to address his problems openly in song. "I was bullheaded about my career. I didn't want to talk about being in prison," Haggard recalled, "but Cash said I should talk about it. That way the tabloids wouldn't be able to. I said I didn't want to do that and he said, 'It's just owning up to it.'" An ardent admirer of Cash ever since he'd seen him perform at San Quentin years before, Haggard couldn't argue with that. Cash helped by introducing Haggard on his television variety show as "a man who writes about his own life and has had a life to write about." Having been frank about his criminal past, Haggard was, paradoxically, forever free.[16]

Prison- and crime-themed songs became a trademark, with "Sing Me Back Home," "Mama Tried," "Branded Man," and "The Legend of Bonnie and Clyde" all reaching the top of the charts. Haggard also demonstrated a soft side with "You Don't Have Very Far to Go" (cowritten by Red Simpson), "Today I Started Loving You Again," "You Still Have a Place in My Heart," "I Just Want to Look at You One More Time," and "I Threw Away the Rose."[17]

Then in 1969, Haggard's music took a sudden political turn with "Okie from Muskogee," a phenomenon that forever changed Haggard's career, thrusting him into the firestorm of the 1960s culture wars. The song, recorded in Hollywood on July 17, 1969, sold 264,000 copies as a single that first year, and the album of the same name surpassed 885,000—making it one of the few country albums of the period to achieve gold-record status. It propelled Haggard to the Country Music Association's 1970 Entertainer of the Year award. Capitol seized on the momentum by pushing back the single Haggard had intended to release next and substituting "Fightin' Side of Me"—a pugilistic sequel of sorts. From a business point of view, it was the right call, and "Fightin' Side" followed "Okie" right to the top of the country charts. Haggard, a regular guest star on television variety shows hosted by Buck Owens, Johnny Cash, Glen Campbell, Barbara Mandrell, and others, had become the darling of the American Right, his message of blue-collar (and Okie) pride resounding with the great American middle class.[18]

That year, Haggard's hit streak having continued unabated, he released "If We Make It through December." Again, he'd drawn on real-life drama for inspiration. Haggard had asked Roy Nichols one day how things were going with his wife, with whom Nichols had been having troubles. "Well, we might be okay if we make it through December," Nichols replied.[19]

Haggard took that poignant line and grafted it with the uncertain economic days of that difficult autumn to tell the story of a working man who'd lost his job and was thinking about his family at Christmas. The song sold 468,000 copies in six months, becoming the biggest hit of Haggard's career—and the first to cross over to the pop charts, where it peaked at number twenty-eight. By that Christmas Haggard had turned pessimistic and bitter about Richard Nixon because of Watergate and the many economic troubles he'd seen across the country. Gas was getting tough to buy, families were struggling, and automobile manufacturers were laying off workers. But he was at the apex of his career.

Good Times, Bad Times

At about that time, Haggard built a $700,000 mansion along his beloved Kern River. The place was surrounded by 180 acres of grassland in the shadow of the Sierra Nevada foothills just east of

Bakersfield. Among his many toys was a $50,000 model railroad that ran through the living room, across the sun deck, and then out onto a trestle above the rear patio. Haggard threw parties and held recording sessions, including one for Bob Wills's reassembled Texas Playboys. Haggard mastered the fiddle over an intensive, protracted six-month cram session especially for the occasion. Wills died a few months later, willing Haggard one of his prized fiddles—and an old cigar butt that Haggard still keeps under glass.

Haggard stayed with Capitol Records until 1977 and then moved to MCA Records. His first two singles for the record label, "If We're Not Back in Love by Monday" and "Ramblin' Fever," made it to number two, as did two later hits, "I'm Always on a Mountain When I Fall" and "It's Been a Great Afternoon." He dabbled in acting, appearing in the Clint Eastwood film *Bronco Billy*, and two songs from the soundtrack charted.

In 1981, Haggard published his autobiography *Sing Me Back Home* and left MCA for Epic Records. He began producing his own records, and his first two singles, "My Favorite Memory" and "Big City," went to number one. His duet with George Jones, "Yesterday's Wine," was also number one, as was his 1983 duet with Willie Nelson, "Pancho and Lefty." He scored another number one hit in 1987, at the age of fifty, with "Twinkle, Twinkle Lucky Star."

Amid it all, Haggard endured significant financial problems, including trouble with the IRS, a problem he chalked up to having given too many people too much access to too much of his money while he concentrated on his music. "I had earned maybe a hundred million dollars in twenty-five years," he wrote in *My House of Memories*, his second autobiography. "By 1990, I was practically broke."[20]

That year he changed to Curb Records, a move he eventually regarded as among the bleakest periods of his career. "There is nothing more frustrating than to be a recording artist who isn't recording or who, if he is, isn't getting his recordings released," he wrote in *My House of Memories*. "The deejays in the world lost track of me because there was nothing new to play. Patty Hearst could've been on Curb. For that matter, Amelia Earhart may be there now."[21]

When his contract ran out, Haggard happily skipped over to Anti, a subsidiary of the Epitaph punk-pop label. By that time Haggard had long since sold his Kern River Canyon mansion and moved to the Lake Shasta area of Northern California. He shares the two-hundred-acre spread, which he calls Shade Tree Manor, with his fifth wife, Theresa Lane, whom he wed in 1993. There, they raised their two children to adulthood. "People who haven't been around me in years wouldn't know me," he wrote.[22]

On the woodsy, out-of-the-way property he calls Shade Tree Manor, Haggard built a veritable petting zoo for the kids and a first-rate recording studio, adorned with assorted memorabilia, including some of Lewis Talley's dusty, half-empty bottles of bourbon and printed words of inspiration, courtesy of Roger Miller: "We Shall Over Dub."[23]

In those days, during his midfifties, Haggard did a lot of grousing about country music's cookie-cutter hat acts and particularly about the lack of respect the industry accords its elder statesmen. He doesn't have that gripe anymore, given the accolades he began to collect in his midseventies. The John F. Kennedy Center for the Performing Arts recognized him for "lifetime achievement as an artist" in December 2010, and in 2014 the Nashville-based television network CMT bestowed upon him nothing less than its Artist of a Lifetime award, an honor that presumably takes in all fields of human artistic endeavor. And yes, there is that word "lifetime" again. Auspicious laurels indeed, but Haggard has said he has no intention of retiring, and he reiterated those intentions in mid-2015 with a top-selling reunion with his old *Pancho and Lefty* partner, Nelson—*Django and Jimmie*.

Car Thief to Poet Laureate

It's been quite a ride. Between 1966 and 1987, Haggard and his band recorded thirty-eight songs that reached number one on the *Billboard* country charts and another thirty-three that reached the top ten. By the time "If We Make It through December" hit number one, Haggard had sold more than 8 million albums and 3.5 million singles worth $44.5 million. His songs have been recorded by artists as diverse as the Everly Brothers and Elvis Costello, and one song alone, "Today I Started Loving You Again," has been recorded by more than four hundred performers. Haggard rose from working as a forty-dollars-a-week sideman to the biggest star in the country music universe to one of the most revered poet laureates of American music.

Smoke and flash didn't put him there; he's never been the type for rhinestones or hand-tooled boots. Neither was it simply the pretty melodies that propelled his success, although they contributed mightily. "He'll tell you he's a country singer, but to me the essence of rock 'n' roll is a cry for freedom and rebellion," producer Don Was, who has worked with Bob Dylan, the Rolling Stones, and Bonnie Raitt, told *Newsweek* in 1996. "And I don't know anyone who embodies it better. Every aspect of his life is a refusal to submit."[24]

Maybe that's why rock and folk-rock audiences were so responsive on concert tours that paired Haggard with the Rolling Stones in 2005 and with Bob Dylan in 2006. There was always something about that rebel spirit, that core of obstinacy, that set him apart. Haggard the poet once tried to summarize what might be learned from listening to his songs. "That I'm a contrary old son of a bitch, I guess," Haggard said.[25]

But Haggard wasn't always a hero in his hometown. In fact, to some he was something of a pariah. An effort in 2000 to name Bakersfield's then-new Amtrak station in his honor had wings for a short time, owing to Haggard's association with trains, but it fizzled. Some, including the city's then-mayor, a former police chief, openly scoffed at the idea.

Merle Haggard enjoys himself with Marty Stuart prior to a symposium at
California State University–Bakersfield in 2009.
(Photo courtesy of the Bakersfield Californian/*Felix Adamo.)*

Haggard, the Central Valley's "poet of the people"? Hardly.
Most of the San Joaquin Valley's literati would agree that that honor
goes to Fresno's William Saroyan, a novelist-playwright admired
by a vast legion of fans despite having lived what detractors might
characterize as a life tainted by periodic lapses of good judgment.
Saroyan's excesses, like Haggard's, were legendary. His long-
suffering mother became accustomed to seeing him "staggering
home," as he once put it, "loud and drunk at daybreak." One year,
at the height of his popularity, he embarked on a European tour,
intent on earning enough money to pay off the tax man, who'd
been dogging him for fifteen years. The trip was a huge success,

and he earned tens of thousands of dollars. The government didn't see a dime of it. "I certainly didn't gamble away every penny," Saroyan wrote in his autobiography years later. "I drank some of it away, and I bought a raincoat."[26]

Haggard might have penned something very much like that if it rained more often in Las Vegas. Yet Fresno saw fit to name the William Saroyan Theatre in the writer's honor, erecting a bronze bust of Saroyan at the entrance to the building. Saroyan, rascal that he was, was a native son to be proud of.

For decades, Haggard got no such love from Bakersfield. Invariably, he was compared unfavorably to Owens, whose generosity and civic involvement were considerable. And Haggard, after all, had moved away decades ago to Lake Shasta, 450 miles to the north. But many in Bakersfield realized that people such as Haggard proved the city was a place that spawned producers of culture, not simply consumers of culture. People such as Haggard proved that the wellspring of poetry and grace (along with other, more pedestrian forms of expression) bubbled forth in Bakersfield too.

Finally, in 2008, good sense prevailed, and a portion of Seventh Standard Road, including the entrance to the county's main commercial airport, was renamed Merle Haggard Drive. Haggard now had a freeway off-ramp with his name on it, just four miles north of Buck Owens Boulevard.[27]

Bakersfield started seeing a lot more of Haggard after that. He took an interest in the Ronald McDonald House at Bakersfield Memorial Hospital, among other causes, and he autographed guitars for most every legitimate charity that asked to auction one off. In 2013, California State University–Bakersfield's School of Arts and Humanities awarded him an honorary doctorate. (Owens received a posthumous president's medal the same day.) "It's nice to be noticed," Haggard, mortarboard askew, told the crowd. But he was never one to sit still in school, and he wasn't about to now. With the audience distracted by the imminent recitation of the graduates' names, Haggard slipped out the back, just as he had done so many times before, so many years ago.[28]

Snapshot
The Man in Black Needs Cash

Gene Torigiani was a twenty-six-year-old accordion player the day in late 1964 that greatness walked into his music store—hungry, dirty, and a tad irritable. Johnny Cash needed some cash.[1]

The country music singer, not yet the instantly recognizable celebrity he became after ABC-TV gave him his own show in 1969, wanted to write a check. But on that day in the dusty little oil town of Taft, thirty miles west of Bakersfield, the only thing he was carrying that remotely resembled an ID was a wrinkled, yellowed Columbia Records recording contract. The off-the-interstate town of Taft was home to the very sort of working-class people Cash professed to admire, but that wasn't doing him any good that day. Cash, just forty miles away from the Blackboard, ground zero for the burgeoning Bakersfield Sound, but two years away from making the acquaintance of its two best-known evangelists, was in a dark place—a dark, hungry, supply-depleted place.

Cash parked his dusty old station wagon in front of Hall's Market and walked the aisles, gathering wine, dog food, bologna, french bread, and other supplies. But Cash carried no identification, and he was turned away at the check stand.

So the singer, dressed in black, walked across the street to Gene's Music, where Torigiani sold musical instruments, records, and sheet music. The store was also the unofficial headquarters for Torigiani's dance band, which played weekends at the White Elephant restaurant and lounge a few blocks down Center Street. Cash pulled out his checkbook and his crumpled recording contract. He needed $250 for supplies, he said. Torigiani, finding it hard to believe a recording star could possibly be in his store under such circumstances, told him he couldn't help. Cash shrugged his shoulders and stumbled out the door. But Torigiani wasn't sure he'd done the right thing. He went over to the store's rack of record albums and pulled out Cash's latest album, *Bitter Tears*, which featured the singer's controversial new song, "The Ballad of Ira Hayes." There, pictured in a black sleeveless shirt, was the same tousled man who'd just been in the store.

Torigiani and Dan Keel, a customer who'd witnessed the whole exchange, ran out the door to see if they could find him. They spotted Cash's station wagon outside Topper's Bar, its cargo area piled with clothes and junk, including a couple of rifles. A large dog sat patiently in the front seat; another was in the back. Torigiani went inside and convinced Cash to come with him to the Bank of America branch next door to the music store. Sufficiently encouraged by Torigiani's assurances—but just barely—the bank manager cashed Cash's check. Cash went back to the market and stocked up.

Then he walked back into Torigiani's music store and looked over the merchandise—in particular a row of guitars hanging on display. "How much is this one?" he asked, pointing to a nylon-stringed flamenco that sold for one hundred dollars. It wasn't the type of guitar Torigiani would have expected Cash to be interested in, but Cash grunted, "Give it to me," and handed over a one-hundred-dollar bill. Then he turned and walked out of the store. No "thank you." No other words at all.

Cash's visit was the talk of Taft for three months afterward. Word was he spent a lot of time south of the Cuyama Valley, fishing, drinking, and writing songs. A deputy sheriff told Torigiani that long before the check-cashing episode, Cash had been occasionally rousted while sleeping in his car in front of a Maricopa liquor store. But he never came near Taft or Maricopa again, as far as Torigiani knew—except for one well-documented day later that year.

In those days, Cash, his first wife, Vivian, and their daughter, Rosanne, lived in Ojai, about seventy-five miles south of Maricopa on Highway 33. The marriage was tumultuous, mostly because of Cash's amphetamine abuse. When things got unbearable at home, as Cash wrote in his 1997 autobiography, *Cash*, he would "head out to the desert in [his] camper, and stay out there, high, for as long as [he] could. Sometimes it was days." Cash's well-traveled camper had a nickname: Jesse, in honor of the outlaw Jesse James. Cash painted the inside of the windows black so that he could sleep peacefully during the day and also, he wrote, "because [he] just liked to spray-paint things black."

Johnny Cash, Merle Haggard, Buck Owens, Glen Campbell, late 1960s.
(Photo courtesy of the Buck Owens Private Foundation, Inc.)

The camper met its final, fiery end in the mountains south of Cuyama. It had developed an oil drip from a cracked wheel bearing, and when Cash stopped along the road, the hot oil ignited some dry grass. While Cash fished some distance away, trying to create an atmosphere of innocence, the fire spread across 508 acres of the Los Padres National Forest, including part of a California condor preserve. The federal government sued him for $125,000, and Cash settled for $82,000.[2]

Cash's self-destructiveness subsided after his marriage to June Carter Cash. By the time of his death in September 2003, at age seventy-one, he was considered a cultural icon who had infused American music with an emotional honesty and political courage exceedingly rare for the time. Torigiani abandoned his music store in 1972 and a year later signed on as a salesman at Weatherby's Furniture in Bakersfield—a business that, coincidentally, was closely associated with Herb Henson, the store's most recognizable pitchman. Torigiani, who eventually became the store's sales manager, worked there for more than forty years. He followed Cash's career closely after that day in Taft, applauding the personal high points but never forgetting his personal glimpse at the man's lows.

CHAPTER 8

The Two
Defining Songs

The Streets of Bakersfield

E very city of consequence has an anthem: "New York, New York"; "My Kind of Town (Chicago Is)"; "I Left My Heart in San Francisco." Sometimes cities can be considered to be "of consequence" mainly because they *have* a song: Luckenbach, Texas; Winslow, Arizona; Muskogee, Oklahoma; Lodi, state of stuck. One can make a case that Bakersfield fits into the first category. One can make a better case that it fits in the second. Either way, love it or hate it, "Streets of Bakersfield" is permanently, undeniably tattooed onto the town's civic visage.[1]

That became clear, if it wasn't already, one night in June 2005 on the street in front of Buck Owens's dinner club. Here were 150 people, standing under the giant Bakersfield arch, howling to the familiar strains of "Streets of Bakersfield" for the taping of a CMT television special. Those 150 volunteers weren't merely resurrecting the recycled tune that had rejuvenated Owens's career seventeen years before. They were singing Bakersfield's de facto anthem. When Homer Joy wrote "Streets of Bakersfield" in the early 1970s—in ten minutes flat, no less—he was just getting something off his chest. It turned out he changed his life forever that day in his Oildale motel room—Buck Owens's life too, really.

Owens never forgot the story of the day the song landed in his lap—his version of the story anyway. "My secretary came into my office and says, 'He's here again,'" Owens told me one day in his oaken office above the Crystal Palace stage. "'Who?' I said. 'Homer Joy,' she says. 'Well, who's that?' I said. 'Same guy who was here yesterday,' she says. 'In fact he's been here several times. Six, eight, ten, twelve times.'"

"I finally looked at his songs," Owens said. "I could tell he had talent. But I did not sign him to a writer's contract. At that time I didn't need any new hassles. But I told him I liked 'Streets of Bakersfield.'"

Joy remembered the story a lot differently. For one thing, he recalled having signed a contract with Owens's publishing company two years before, in February 1970. He had flown down to Bakersfield from his home near Spokane, Washington, one day in 1972 at the behest of Bob Morris, who then managed Owens's music-publishing business. K-Tel Records, the purveyor of cheesy soundalike cover records promoted with equally cheesy TV commercials, wanted an album of Hank Williams songs. Did Morris know anyone who could sing like Hank? Sure he did: Homer Joy. But Joy wasn't keen on the idea. It was a paycheck, sure, but he was more interested in writing and recording his own material. So Joy struck a verbal deal with Morris: if Joy agreed to cut the songs for the K-Tel project at Owens's recording studio on North Chester Avenue in Oildale, he'd also get to borrow the Buckaroos and the studio to record a few of his own songs.

But after Joy laid down the K-Tel tracks, the circumstances changed. The Buckaroos were no longer available, Joy recalled, because Owens and the band had to leave soon for Japan or some other exotic locale. Joy's recording session would have to wait. "I was mad," Joy said. "And I just started walking toward the motel I was staying at, there in Oildale. I'd just bought a brand-new pair of boots that weren't broken in yet, so my feet were hurting, and that made me even more mad. I just sat down in that motel room and wrote that song in about ten minutes. I didn't want to be Hank Senior. I wanted to be me. 'You don't know me, but you don't like me.' You know?"

Joy went back the next day and pleaded his case with Morris

once again. "I ain't leaving till I get in that studio," Joy said. "Now Bob is finally getting miffed at me. He says, 'Okay, Homer, if you were going to do a session, what would you do?' And I sang 'Streets of Bakersfield,' sort of as a protest. He said, 'Wait a minute,' and he went and got Buck. Buck listened to me sing it again. Then he said, 'Call the Buckaroos. We're going to do a session this morning.'"

Neither man ever seemed bothered that the other's recollection was so different. "No two people," Owens conceded, "remember the same story the same way." This much is certain: on November 6, 1972, Buck Owens and the Buckaroos recorded "Streets of Bakersfield." On May 14, 1973, it was released as part of Owens's album *Ain't It Amazing Gracie*. "It was just an album cut," Owens said. "That's all it was ever planned for."

By 1987, Owens's career had crested, his remarkable string of country-radio hits relegated to the oldies bin. When Don Rich was killed, Owens had effectively retired as a recording artist. A whole new generation had come to know him as the cohost of *Hee Haw*, and his recording career had practically become a footnote.

But in late 1987, CBS asked Owens if he'd like to participate in a broadcast of the Country Music Association's 1988 awards show. The producers wanted him to pair up with Merle Haggard and perform a song that evoked the Bakersfield experience. About a week before the show, though, a CBS producer telephoned to say that Haggard had been forced to cancel. "He says, 'Is there anybody else you can bring?'" Owens recalled. "I say, 'Well, there's this boy who lives down the road named Dwight Yoakam.' His big song at the time was 'Guitars and Cadillacs.' I'd sung with him at the fair. The guy tells me, 'Well, bring a song you can sing together too.'" Owens, thinking those watching on television might like to hear something they had not heard before, rummaged through his catalog and emerged with one of his more obscure songs: "Streets of Bakersfield." Owens gave Yoakam a tape of the song and asked him to learn it—quickly.

Their performance was the highlight of the show. NBC producers planning the upcoming Academy of Country Music Awards show called and asked if Owens and Yoakam could reprise the song six weeks later in Los Angeles. They did. "The reaction was amazing," Owens said. "But people went crazy over the fact that there was no record. We hadn't recorded it. I got letters from deejays in Canada who wanted to play it on the radio from a tape they'd made off the TV. I told them, 'Well, that's up to CBS, but it's okay with me.'" Owens and Yoakam got the song on record as quickly as they could, released it July 16, two months after they'd performed it at the Country Music Awards, and then watched it hit number one within a matter of days. The song thrust Owens back into the spotlight. He must have enjoyed it because he soon ratcheted up vague, long-dormant plans for a dinner club, and within a few years he was performing regularly again at the Crystal Palace.

He returned to touring—on a limited basis, but with all the exuberance of his youth. Yoakam tells of the opening night of a 1988 tour with Owens: Buck came onstage and played "Act Naturally." "Holy moley ... He took the guitar riff and ran with that lead, and it was like an F-100 Saberjet went past at strafing height. He was like the loudest thing on the stage." Buck was back.[2]

"Streets of Bakersfield" has had phenomenal staying power. It's been covered by other artists at least eight times—once by Joy and several times, individually and as a duet, by Owens and Yoakam. Joy once figured the various versions had sold fifteen million copies. And every time someone else bought a copy of the song, or it was played in a restaurant or performed on a stage, Joy got paid. He even received a royalty check when the opening line, "You don't know me," turned up in the liner notes of a CD by the Bakersfield scream-rock band Korn. By 2005, Joy figured he'd made close to $250,000 on it, some of which had arrived in unexpected chunks. The song's sales didn't track the way songs normally track: the Owens-Yoakam version came out in 1988, yet one of its biggest sales years was 1997. How does that happen?

Joy had some tough times along the way, the sort of tough times that make for authentic jukebox fodder—a drinking problem, a divorce, and maybe worst of all, songwriter's block. "I had just dried up in the songwriting business, and I was having a hard time with my [first] marriage," Joy said.

So Buck calls me up and tells me to come to Bakersfield and see him. Studio time is held against your royalties, and I owed Buck $35,000 in studio time. He sat me down, showed me the bill, ripped it up, and threw it in the wastebasket. He said, "Whatever's dragging you down, don't let it be that anymore." And he did it again a second time for $17,000 ... Buck Owens has never taken a nickel out my royalties for anything. I can't say enough good about him.

Those songwriting royalties helped Joy and his wife, Suzan, buy the Cowboy Depot, the finest steakhouse in Caddo, Oklahoma—a town of three hundred about forty miles from Owens's boyhood home of Sherman, Texas. "I tell Buck I'm living his life in reverse," said Joy, who also lived for a time in Mesa, Arizona, another of Owens's stomping grounds.

Perhaps ironically, Joy never resided in Bakersfield, unless one counts three brief stays: a few unhappy weeks there as a child, two months in a trailer near Weedpatch in the 1980s, and just a few years before his death, a triumphant return to soak up some love following that CMT special. "When we left Arkansas in 1949, the first place we came was Bakersfield," Joy said.

We were flat told by people they didn't want no more damned Okies. They wouldn't even let their kids play with us. We left Bakersfield. And that was the first roots for "You Don't Know Me, but You Don't Like Me." But every time I came to Bakersfield after that over the years, seems like I'd meet somebody who knew somebody I knew mutually. Every time I came to Bakersfield, it was almost like going to a friend's house.

Joy and his wife finally sold their restaurant and took his country-gospel show on the road. But he was slowed by a bad heart. Two open-heart surgeries, three defibrillator implants, twelve inserted stents, and a 2006 heart transplant took their cumulative toll, and in 2012, at the age of sixty-seven, he died. Given his many health problems, Joy was probably lucky to have lasted that long. Maybe he had something else in common with that twangy shuffle of his—the unlikely anthem that, forty years after he penned it in an Oildale motel room, was still refusing to slip into musical oblivion.

Buck Owens and Dwight Yoakam in the Buckmobile during shooting for the music video for "Streets of Bakersfield," 1988.
(Photo courtesy of the Buck Owens Private Foundation, Inc.)

Okie from Muskogee

More than a few times in his long and productive career, Merle Haggard would be onstage, warbling in his fine baritone, when some yokel in the back would bellow, "Play Okie!" And almost without fail, Haggard, writer of hundreds of gentle and poignant jazz-country ballads, would oblige. Sometimes Haggard's most famous, profitable, and career-solidifying song, the one that expressed disgust with smoking marijuana, burning draft cards, and those "hippies out in San Francisco," must have seemed to him an insufferable relative who just didn't know when to go home. But his audiences never seemed to tire of it.[3]

Haggard was already a well-regarded and successful star when he released "Okie from Muskogee"; by the end of the song's four-week run atop the country music charts, he was much more than that. The populist anthem that Haggard has said he too wrote in ten minutes was, and remains, a signpost on America's difficult and still-unfulfilled journey through one of its most trying eras. It also established Haggard as a simple poet of the white underclass. Almost immediately upon the song's ascent to number one in November 1969, "Okie from Muskogee" was regaled as the voice of the silent majority, a revitalizing tonic for conservatives who had grown defensive and angry over Vietnam and the counterculture movement it had helped spawn.

Of course, Haggard had been covertly political for most of his career, so covert that perhaps he did not fully realize it himself. The songs "I Take a Lot of Pride in What I Am," "Hungry Eyes," and "Workin' Man Blues," among others, had already firmly positioned Haggard as a man with working-class, anti-elite, populist sentiments. To a great extent, "Okie" tracked that same course. Sociologists, historians, and assorted pundits have long debated the song's meaning and intent. Was it a parody or a sincerely indignant jab at the LSD-tripping left? At various times Haggard has endorsed each interpretation, but its origins suggest the former.[4]

Haggard's tour bus was heading east through Oklahoma in mid-1969 when he and his bandmates spotted a road sign: "Muskogee 19 miles." A band member joked that they probably didn't smoke marijuana in Muskogee, and before the town was visible on the approaching horizon, Merle had written the song. But Haggard confesses he had no inkling what he'd created until he played it publicly for the first time on that same road swing: his unveiling, at a club for noncommissioned army officers in Fort Bragg, North Carolina, inspired a response so passionately rowdy that Haggard, then thirty-two, later admitted he'd momentarily feared for his life.

The song, recorded at Capitol Studios in Hollywood on July

17, 1969, and released in August, made Haggard one of the hottest concert commodities in the country. The *Los Angeles Times* described one scene in Anaheim, California, where 9,100 fans gave him a standing ovation for both "Okie from Muskogee" and its follow-up, "Fightin' Side of Me." "The audience roared its approval several times during each song, particularly when the title lines were sung," wrote the reviewer.[5] As a single, "Okie" sold 264,000 copies the first year, propelling Haggard to 1970 Entertainer of the Year awards from both the Academy of Country Music and the Country Music Association.

Some critics decried the song's ultraconservatism; others, as historian Peter La Chapelle has noted, tried to rehabilitate the song by reading it as a working-class assault on middle-class snobbery and elitism.[6] It became perhaps the most parodied song of the Vietnam era, inspiring left-of-center knockoffs by Kinky Friedman and the Texas Jewboys ("Asshole from El Paso"), Jesse Colin Young and the Youngbloods ("Hippie from Olema"), Commander Cody and His Lost Planet Airmen, and Arlo Guthrie.[7] So many country, rock, and country-rock groups released transmogrified versions of "Okie" that *Rolling Stone* magazine kept score: as of March 1971, the song had been recorded twenty times, with the tally standing at "Honkies, 12, Hippies, 8."[8]

Conservative politicians understood they had a natural constituency in country music fans, and their efforts to exploit it during the Vietnam War era occasionally focused on Haggard. Sometimes Haggard allowed it. Of course, he gratefully accepted Gov. Ronald Reagan's 1970 pardon for the crimes that had eventually led to his incarceration at San Quentin State Prison in the late 1950s. And he accepted Richard Nixon's invitation to the White House in 1973 to sing at wife Pat's staid birthday party. But Haggard refused to endorse George Wallace when the Alabama governor and presidential aspirant—who was already campaigning with country stars Ernest Tubb and Marty Robbins—asked for his support in 1972. Years later he rejected similar overtures from US Senate candidate David Duke, a former Klansman.

Eventually, Haggard came to the conclusion that antigovernment protest "wasn't un-American" after all. Those young Vietnam-era protesters could "see through our bigotry and our hypocrisy ... I believe history has proven them right." If that wasn't a full-on repudiation of his famed song's at-face-value political message, it was close.[9]

But "Okie" wasn't just a political message. In the context of Haggard's lifelong body of work, it's clear that when he saw protesting college students, he didn't just see disrespect for flag and country; he saw class distinction and privilege. He saw trust-fund snot noses who'd never stooped over a row of cotton in their lives, never seen dirt under their own fingernails. The marijuana was one thing—and maybe not such a big thing at that—but the naïveté was quite another. If the literal weight of the lyrics is an indication, the song was less about Vietnam than about class dignity. "I'm proud to be an Okie" is, after all, the song's most repeated line.

Eventually, however, Haggard began expressing misgivings about the song's tendency to brand him a reactionary, and he started characterizing it as simply a statement of Okie pride. When Haggard spoke at the Oildale and Beyond history symposium at California State University–Bakersfield in November 2009, that was the interpretation he shared with the actual central California Okies who dominated the audience. Okie, he told them, is more a declaration about cultural autonomy and collective self-worth than a volley of class animosity.[10]

Maybe Haggard's political soul is best revealed in a lesser-known song, "Somewhere in Between," recorded a short time after "Okie" but never released: "I stand looking at the left wing, and I turn towards the right, and either side don't look too good, examined under light. That's just freedom of opinion, and their legal right to choose. That's one right I hope we never lose."[11]

Politics is one thing, performance quite another. Haggard will hear cries of "Play Okie!" as long as his voice gives him confidence enough to stand behind a mike. Will he actually play the song? Probably. But then, Okies can be temperamental.

CHAPTER 9

The A&R Man

Ken Nelson just couldn't help himself sometimes. His black and white cat, K. C., would saunter across the kitchen floor, and Nelson would reach down and gently grab a handful of fur. And then, self-consciously silly, he'd belt out one of his favorite Buck Owens hits: "I ... got ... a ... tiger by the tail, it's plain to see ..."[1]

For him, this was no simple, whimsical jukebox flashback. "I've Got a Tiger by the Tail"—a song for which he'd trade his flat, Midwest vowels for an impish, exaggerated Oklahoma twang—had a special significance. He had been present at the recording session. As a top staff producer for Capitol Records, the label most strongly associated with the Bakersfield Sound of the 1950s and '60s, Nelson played a vital role in capturing and preserving the raw edge his performers brought into the studio. By 1965, with "Tiger" hitting number one and Capitol artists Owens, Merle Haggard, Bonnie Owens, and Kay Adams pulling off a virtual Bakersfield sweep at the inaugural Academy of Country Music Awards in Los Angeles, Nelson did indeed have a tiger by the tail.

But as much as fiddles, steel guitars, and Fender Telecasters were part of his life, Nelson—Capitol Records' country and western A&R man for nearly three decades—was really a numbers man. To be sure, he more closely resembled an accountant than a record producer, with his thick, black Buddy Holly spectacles and his preference for cardigans and sweater-vests. He certainly boasted the sort of numbers any businessman would be proud of: more than

141

170 artists passed through his studios to record literally thousands of songs, including more than one hundred number one hits.

From his primary base in Hollywood, Nelson orchestrated the conversion of the Bakersfield Sound from regional honky-tonk phenomenon to its position, in the mid-1960s, in the middle of the country music mainstream. Besides Buck Owens and Merle Haggard, his top artists included Glen Campbell, Tommy Collins, Rose Maddox, Ferlin Husky, Jean Shepard, Wanda Jackson, Wynn Stewart, and Red Simpson—in short, almost every major artist to ever pass through the San Joaquin Valley.

Minnesota-born and Chicago-bred, Nelson was an entertainer himself in the 1930s. He played banjo and sang in a trio called the Campus Kids but eventually left to pursue a solo career. That ill-timed expedition led nowhere. In the meantime, the Campus Kids landed a regular gig on *Fibber McGee and Molly*, a long-running radio program of national renown. Nelson, undaunted, soon landed a job as the host of a prominent classical music program on Chicago's WAAF. He was efficient and professional, if prone to occasionally butchering pronunciations: maybe "Tchaikovsky" would come out "Chai-cow-ski" instead of "Chai-koff-ski," or "pianissimo" would get the emphasis on the wrong syllable. Finally, a listener, a helpful woman of French extraction, phoned the station and said she couldn't take any more. Could he use a little help in the booth pronouncing these names? Nelson agreed that he could, and for a month she sat in with him as he did his show. The man who would later be closely associated with Buck and Merle became a credible advocate for Bach and Mozart and in short order was Chicago's top classical program host.

In the late 1930s, Nelson moved to Chicago's WJJD and WIND, where he created the wildly popular hillbilly music show *Suppertime Frolic*. The job required that he audition performers as well as schedule them for his several weekly music programs, meaning that Nelson was evaluating country music talent well before he'd reached the age of thirty. Among the artists Nelson brought to the airwaves was a guitar player billed as "Rhubarb

Red"—Les Paul, who would later become one of the country's foremost guitarists and guitar makers.

After serving a year in the army during World War II, Nelson returned to Chicago and resumed his old radio job. But one day in the early 1940s, it all changed: producer Lee Gillette, Nelson's old friend and singing partner from the Campus Kids, asked him to help out over at Capitol Records' recording studios by producing a bluegrass session for Uncle Henry's Kentucky Mountaineers. A strike by the musicians' union was looming, and record companies everywhere were trying to cram as many sessions into as little time as possible to minimize its impact. "I was scared to death, but I suppose it went all right," Nelson remembered. More production work followed, including a session with the Dinning Sisters that resulted in Nelson's first hit, "Buttons and Bows." A new career had been launched.

In 1948, Capitol Records created a country music department, independent of its pop-music division, and Nelson, with the support of Cliffie Stone, became one of its most influential executives. Nelson's job was A&R—artists and repertoire—and he was well suited for it. He developed an uncanny knack for finding talent. In 1951, while riding in a car from Louisiana to Dallas, he tuned in to Webb Pierce's New Orleans–based radio program and heard a voice that was unfamiliar to him. He listened for the announcer to identify the singer, to no avail, so Nelson ordered the driver, another fledgling performer, to turn the car around, and they drove all the way back to New Orleans. Without tipping his hand, Nelson coaxed the singer's name out of the on-duty disc jockey: it was Faron Young. Nelson located the golden-throated nineteen-year-old the next day and signed him on the spot. During his career, Young made more than thirty albums and became a movie actor, a *Grand Ole Opry* regular, and eventually, the publisher of the Nashville-based trade publication *Music City News*.

The Faron Young signing may have been a bit of a fluke, but it was not unusual for Nelson to travel the highways from Texas to Carolina in search of the right sound. "I used to take buses through the South and listen to the jukeboxes to see what people were listening to," said Nelson, who didn't get a driver's license until 1961, at age fifty. "Most of the country records were selling in the South, and I wanted to see what they liked. I might be going from LA to Nashville, or Atlanta, or Cincinnati—I recorded in all those cities—and I knew I could get a good feel for things by stopping in the bus stops and the restaurants."

Nelson kept a black binder with names, dates, and places, the chronicle of a career that included sessions with Roy Acuff, Sonny James, Ray Stevens, Tex Ritter, Speedy West, Jimmy Bryant, and Roy Rogers and Dale Evans ("Dale was the boss—no question about it," Nelson noted). One of the entries in that black binder recorded a landmark date: August 30, 1957, the day Nelson signed Buck Owens. Of course, he'd known Buck for some years, from Owens's frequent work as a session guitarist behind Collins, the Farmer Boys, and others. Buck had tried long and hard to get himself a recording contract of his own, but Nelson hadn't seemed all that interested. "I was, you know, 'Go away, boy. Ya bother me,'" Nelson said, feigning mild irritation.

Buck remembered it differently: he said he never personally asked Nelson about joining Capitol, although he had others ask on his behalf. In any case, with Columbia Records now knocking on Owens's door, Nelson quickly changed his tune. Owens suddenly looked like a hot commodity, so continued indifference on Nelson's part, real or phony, clearly could have proved costly. Decades later, Nelson remained convinced that Owens would have been a major star on any label.

There was no logbook entry for it, but Nelson never forgot one memorable recording session—September 12, 1963, the live concert at the Bakersfield Civic Auditorium honoring the ten-year anniversary of Cousin Herb's television program. It was at that concert, which resulted in the album *Country Music Hootenanny*, that Nelson first noticed Merle Haggard, then a singer-guitarist in Henson's backup band. "After we were done, I walked up to Merle and asked him if he'd like to sign with Capitol," Nelson said. "He just said, 'No.' I said, 'Well, wh-wh-why?' He said he had a contract with Tally Records. That was this little label he had with Fuzzy Owen. I'd never even heard of it at the time, but over the next few months I started to see it on the chart." Nelson eventually convinced Fuzzy Owen to sell Haggard's Tally masters to Capitol, and Haggard's association with the label spanned twenty-five years.

Some good ones got away. Nelson had an opportunity to grab Willie Nelson, whose records weren't selling particularly well on the RCA Victor label, but he elected to pass. Many years later, Willie quit shaving and grew his hair long. With his new-look bandanna and ponytail, he went on to a huge career. Looking back at it, though, Nelson didn't feel too bad. "He got big years later— many years later," the producer said. "I'm not sure we would have waited, even if we'd known."

As a producer, Nelson's style was relaxed, to say the least. He often sat back quietly behind the recording board, doodling on paper, his mind seemingly far away. But if he heard a sour note or a missed beat, he'd stop everything and make the musicians start over again. "But if it was good, Ken would say, 'A joy to hear and a sight to behold,'" remembered Bonnie Owens. "If he said that, we all knew it was good. But he never tried to tell Merle how to sing. They made a good team."

Capitol Records producer Ken Nelson ushers Buck Owens through the Tokyo airport, 1967.
(Photo courtesy of the Buck Owens Private Foundation, Inc.)

Indeed, for the most part, Nelson was a hands-off producer. He demanded that his artists be practiced, prepared, and professional, but otherwise he let them be. Nashville producers might make demands about specific material, instruments, or musicians, but Nelson was much less likely to call those shots. In that way, by preserving the musical fingerprints of his West Coast artists, he preserved for history a sound that other producers just couldn't seem to capture.

The value of Nelson's approach as a producer became clear to Haggard in April 1966. He was itching to record a follow-up to "Swinging Doors," but Nelson wasn't available. Haggard and the Strangers, not willing to wait, simply packed up and went to Nashville, where they found themselves another producer. The results were abominable, and the tapes were buried. Haggard—back in Hollywood with Nelson and coproducer Fuzzy Owen in the booth—recut "The Bottle Let Me Down" with honky-tonk guitarists Glen Campbell and James Burton playing alongside Roy Nichols, and they deemed it a keeper.

Nelson's country music record collection was sizable, but his personal tastes were more sophisticated. He preferred George Gershwin, Jerome Kern, Rodgers and Hart—classic Tin Pan Alley and American Songbook—and piano pop-jazz. In another life, Nelson might have been a great lyricist: he would still get a lump in his throat from Rodgers and Hammerstein's "Oh, What a Beautiful Morning" or, for that matter, Tommy Collins's "If That's the Fashion."

Nelson retired in 1976 and settled down in tiny Somis, California, a few miles east of Ventura, where he and his wife June had built a house in 1972. After her death in 1984, Nelson occupied himself with his autobiography; *My First 90 Years Plus 3* was published in 2007. He died the following year, thirteen days shy of his ninety-seventh birthday.[2]

In 2001, Nelson was voted into the Country Music Hall of Fame, joining his Nashville-based contemporaries, Paul Cohen and Owen Bradley of Decca Records, Don Law of Columbia, and Steve Sholes of RCA. That the bestowing of the honor took so long irked many of the musicians whose careers he had helped shape—and not just because Nelson was a founder and two-time president of the Country Music Association. "It's really a slap in the face at Ken Nelson," said Jean Shepard, whose 1953 duet on Capitol with Ferlin Husky, "A Dear John Letter," was one of the first country songs by a Bakersfield-area artist to go to number one. "I don't know if he didn't fit their mold, or what."[3]

No, Ken Nelson didn't fit the mold, but then that's what made him—and the Bakersfield Sound he helped create—a "joy to hear and a sight to behold."

CHAPTER 10

The Mentor, the Muse, and the Protégé

When music fans think of the Bakersfield Sound, they typically visualize its two best-known practitioners, and with good reason. No one else who came out of the Central Valley during that quarter-century explosion of aptitude and creativity remotely approached Buck Owens or Merle Haggard in terms of record sales or general recognizability. But pop-culture fame is a mysterious and random thing. Sometimes the dichotomous outcomes we label as successful and unremarkable are as much matters of timing and the elusive quest to satisfy fickle consumer tastes as they are matters of talent and work ethic.

Among the performers who spent substantial portions of their careers in Bakersfield banging on that door, three came very close to breaking through—just not to a degree that justifies "enduring fame" status. Nonetheless, they are important figures in the development and popularization of the Bakersfield phenomenon. They sold records, certainly, but they also contributed to an atmosphere that made others' superior achievements possible and almost even expected. One was a mentor, one a muse, and one a protégé, and they mattered.

The Mentor: Tommy Collins

Tommy Collins played poker with the devil and wrote hymns alongside the Lord. He saw the world from the stage of countless auditoriums and tasted his own emptiness in a bitter mouthful of gin. He gave up on country music to preach the Gospel and then gave up on God for booze, women, and drugs. He gave up on his family and his career too—and they on him. But as Haggard sang in "Leonard," a 1980 track about his old mentor, musical collaborator, and fishing buddy, Collins had a way of inspiring people.[1]

Along the way, Collins wrote three hundred songs. His first big hit, "You Better Not Do That," recorded in 1953 and featuring young, unknown Buck Owens on lead guitar, was of the first commercially successful recordings to deliver what came to be known as the Bakersfield Sound. Then, and forever after, Collins insisted on getting that distinctively twangy Fender Telecaster sound on his records, preferably with Owens providing it.

Collins saw two hundred of his songs make it onto vinyl, but it wasn't until 1987 that he finally received his first gold record—for a songwriting credit. Given his biographical cache of success and defeat, joy and anguish, it must have seemed inevitable to those who knew him best.

By the time Collins—born Leonard Sipes in rural Oklahoma—moved to Bakersfield in 1952, he already knew his way around a recording studio. Despite his tender years, he had produced some studio work back in Oklahoma City and, in 1951, had waxed a few inconsequential sides for Fresno-based Morgan Records as Leonard Sipes and His Rythmn Oakies (yes, with an "alternative" spelling for the first word and a bonus "a" in the second). Those records didn't sell much to speak of, but they did garner some attention, and in 1952, having been introduced by Ferlin Husky to Ken Nelson and Cliffie Stone of Capitol Records, Collins landed a deal—not a recording deal, unfortunately, but a deal nonetheless. Stone liked Collins's material enough to bring him on as a writer for his publishing company, Central Songs.

Tommy Collins and Buck Owens pose with the queen of the *Grand Ole Opry*, Minnie Pearl, circa 1965. This photo still hangs in her preserved dressing room at the Opry.
(Photo courtesy of the Buck Owens Private Foundation, Inc.)

Nelson thought Collins had potential as a performer in his own right, but he had one reservation: the name Leonard Sipes didn't strike him as particularly marketable. He gently badgered the singer about changing it, without apparent success, but on July 9, 1952, Husky settled the matter. Husky was in the studio, recording a Collins composition called "Are You Afraid," and Collins was hanging about the studio, listening. During a break, the musicians asked for some sandwiches, and Collins volunteered to go out to get them. One of the musicians wanted a cocktail too—a Tom Collins. Husky announced, "That's it, that's your new name. Only we'll call you Tommy." Husky, who was then calling himself Terry Preston, clearly had stage-name creation credentials, so the rechristening was immediately celebrated as a done deal. And so it was that the man whose life and career would repeatedly convulse from alcohol abuse came to be named after a concoction of lemon juice, sugar, carbonated water, and gin.

The other crucial prefame moment in Collins's career came at the Blackboard in 1953. He was playing at a Sunday jam session when he caught sight of a young woman: from their vantage points on the bandstand, both he and bandmate Owens took immediate notice of pretty Wanda Shahan. Afterward Collins made it a point to meet the young divorced mother, and three weeks later, the two drove to Las Vegas and were married.

Later that year Collins signed that long-anticipated recording deal with Capitol Records. At his first studio session, on June 25, 1953, Collins cut four songs, including one of his most memorable: "You Gotta Have a License." At his second session, on September 8, 1953, he cut four more, including "You Better Not Do That" and "High on a Hilltop." Collins's studio band for both sessions was the definitive Bakersfield ensemble: Owens and Husky on lead guitars, Lewis Talley on rhythm guitar, Fuzzy Owen on bass, and Bill Woods on fiddle. "You Better Not Do That" climbed quickly to number two on the *Billboard* charts. The Bakersfield Sound had cleared the runway and was airborne.

The rewards were frequent and numerous. Collins performed on the *Houston Jamboree*, *Ozark Jubilee*, and *Grand Ole Opry*. A poll of America's disc jockeys voted Collins "Most Promising Country and Western Artist," and similar honors came from *Billboard*, *Cashbox*, and *Down Beat* magazines. In 1955, Collins guest-starred at the *Big D Jamboree* in Dallas, at the *Ozark Jubilee* in Springfield, Missouri, and on a touring swing through Florida. The promoter of the Florida tour put him onstage right after a singer whose name Collins had never heard before: Elvis Presley. The kid from Tupelo, Mississippi, borrowed Collins's Martin guitar one night, and when he handed it back, only four strings were still intact.

That tour provided Collins with a front-row seat for Presley's historic emergence. "Nobody knew who he was yet," Collins said, "but they found out at one show in Jacksonville, Florida, at a baseball stadium. Andy Griffith was the show's headliner, and he and I were standing there together, near a dugout, watching while people tried to get up on the stage with Elvis. Andy turned to me and said, 'It's an orgy.' That's the show where Elvis broke loose."

About the same time, Collins began to sense another voice calling his name, pulling him in a direction away from music. Maybe the drinking had finally taken its toll on his conscience, or something in Collins's religious upbringing stirred inside, but in January 1956, at the Central Baptist Church in Bakersfield, Collins publicly declared his acceptance of Jesus Christ as his life's guiding influence. This sudden spiritual awakening turned Collins's life completely around, to the surprise and chagrin of some of his music industry confederates. Collins himself could hardly believe it either, but it felt so real he became convinced that God was calling him to the ministry.

So while Presley was grabbing the record-buying public by its lapels with his first RCA recordings, including "Don't Be Cruel," Collins was at Capitol's studios in Hollywood recording original gospel tunes such as "Upon This Rock."

In January 1957, Collins moved Wanda and their three children (two from Wanda's first marriage) to Berkeley, California, where he enrolled in the Golden Gate Theological Seminary. Ken Nelson and his wife, June, drove all the way up from Los Angeles to try to talk him out of quitting the music business, but Collins held fast.

Collins didn't always know his New Testament from his Old Testament, but he graduated and took his first ministerial job at a Southern Baptist church in Colfax, California, a gold-rush mountain town east of Sacramento. He soon moved on to nearby Lincoln for a little over two years. Then, in the early 1960s, he took a job as an interim pastor in Mettler, just south of Bakersfield. But finding himself going "spiritually cold"—and financially bereft—he started selling Kirby vacuum cleaners to make ends meet.

In 1963, Collins quit the ministry and re-signed with Capitol

Records, and in April 1964, he began recording with Haggard, who had seen Collins perform years before at the Rainbow Gardens. Also in that first session with Haggard was Glen Campbell, then a prolific studio guitar player whom Collins had met the year before at Cousin Herb Henson's ten-year anniversary show. (Henson, who'd had premonitions of his own death, had told family members that if anything went wrong, he wanted Collins to officiate at his funeral. Collins somberly obliged.)

Collins's second contract with Capitol didn't result in the kind of sales the two parties had hoped for, and so they parted ways, and Collins signed with Columbia Records in 1965. That relationship—which lasted until 1968—wasn't much better. "I had selected the musicians to be on my Capitol sessions and I've often wished that I had done that when I got on Columbia and recorded in Nashville," Collins said. "With all due respect to [lead guitar player] Grady Martin, who is a genius, and Ray Edenton, a fine rhythm player, it was very difficult to keep the Buck Owens sound going. One time I did talk [Columbia A&R man] Don Law into hiring Fred Carter, a lead guitar player who played a Fender Telecaster ... but I got this feeling: 'Here's the way we do it in Nashville.'"[2]

At about the same time Collins first moved to Columbia, Owens called to tell him he wanted to cut an album of Collins's songs, many of which he had helped Collins record earlier. The result was the Capitol album *Buck Owens Sings Tommy Collins*, which contained twelve cuts, including "High on a Hilltop" and "If You Ain't Lovin' (You Ain't Livin')."

So it seemed only natural that Buck called again in the late 1960s and invited Collins on a North American tour that included Haggard and Rose Maddox. Collins opened each show and performed well, but one day in Des Moines, Iowa, he abruptly quit the tour. He had overslept that morning in his hotel room in Minnesota, and the tour bus had left for Iowa without him. Collins had to hitch a ride to Des Moines with a disc jockey. Collins asked Owens for an explanation and then demanded his paycheck and announced he was quitting. Collins's timing couldn't have been worse. On his way home to Bakersfield, a friend mentioned to him news of a new television show Buck would be starring in, something called *Hee Haw*.

That was typical of the way things were going in his career and in his personal life as well. Collins had had moderate success with the album *If You Can't Bite, Don't Growl*, but a long drought followed. His last session with Columbia was in March 1968. By that time he had a serious drinking problem and, as his marriage began to fray at the seams, an increasing tendency to stray. "The drinking came first, from pressures on the road, always traveling, getting uncomfortable," Collins said. "And then, too, my divorce [from Wanda, in 1971]. After that, I didn't care much what happened." In addition to gin, whiskey, and beer, Collins developed a fondness for diet pills and Mexican-made Benzedrine pills—bennies, whites, or cross-tops, depending on the part of the country. "I got to gambling with the musicians, and [I was] up all hours of the night, even one night before a session. I just didn't care anymore," he said. In 1976, Collins, who had lived in Bakersfield for twenty-five years, moved to Nashville for good, and after a few failed attempts at quitting drugs and drinking, he finally entered a rehab program. "There, I kinda saw the light, that if I didn't straighten up, I was going to drink myself to death," Collins said. "Then I went back to church, when I finally got my mind right. Righter than it was, anyway."

He took his last drink in December 1982, and in 1987 he finally earned his first gold record—platinum, technically, in today's vernacular—when George Strait's album *Ocean Front Property*, containing Tommy's song "Second Chances," sold its millionth copy. Collins's biggest songs as a recording artist—"You Better Not Do That" and "Whatcha Gonna Do Now?"—had been produced before 1958, when the Recording Industry Association of America (RIAA) began certifying gold records, and his biggest sellers as a writer, primarily for Haggard, were similarly unrecognized because the RIAA did not honor songwriters with gold records at that time. He figures one of those Haggard recordings represents the "gold record on the wall" that Haggard referred to in the 1980 song "Leonard."

"I don't know what Merle was talking about, really," he said. "And I don't know if I forgot to ask him or if I just decided not to ... He may have been referring to my song 'Carolyn' from Haggard's best-selling album *Someday We'll Look Back*." In any case, Collins, who made ten albums over the course of his long, often-interrupted career, had to wait thirty-three years for his own gold record. Collins's final hit record was yet another version of "If You Ain't Lovin' (You Ain't Livin')," recorded by George Strait in 1989.

Collins was nominated for the Nashville Songwriters Hall of Fame on six occasions, twice by Marty Stuart, the singer, songwriter, and music historian. "Tommy comes from that same Hank Williams vein," Stuart once explained. "There's not a lot of space between the initial, raw emotion and what comes out on paper." That sixth nomination finally paid off: on September 19, 1999, Collins was inducted. By that time his writing output had stretched to three hundred songs, including twenty-two for Haggard.

Collins was a Southern Baptist deacon in the last years of his life, and he often sat in church with Dallas Frazier, his old friend and roommate from the Ferlin Husky days. By that time, Collins, married four times and divorced three times with three grown children of his own and two grown adopted daughters, had stopped preaching, choosing instead to serve by making regular visits and phone calls to parishioners. In a rare exception to his no-preaching preference, he donned the vestments and officiated at the 1993 wedding of his old friend Haggard.

For a time it seemed possible that Collins might live out his days alone on a single green acre about halfway between Ashland City and Pleasant View, Tennessee. But in August 1998, Collins brought home a new bride, Hazel. Almost until the day he died in March 2000 at the age of sixty-nine from emphysema, Collins continued playing and composing on the acoustic guitar Husky had given him in 1986. Hazel might never have seen Collins at the pinnacle of his career, but she was with him for a time of rare peace.

The Muse: Bonnie Owens

She was married to the two best-known instigators of a twenty-five-year music phenomenon. She sang in the two smokiest, twangiest honky-tonks of the era. She even served drinks to the fruit pickers and oil-field workers who truly made the Bakersfield Sound what it was. Bonnie Owens, married (at different times, years apart) to both Buck Owens and Merle Haggard, had a front-row seat for a wild, influential chapter in American music history, and she was grateful for it.[3]

Bonnie Campbell was born in Oklahoma City to a pair of sharecroppers, one of eight children. She first got to know Alvis Edgar "Buck" Owens Jr. at the Mazona Roller Rink in Mesa, Arizona, in about 1945. "He was a pretty good roller skater," said Bonnie, just fifteen or so at the time. "But I liked him because he played guitar." The two dated, but Buck, who was six weeks older, was surprised nonetheless when he showed up for his daily fifteen-minute radio show, *Buck and Britt*, costarring Theryl Ray Britten, and encountered Bonnie. "What're you doin' here?" he asked, assuming she'd come to watch him. "Singin'," she answered. He didn't even know she could carry a tune.

In 1947, Buck helped Bonnie get a job performing with him on another radio show, this one starring Mac MacAtee and the Skillet Lickers. By January 1948, they were married. Son Alan "Buddy" Owens arrived on the scene five months later, and Michael Lynn Owens, their second son, was born in March 1950. Buck picked oranges, and Bonnie stayed home with the kids, but by 1951, it had become evident that the marriage wasn't working. Bonnie and the two boys left for Bakersfield, moving in with Buck's favorite uncle and aunt, Vernon and Lucille Ellington. Buck arrived soon afterward, closely followed by his parents.

Buck set out to look for work in the local saloons, and it didn't take long for him to hook up with steel guitarist Dusty Rhodes and, four months later, Bill Woods and the Orange Blossom Playboys. It wasn't quite so easy for Bonnie, who had to take a job carhopping at a hamburger joint. Buck's aunt took care of the boys while Bonnie served up chili dogs and chocolate malts. Buck and Bonnie remained legally married, though they were separated, because neither could afford a divorce. "And besides," Bonnie said, "we had one good thing in common. That was Buddy and Mike. We both wanted to make sure they had adjusted minds. It was a friendly parting."

Bonnie eventually graduated from carhopping to waitressing at the Clover Club, where she set down her cocktail tray once or twice a night to perform next to Fuzzy, Lewis, and the others. When Henson landed his *Trading Post* TV show in September 1953, the entire Clover Club band, Bonnie included, became the program's house band. Bonnie sometimes picked up her children from school and brought them to the television station for the live broadcast, which started at five in the evening. Afterward, she'd go home and cook dinner for the boys before leaving for her waitressing job.

Bonnie remained good friends with Buck, touring with his band on at least one occasion in 1963. In 1965, the two crossed paths again, professionally speaking, when the newly formed Strangers (Merle, Bonnie, Fuzzy, Roy Nichols, bassist Jerry Ward, and soon afterward, "girl drummer" Helen "Peaches" Price, from Wynn Stewart's band) signed with Omac Artist Corporation, a booking agency owned by Buck and his manager, Jack McFadden.

Merle and the rest of the Strangers agreed that they could do far worse than to follow in the footsteps of Buck Owens, who by this time was an undisputed chartbuster. Things were never tense among Buck, Bonnie, and Merle, though no doubt their fans wondered about the trio's seemingly overlapping love lives. "There was never animosity with Buck," Bonnie said. "Buck and Merle have always gotten along well ... I was broken up with Buck long before I ever met Merle, and there was a whole lot in between. I can't fathom either one, Buck or Merle, even thinking about it."

Bonnie Owens publicity shot, circa 1970.
(Photo courtesy of Bonnie Owens.)

Bonnie had done some songwriting before she married Haggard, but under his tutelage, she began to blossom. She wrote whole songs, partial songs, and small pieces of songs—and on one occasion even got composer credit for writing nothing at all. "Merle wrote every verse of the song 'Today I Started Loving You Again,' but he had another verse there that I thought didn't add anything," Bonnie said. "In fact it took something away. I talked him out of putting in those four lines, and he gave me half-writer credit."

Their marriage lasted until 1978, although it was as good as over in 1974, when Bonnie stopped touring with the Strangers. The two separated for good in 1975, with Merle doing his best to romance Dolly Parton, whose "In the Good Old Days (When Times Were Bad)" he had recorded seven years earlier, at Bonnie's suggestion. But when Merle married Leona Williams in October 1978, the ink on his divorce decree barely dry, Bonnie was a bridesmaid. She eventually resumed touring with the Strangers. "I had a lot of fun being married to Merle, but we never should have been married," Bonnie said. "We were too good a friends. I was older, seven years older, and there was like a big sister thing going on. But there was a lot of mutual respect too."

Even after Bonnie married Ridgecrest native Fred McMillen and moved to rural Missouri, she remained a touring member of the Strangers, flying from Springfield to whatever city kicked off the tour; she'd then hop aboard the band's tour bus and, after each show, sleep in her own hotel room. Fred understood.

She was always thoroughly and genuinely modest about her own contributions and her own career, which included six solo albums and two duet albums with Haggard, including one of gospel songs, as well as Haggard's staggering catalog of recordings, most of which include her backing vocals. "I was a follower; Buck and Merle were leaders," she said. "I did what was needed, and I did what I could. It was a great time though. We thought we were as big as Nashville. We didn't have their recording studios, and we didn't have the big radio stations, but we had the thing that was more than anything: we had the music." They also had unique history in the love and marriage department. As Bonnie once admitted, her diary could have been a hot seller, given her intimate association with Bakersfield's two most prominent stars.

In the last years of her life, Bonnie suffered from Alzheimer's disease, and she moved from Missouri back to Bakersfield. She died April 24, 2006—exactly thirty days after the death of her first husband, Buck Owens—without a single enemy in the world.

The Protégé: Red Simpson

A truck driver once asked Red Simpson about his experiences behind the wheel of a big rig. Simpson, Capitol Records' Bakersfield-bred answer to Red Sovine, fessed up: he had none. Well, the trucker inquired, what could have inspired Simpson to record such songs as "Roll, Truck, Roll" and "(Hello) I'm a Truck"?

"M-o-n-e-y," Simpson answered.[4]

Simpson probably fooled a lot of truckers during his seventeen-year run aboard Phantom 93308 (Local humor: that's Oildale's ZIP code). He posed for the cover of his first Capitol album, released in 1966, wearing a black knit cap rolled up above his ears, longshoreman style. He sang in a baritone that sounded as if it had been cured in black coffee and twenty years of Lucky Strikes. He seemed as authentic a long-haul driver as might be found at any truck-stop lunch counter. But he was merely playing a role developed by his producer, Ken Nelson.

Nelson had wanted Merle Haggard for the part, but Haggard's cocksure street-poet persona had just dented the national consciousness, and he wasn't about to switch gears now (although almost a decade later, in the midst of the CB radio craze, Haggard recorded one of the definitive trucking numbers of all time, the theme song for the 1974 TV series *Movin' On*). Enter Simpson, a friend of Haggard's who'd been penning ditties since the age of fourteen. He was known around the clubs as "Suitcase Simpson" for the aluminum briefcase, supposedly packed with original songs, dozens of them, that he lugged around in the hope he'd bump into a singer in need of a good song. (Though the briefcase, a very real artifact of Bakersfield lore, eventually made it into an exhibit case at the Country Music Hall of Fame and Museum in Nashville, Simpson finally admitted the story was somewhat apocryphal.) One day in the mid-1990s, Simpson took out a list of his published compositions and rolled it out on the street of his Bakersfield mobile home park. The printout stretched forty feet.

Simpson, born in Higley, Arizona, in 1934, was just following the path that his brother Buster had laid out for him. For Buster Simpson, music had offered a way out of Little Okie, the village of

160

shacks and dirt-floor tents off Cottonwood Road where cotton- and potato-picking families consoled one another in their mutual poverty. The family of John and Lillie Simpson, who had brought their brood of eleven children out west from Rush Springs, Oklahoma, in 1929, was just such a clan. Joseph "Red" Simpson, the twelfth and final hatchling, arrived during the family's eight-year layover in Arizona. Brother Buster played guitar and stand-up bass in the clubs in and around Bakersfield in the late 1940s and early '50s, most notably with Bill Woods and Billy Mize in an early incarnation of Woods's Orange Blossom Playboys. Red idolized them.

One hot afternoon, the band stopped by Red's sister's house on the way to a show, and there sat freckle-faced Red on the front steps, sweat pouring across his face. He looked up at Woods and said, "When I get big, I'm going to be a big star like you guys." Woods couldn't bring himself to tell the kid they were playing for ten dollars a night at the Clover Club and hosting a radio show for free, just for the publicity.

Red learned the truth soon enough. At eleven, he started hitting the clubs too—the all-ages clubs, anyway: Rainbow Gardens, the Pumpkin Center Barn Dance, the Rhythm Rancho, the Beardsley Ballroom, and the open-air Roundup. Red shined shoes out in front and asked performers such as Woods and Tommy Hays to show him chords on the guitar. Sometimes they'd let him get up and sing.

Simpson saw famed singing cowboy Tex Ritter one day in 1948 outside the Rhythm Ranch and offered to shine Ritter's dark green cowboy boots. Ritter's boots looked black to Red, so that's the color he put on them. "I got through, and I said, 'How's that, Mr. Ritter?' He grabbed me by the hair of the head and said, 'Boy, you just ruin't my favorite pair of green boots,' and I ran off, about ready to cry. Then he said, 'Come back over here, boy.' So I went back over there, and he handed me a dollar and said, 'Well, that's a pretty good shine after all.'"

Buster, twenty years older than Red, had told his little brother that once he reached twenty-one, they would start a band together, but that day never came. Buster went to Idaho in 1952 to pick up some money doing drywall work, and one day a doctor called the

Simpson home to say he was seriously ill. Buster didn't last much longer. It was Hodgkin's disease.

His brother's death crushed Red's heart, and suddenly adrift, he joined the US Navy. He was just eighteen when he shipped off to Korea. Aboard the USS *Repose*, a hospital ship, he met some fellow sailors who played music. They formed the Repose Ramblers, and every night aboard ship, right before the evening movie, they sang and picked for thirty minutes. The captain, P. J. Williams, liked them so much he bought them western shirts and sent them onshore to perform—at the Officers' Club at Inchon one day and at a Korean orphans' home on another.

Whenever Simpson came home on leave, he'd head over to see Woods, who by this time had become his mentor and surrogate big brother. They'd sit around and write songs. "The music just lured him," Woods said—so strongly, in fact, that Simpson went AWOL for a week or so on one occasion and ended up in the brig aboard ship all the way from San Diego to Hawaii.

Simpson mustered out of the Navy in 1955 and, swearing off cotton-picking, went to Bakersfield College on the GI Bill to learn sheet-metal work. What he really wanted to do was get onstage and pick guitar in the Bakersfield area's many nightclubs. But Bakersfield was full of great bands and talented players, and none of the top acts had openings. "I wanted to play at the Blackboard or the Lucky Spot, but all I could get was the Wagon Wheel in Lamont for five dollars a night," he said.

Red eventually started studying piano, getting tips from Buck Owens, George French, and Lawrence Williams, and in 1956, when Williams left Fuzzy Owen's band at the Clover Club, Owen offered Simpson the job. After working for next to nothing for so long, Simpson was finally playing for what the boys called "whiskey money."

In 1957, Simpson took a stab at a side career driving a Good Humor Ice Cream truck. He wasn't any good at it: he made just nineteen dollars in two weeks because he couldn't stand to see penniless kids watch longingly while their friends gobbled down pineapple-orange missiles and fifty-fifty bars. But he did get a song out of the experience. One day, while he was cruising past Buck Owens's house, an idea for a song came to him. He finished the route, went back to Buck's house, and sang what he had written. Owens got out his guitar and finished the song "Someone with No One to Love." Later that year, the Farmer Boys recorded the song for Capitol Records. By the following year, Simpson had signed with Stone's publishing company, Central Songs.

RED SIMPSON
"HELLO I'M A TRUCK"

TURQUISE RECORDS
Eagle Feathers Publishing

Artist Management:
JIMMIE ADDINGTON ENTERPRISES
P.O. Box 1921
3650 Rosedale Hwy.
Bakersfield, CA 93308
(801) 323-3038 or 323-0541

Red Simpson publicity photo for "(Hello) I'm a Truck."
(Photo courtesy of the Kern County Museum.)

Over the next few years, Simpson cut singles on three small labels: Lewis Talley's Tally Records and Leon Hart's Millie Records (both based in Bakersfield) and Los Angeles–based Lute Records. Then, in 1966, at the ripe old age of thirty-two, he caught his big break.

Truck-driving songs were all the rage on country music radio, with the likes of Red Sovine, Dick Curless, Dave Dudley, Jerry Reed, and Kay Adams having established themselves as truck-stop staples. Ken Nelson wanted a slice of that pie for Capitol, and he chose Simpson to play the part. It was a good choice: "Roll, Truck, Roll" proved Simpson indeed had an aptitude for truck-drivin' songs. He cut three more albums for Capitol in the next two years (*Man behind the Badge, Truck Drivin' Fool,* and *A Bakersfield Dozen*) and was given the opportunity to tour the country.

In 1966, he opened shows for Owens, including Buck's March appearance at Carnegie Hall. He appeared on a half-dozen installments of the syndicated TV program *Buck Owens' Ranch Show.* Later that year, he toured US military bases in Germany and France, and in 1967 he went on tour as an opener for Haggard. The two wrote songs together on the bus and in hotel rooms. But in 1968, after four albums, Capitol cut Simpson loose. Simpson says he didn't care much—"I still had a lot of booking power off the records I'd had," he said. That booking power had to carry him a long time because Red didn't record another album until 1971, after he happened to run into Visalia native Gene Breeden up in Vancouver, Washington. Breeden was starting his own label, Portland Records, and he was looking to add artists and then land a Capitol Records distribution deal. Breeden even told Simpson he had a song for him to record. "He told me, it's called '(Hello) I'm a Truck.'" Red replied, "Hello, I'm a what?" But he gave it a listen and realized it was a pretty good song. Indeed it was, as far as the record-buying public was concerned, because it reached number four in December 1971. All told, "(Hello) I'm a Truck" spent seventeen weeks on the country charts and hit number one on radio playlists around the country. Ken Nelson, who hadn't always had the greatest faith in Red's ability to sell records, was amazed by the song's success.[5]

Simpson's final entry on the charts, "The Flying Saucer Man and the Truck Driver," on Key Records, sputtered to number ninety-nine in 1979. He toured for three more years and then quit the road.

Simpson and Haggard, three years apart in age, both had hung out as kids in places like the Rainbow Gardens but never got around to meeting each other until the early 1960s. Simpson, who has a one-liner for every occasion, reasons that it's probably a good thing they didn't meet earlier. "We'd [have] both been in jail," he says. Haggard managed to find the inside of a few cells on his own, of course, and Simpson had some close scrapes. The "hillbilly hippie," as Haggard called him, never minded a drink or two. "I had three cars back in 1979," Simpson said. "I didn't need any DUIs, so when I went out drinking, I'd catch a ride home with somebody else. But after three days of doing that, I had three different cars parked at three different bars. It took some doing to get them all home."

Simpson figures he has cut a dozen or more albums, and his work has turned up in another half-dozen compilation albums built around truck-driving themes. Simpson counts two songs recorded by Haggard as among his best: "Lucky Ol' Colorado" and "You Don't Have Very Far to Go" (cowritten with Haggard). "Very Far" is among his most profitable, having been recorded three times by Haggard and by such luminaries as Rosanne Cash, Connie Smith, Jeannie Seely, Roy Clark, Billy Mize, and Bonnie Owens. Other Simpson songs have been recorded by Wynn Stewart, Alan Jackson, and of course, Buck Owens.

Simpson enjoyed a second brush with fame in the fall of 1995, when Junior Brown—known for his wizardry on the "guit-steel" double-neck, hybrid guitar—brought him to Austin, Texas, for a duet recording of "Semi-Crazy," a Brown composition in the Simpson trucker tradition. During that session, Simpson sang with Brown on "Nitro Express," a song Simpson had covered once before on his 1966 album *Roll, Truck, Roll*.

Simpson continued to stay busy well into the twenty-first century, playing regular one-man-and-a-keyboard gigs at Trout's, the Fairfax Grange, and the Rasmussen Senior Center, whose members often follow him from engagement to engagement. "Now remember, girls, no dancing on the tables," he teases them between songs. "And don't forget the bikini contest next week. I won't be here."

Those truck-driving songs are Simpson's irrefutable legacy. They're not necessarily what he envisioned when he was a redheaded kid hanging out in front of the Rhythm Rancho, dreaming about the big time. But as music careers go, his certainly had its share of satisfactions. And it sure beat alternate scenarios. That point was made abundantly clear one night in 1974, the last time Simpson performed at Nashville's *Grand Ole Opry*. Tex Ritter was the emcee who introduced him. "He went for about ten minutes telling about this kid who shined his favorite green boots black," Simpson said. "Then he said, 'I'm sure glad the boy is recordin' 'cause he never could shine shoes.'"

Simpson got to tell that story more than once in March 2012 when he was asked to headline the grand opening of the Country Music Hall of Fame and Museum's two-year exhibition on the Bakersfield Sound. He returned several times during the exhibit's two-year run and basked in the warm, loving attention with grace and good humor. Buster would have been so proud.[6]

Snapshot
Millennium Eve

Dwight Yoakam is sitting on a blue yard-sale sofa in Los Angeles, sans hat, his head surrounded by a wispy halo of thinning hair. He sets his iced tea on the coffee table and leans forward, resting his forearms on two boney, denim-clad knees. He is pondering a visitor's question: what's the most vivid memory you have of working with Buck Owens? We're talking about Yoakam's mentor, the man whose style he adopted, adapted, and presented to a nation of young, receptive ears just about the time it seemed as if the Bakersfield Sound might be relegated to the dusty one-dollar bin in the back of the record store.[1]

The moment comes to Yoakam in a flash. He recalls a day, the last day of 1999. Yoakam was at the Crystal Palace in Bakersfield, kicking back in the lavishly upholstered owner's suite. The last remnants of the twentieth century were dissolving into a glorious, gray-purple swirl on the western horizon. Seated across from Yoakam, guitar at his side, was Owens, the club's resident legend. The two were killing time before their performance together in what had been advertised as the Palace's Millennium Eve show.

Maybe it was the arrival of that much-anticipated chronological milestone, four new digits on the cosmic odometer heralding a new century. Maybe it was the realization that Yoakam's host and musical mentor had turned seventy just four months previous. Whatever it was, Owens too must have sensed that the time was ripe, because when Yoakam suggested they collaborate on writing a song, the head Buckaroo immediately grabbed his guitar. Until that day, Owens had always rejected such an idea. "You're not old enough," he would tell Yoakam. "I got underwear older'n you." Not this time. "Well," Owens confided, "I got this thing in my head."

"And he started that melody," Yoakam remembers, "just the first couple of chords in the melody for what became 'The Sad Side of Town' … And then he said, 'I got another idea here too.' I said, 'Nuh-nuh-nuh-nuh-*no*, I don't want to hear anything else. That. Let's write that.'" Yoakam and Owens mapped out the first few changes, established a mood and a general direction, and then turned their attention to the show they were about to play.

Some two months later, Yoakam drove north again from his home in Los Angeles, and the two sat down in Bakersfield and picked up where they'd left off. Yoakam, who collects titles and random lyrics in search of songs they might one day fit, offered up one such fragment: "The Sad Side of Town." Owens liked the sound of it. "Dreams are better left alone is what we've found / when you're living on the sad side of town."

In the spring of 2000, Yoakam and his longtime producer-guitarist, Pete Anderson, cut the basic track for "Sad Side" and invited Owens down to LA to add his own harmony. Eventually, Owens also sang lead vocals on two additional songs, both featuring norteño accordionist Flaco Jiminez. They became bonus tracks on *Tomorrow's Sounds Today*, Yoakam's fourteenth album, released in October 2000. The record was vintage Dwight: mostly upbeat, with a shamelessly pervasive twang and those wisps of mystery and danger that have always been hallmarks of his best work.

And there, alongside Yoakam's trademark swivel, was the classic, proud Buck of another era. Anderson later jokingly told Owens, "Every now and then, we do an album of Dwight Yoakam imitating Buck Owens imitating Dwight Yoakam imitating Buck Owens. This is the best one we've done yet."

That Yoakam was there for some of the most memorable days of Owens's December says a lot. After having introduced himself a few years before with a random, weekday office call, Yoakam was there for, and indeed was instrumental in, Owens's latter-day resurrection as a mainstream force with "Streets of Bakersfield." He was there the night that great Gregorian timepiece tolled with four new digits, and together they glimpsed the shadow of Owens's mortality. And he was there at the end, at the church, on the altar with his guitar, that cool spring morning in 2006.

CHAPTER 11

The Next Wave

D wight Yoakam didn't hold Buck Owens in high esteem simply because he had grown up listening to his music amid the stew of rock, pop, R&B, and country that dominated AM radio and Yoakam's diverse, adolescent record collection in the 1970s. Yoakam identified with Owens's route to success too—literally, the physical and emotional journey from old home to new, the preservation of the culture, the sustaining pride in his people.[1] He too had lived the migrant's existence.

When he was one year old, Yoakam's family moved from the coal mines of Appalachia to the factory region of the upper Midwest—from Pikeville, Kentucky, to Columbus, Ohio. He remembers riding those ninety miles with his family along Route 23 on holidays and occasional weekends, back into Floyd County, Kentucky, to visit his coal-miner grandfather, Luther Tibbs. "We were taillight babies," Yoakam once told me. "On weekends there were Michigan and Ohio license plates lined up going down Route 23 … crossing [the Ohio River] at Ironton, Ohio, and Ashland, Kentucky, to visit family—going home, as my mom called it. And I remember sitting on my gramp's porch in the holler with that guitar of mine, my ear to it."

Born in Kentucky, raised in Ohio, matured in California—substitute Texas for Kentucky and Arizona for Ohio, and that's Owens's story as well. Substitute Yoakam's naive, punk rebelliousness for Owens's mulish insistence that country music might just exist outside of Nashville's definition, and that too is Owens's story.

Yoakam admits that his willingness to embrace, even flaunt, a consciously cultivated outsider identity got him into trouble with the Nashville establishment perhaps unnecessarily. "Over the years, Nashville came to realize that my naive candor early on—which created some animosity on the part of some folks—was just that, naive," Yoakam said.

> *I was naive enough to be overly candid about my thoughts and observations on the industry. I learned a couple albums in ... that my opinions and observations on the industry were not pertinent to what I needed to do as an artist, so I just really began to focus solely on what I was doing at the time. And I quit ever trying to second-guess what the industry was going to do, or what radio wanted or needed, and/or what the taste of the public would be, as fickle as it can be at any given time.*

Those words might have just as easily come out of Buck's mouth in 1966. Cautious marketability versus individualism of a near-reckless nature: that was West Coast country forty years before too. It was no small wonder, then, that when Owens passed the torch to a new generation of boisterous, nonconforming troubadours, Yoakam was front and center.

Early on, Yoakam seemed to be rejecting Nashville not only with his words but also with his choices. "I went to Nashville for a brief time," he said, "and I realized that 1976–77 Nashville was not really an environment that was going to be conducive to what I needed to do to grow into who I was going to be. I came west, young man; I came west. I wasn't necessarily real clear on what I was going to be. I had an instinct about what this music could still be and what I could maybe do with hillbilly music."

In 1977, Yoakam realized, echoes of Haggard and Owens still lingered in California. Emmylou Harris remained a powerful presence in Los Angeles. "She drew me here along with the legacy that Buck and Merle had delivered to her. The [musical breakthroughs of] the late '60s, early '70s, that had given birth to country rock—Gram Parsons and the Byrds, leading to the Flying Burrito Brothers, leading to Emmylou Harris, and leading to Linda Ronstadt, and leading to the Eagles, and everything in between— just drew me here."

Buck Owens and Dwight Yoakam perform at the Kern County Fair, September 23, 1987. Yoakam, then thirty years old, had walked into the offices of Buck Owens Productions three hours earlier to meet the legendary performer and ended up coaxing him into performing for the first time in years.
(Photo courtesy of the Buck Owens Private Foundation, Inc.)

The LA punk scene of those early days—including the bands X, the Blasters, and the Violent Femmes, to name a few that crossed paths with Yoakam—didn't rub off on him so much as it reinforced the extended kinship he recognized between primal hillbilly and primal punk.

You go back to pure, traditional country music,
you go back to mountain music, you go back to the
Louvin Brothers doing "Knoxville Girl" ... [and

you find] an emotional abandon ... that then gave
birth to honky-tonk music and ... had an affinity
to rock 'n' roll. Look, it's one of the parents of rock
'n' roll. That's the child reawakening the parent.
That rock 'n' roll aesthetic came, in part, vis-à-vis
the early hillbilly aesthetic. They were the outsiders.
They were the outcasts. They were not of culture's
and of society's musical taste.

That devotion and passion for his hillbilly heritage cost him in terms of industry recognition, however. It took the CMA thirty years to give Yoakam any honorary hardware—and even then it was 2007's International Touring Artist Award, not an award for any one song or album. (He has two Grammy Awards, however, and has been honored by the Los Angeles–based Academy of Country Music.) The oversight appears not to have fazed him in the least. "I've been lucky," said Yoakam. With fifteen Grammy nominations, in addition to the two Grammy wins, and an Americana Music Award for artist of the year, among many other honors, that much is evident.

Yoakam swears he'll never dumb down, or pop up, his music to satisfy the tastes of radio program directors or anyone else. He's in it for himself, in the musical sense. But his approach is not purely a matter of principle.

"You can't predict when your moment and an audience's moment may intersect," Yoakam said. "Jim Ed Norman, [then] president of Warner-Reprise Nashville, said to me ... after the large success of [1993's] *This Time*, he said, 'You know, as an artist you still just have to sail your course and set your compass heading and maintain it, and allow the sea to rise to meet you. You can't force the bow of the boat down into the sea, or you'll risk a shipwreck.'"

Yoakam has stuck with that advice too, "much to the chagrin of Buck at times," he said, acknowledging the man he honored, postmortem, with 2007's *Dwight Sings Buck*. "But Buck knows Buck didn't listen to anybody but himself [either], and he knows that if we have an affinity to one another, it lies therein ... He understood that I had to walk my own path. He understood it because he had journeyed down his own road also."

Perhaps it was Yoakam's unabashed embrace of all things Buck—and of course, the raging commercial success that came with it—but a subgenre of bands and music honoring Buck, Merle, and even Wynn Stewart and Red Simpson followed. A few of them are even worth celebrating.

Cookie-Cutter Cowboys

But first, a few words about those who may not be particularly worth celebrating. In his line of work as a country music radio station proprietor, Buck Owens saw many of them, so many he appropriated a joke that described the industry's star-of-the-moment development process. It goes like this:

The agent goes in to see Bob, the record company executive.

Agent: Bob, I'm saying to you, I have got an artist for you.

Boss-Man Bob: Yeah? How tall is he?

Agent: Oh, he's six foot.

Boss-Man Bob: Yeah? How's he built?

Agent: Great. Slim, good build.

Boss-Man Bob: Is he good-looking?

Agent: Yeah!

Boss-Man Bob: Does he smile?

Agent: Oh yeah!

Boss-Man Bob: That part about boots?

Agent: Yeah, boots, and he wears a hat too now, Bob. He wears boots and a hat.

Boss-Man Bob (standing up and shaking the agent's hand): You've got yourself a deal.

As the agent gets to the door, the record company boss calls out to him.

Boss-Man Bob: Oh! By the way, can he sing?

You could've heard that punch line coming from three bar stools down, but when Buck Owens was the one telling the joke, you just rode it out. Buck could tell that you knew it was coming too, and that was half the fun of it. It would be sheer embroidery to suggest Owens believed every literal word of the scenario portrayed therein, of course, but by the time he told me this joke in 1997, Buck had seen enough performers with spectacular hygiene and marginal talent to find plenty of truth in it.[2]

Must flavor-of-the-month fame always have such shallow commonalities? Milli Vanilli, the phony pop stars with the ripped abs and immaculate dreadlocks, became lip-synching stars decades before their time—and a quarter century before Auto-Tune. Nothing quite so cynically manufactured has reached that pinnacle of sales prowess since, but sameness and safeness continue to have their place in the industry: style sells, and aptitude is just icing. And that's as true in country music as in any genre. Country didn't become a multibillion-dollar enterprise by taking too many chances too often, and for unique, young performers there has usually been a price for refusing to conform. In the post-hip-hop, new world order, traditionalists and innovators alike risk excluding themselves from country music playlists by being too much themselves. Anyone remember KD Lang? Who says the cloning of humans is still years away?

Hip-hop's arrival marked a moment that saw Nashville's business model pivot in ways it hadn't since Elvis's coronation. The influences of African American culture—in the 1950s, R&B, giving way to rock 'n' roll, and in the 1980s, rap and its progeny—prompted Nashville, consciously or not, to change dramatically.

"You have to understand [the nature of] ... country music's target audience," singer-songwriter Steve Earle once explained. "It used to be music for older people, people who were in their thirties and older. Now it's entirely aimed at twentysomethings who can't get their heads around hip-hop. It's a little uncomfortable to talk about that. It's for people who can't quite go there."[3]

This new ideal, the young, white, trim cowboy, required a certain profile, both musically and stylistically. Talent was still required, originality not quite so much.

There's a fine line between selling cookie-cutter models of commercial success and building on the best traditions of the genre, between mimicking what worked for last year's breakthrough act and infusing some originality into an honored, cherished style. It's tough to explain, but you know it when you hear it. Occasionally, an act comes along that catches fire and defies the logic of the Nashville politburo. Rare folks like that might rise up from the ghetto of the indie, alternative country world and make themselves known to a wider public, but only when their talent and authenticity simply cannot be denied.

In the 1980s, there was no better example than Yoakam, who, like a succession of performers starting with Owens, shunned the assembly line and dared to perch on the fence between rock and country, pop and folk. The Eagles were among a memorable few who were out in front of this, charting three singles from their 1972 debut, *The Eagles*, and two more from their heavily western-influenced follow-up, *Desperado*. But both before and after the Eagles' ascension, the Byrds, the Flying Burrito Brothers, Creedence Clearwater Revival, America, Buffalo Springfield, Neil Young, Crosby Stills and Nash, the Nitty Gritty Dirt Band, Poco, Ry Cooder, Linda Ronstadt, Emmylou Harris, and the Grateful Dead were each in their own way leading mainstream American music toward a dramatic, thematic, stylistic turn. Rock was forever changed; commercial country would embrace this style only a decade or more later.[4]

Imitation and Homage

The Bakersfield Sound has been around long enough now for second, third, and even fourth generations of performers to identify with some aspect of its character: its themes of poverty, alienation, pride, and redemption; its musical styles, both the earnest, urgent freight-train delivery of Buck Owens and the nuanced jazz-folk of Merle Haggard; and especially its rejection of the copycat mentality that has long plagued Nashville and every other capital of genre. To reject the template of the hour is, in a sense, to pay tribute to the Bakersfield Sound, no matter what the theme, the beat, or the instrumentation. Sometimes the homage is subtle. Sometimes it beats you over the head—and the honored artist himself may not even be immune.

When in 1996 Buck Owens first heard the Tex-Mex strains of "All You Ever Do Is Bring Me Down," his ears did a double take. That wasn't his voice on the radio, but it sure might have been: "All you ever do is bring me down / making me a fool all over town." Radio listeners all over the country—even Owens's aunt in Santa Maria, California—thought the same thing, and many phoned Owens's radio station, KUZZ, to say so. A few wanted to congratulate Owens on his new song.

The musicians responsible for this confusion were the Mavericks, the Miami-based band that makes no secret of its collective affection for Owens's "shuffle" style. Raul Malo, the Mavericks' lead singer and primary songwriter, further authenticated "Bring Me Down" by bringing in Flaco Jimenez, whose accordion had added some spice to Buck's 1988 remake of "Streets of Bakersfield." The Mavericks—who formed in 1989, signed with MCA-Nashville in 1991, broke up in 2003, and reunited in 2012—have been "doing" Buck almost since day one.[5]

Buck Owens entered the consciousness of innumerable preadolescent brains through the osmosis of parents' and older siblings' record collections, and he stuck. Consequently, echoes of the Bakersfield Sound turn up in many places; one can hear strains of "Under Your Spell Again" around every corner. Three-time Grammy Award winner Brad Paisley, who tells of running around in circles in his living room as a child, driven to a state of euphoria by Owens's "Tiger by the Tail," is one of the most commercially successful of the flame-keepers. Paisley has said the guitar work on his first two albums was inspired by a philosophy he called WWBOD: "what would Buck Owens do?" By his third LP, 2003's *Mud on the Tires*, Paisley's attitude had become wholly immersed in Buck-think: "what can I get away with?"[6]

Owens, for his part, encouraged that way of thinking, perhaps unconsciously, perhaps not, by reaching out to young musicians in whom he'd heard a gift. Paisley remembers getting a 1999 phone call from Jerry Hufford, Owens's right-hand man at the Crystal

Palace, after he'd sent Owens a copy of his debut album. Hufford told him, "Buck listened to your record, and he loves it ... He wanted to know if you really played all those guitar parts yourself." Paisley responded, "I did. That's all me." Hufford's punch line: "Buck says 'bullshit,' and he'd like for you to fly out here and prove it." Paisley obliged, and the two became good friends, mentor and protégé.[7]

It's not just the literal sound that persists; it's the attitude, the artistic edge, the willingness to lead and not follow—that is what's still alive, just not so much in Bakersfield itself anymore. The Bakersfield Sound never really died, one might say—a big chunk of it up and moved to Texas, perhaps ironically, at about the time of Don Rich's death. The energy and innovation that seized and then abandoned Bakersfield didn't go straight to Austin, however. Singer-songwriter Steve Earle, who left San Antonio for a career in music at age fourteen, has said the vibrancy of early 1970s country and roots music was in Houston, where Lightnin' Hopkins, ZZ Top, Guy Clark, and Townes Van Zandt were based. It was a different brand of country, heavy with blues, rock, and folk, and it heralded changes across the western landscape of country music culture.

"There was this cosmic cowboy thing, this hipster country music," in both Houston and Austin at the time, Earle said in a 2014 interview. "Country rock is a weird thing 'cause it kept coming back under a different name, over and over again. Progressive rock was the term they were using in Austin in 1972."[8]

Specifically, on Austin's Sixth Street, a strip of nightlife every bit as lively and vital as Edison Highway or Chester Avenue was in its heyday. The nearby Continental Club, then as now, is the quintessential Austin saloon, where a neo-Bakersfield Sound—considerably rocked-up in some cases—mixes comfortably with the country, rock, Tejano, folk, and blues that still make up the Texas capital's buoyant musical stew.[9]

"Austin, Lubbock, Dallas, San Antonio—they all seem to connect to the Bakersfield Sound," said Tony Villanueva, the former lead singer of the Derailers, perhaps Buck's favorite Buck-inspired band.

"So many of the Bakersfield guys were Texas immigrants, people who shared that spirit of hard-working people. Hot weather, hard work and hot licks—that was Bakersfield, and that's Texas too."[10]

The innovation and energy of that seminal moment in the early 1970s turned up in Los Angeles too, and Emmylou Harris was the beacon. Her 1975 album *Elite Hotel*, which brought together contributors such as James Burton, Rodney Crowell, Glen D. Hardin, Bernie Leadon, Herb Pedersen, and Linda Ronstadt, was a revelation. The Flying Burrito Brothers of Gram Parsons and Chris Hillman, steeped in "almost a mythical kind of thing," in Dwight Yoakam's words, had opened the door—not that broader mainstream fandom was aware of it—and Harris et al. had walked through.[11]

By 1982 the next chapter had revealed itself—the cowpunk scene had begun. Former punk bands such as Lone Justice and the Dils, who became the groundbreaking but short-lived trio Rank and File, crossed the highway at the crossroads of hillbilly and punk that Yoakam has spoken of. Yoakam seemed to benefit, and by 1985, his star was finally on the rise. Conveniently, Nashville was still largely immersed in the countrypolitan of influential producer Billy Sherrill, who was peddling the easy-listening country of Charlie Rich and the like.[12]

The advent of the Americana music chart represented another such pivot of destiny. Widely credited as having been developed and evangelized by Los Angeles–based sound engineer Clyde Kaplan, Americana emerged as a radio format during the 1990s as a direct outgrowth of the manufactured, assembly-line sound that had come to define commercial music. Yes, yet another backlash against homogenized music.

Americana, known also as alt-country, No Depression, roots rock, cowpunk, or y'allternative, among other nomenclatures, defines itself (at least according to the Americana Music Association) as "American roots music based on the traditions of country." Some of its significant artists—many of whom were well into their careers before the genre was a recognized entity—include Johnny Cash, Solomon Burke, the Band, Jay Farrar, Whiskeytown, Lyle Lovett, Robbie Fulks, the Desert Rose Band, Mary Chapin Carpenter, Son Volt, and Wilco.[13] (Wilco

front man Jeff Tweedy came from authentic Americana stock: he is
Cousin Herb Henson's first cousin once removed. Tweedy was born
and raised in Belleville, Illinois, and Cousin Herb was from East St.
Louis, Illinois, about fifteen miles west.)[14]

Throw Chris Shiflett into that Americana mix. The Foo Fighters
guitarist, having played in an assortment of heavy metal and punk
bands, is all-in with the Bakersfield Sound. His podcast, *Walking
the Floor*, has featured Red Simpson, John Doe, Tommy Hays,
Yoakam, Paisley, Earle, and other figures important to Bakersfield
music, past and present. Shiflett himself has joined the band, so
to speak, with the Dead Peasants, his rootsy side project, and he
seems to have temporarily mothballed his Gibsons and Gretsches in
favor of Fender Telecasters and guitars from the Telecaster family,
including a custom Warmoth Telecaster he dubbed "Shifty."[15]

The Americana format has gained traction in cities across the
United States and Canada over the past two decades—even, finally,
in Bakersfield. It has also inspired the development of a long-running
program called *Bakersfield and Beyond*, based in a community
very much Bakersfield's demographic antithesis—wealthy, liberal,
earthy, western Marin County, California. KWMR's Mike Varley
and Amanda Eichstaedt have won a legion of fans that include
Merle Haggard, Dave Alvin, and Exene Cervenka of X. Much
like Bakersfield circa 1952, KWMR—one of about seventy-five
Americana stations so categorized by americanamusic.net—proves
that authenticity sometimes springs forth from the unlikeliest
places. Sometimes that authenticity wears a hat. Often it doesn't.[16]

Buck Owens's joke about the endless succession of hats and
boots and fit, slender frames still earns smiles because it still speaks
a great and tragic truth about pop fame, no matter what the genre:
pretenders and copycats are just part of the deal, while magic
and genius converge on their own, sometimes without anyone's
help. Bakersfield witnessed that convergence once, more than a
half century ago, as did Houston, Austin, and Los Angeles. And
sometime, somewhere, it will happen again.

AFTERWORD

As the roll is called up yonder, a lot of the newcomers to the pearly gates who've ascended by way of Kern County are answering in Okie drawls. The children and grandchildren of the Dust Bowl era are dying off. The evidence can be found on almost any given day in the obituary pages of the area's daily newspaper, the *Bakersfield Californian*: farmers, teachers, laborers, clerks. Inevitably, it seems, two or three of the recently departed were born in—or were raised by parents born in—Oklahoma, Texas, or Arkansas.

The generation that picked the cotton that clothed our troops during World War II, that riveted together their warplanes and warships, that extracted the oil that powered their machines, is passing on. So too are the people who entertained those workers. Every so often, the people of Bakersfield read an obituary about a guitar player, a drummer, a singer. It's never an outright star, but rather an ordinary, front-porch musician who came to the West Coast to work in a shipyard or on an oil lease or in the orchards—a musician who, seduced by the vibrant, rowdy nightlife of the day, never left.

In one short stretch of 2000–01, for example, the city lost many of the people who had helped develop the music that grew into the country-rockabilly hybrid of Bakersfield honky-tonk: Dusty Rhodes, Roy Nichols, Jerry Ward, Gene Moles, and Tommy Ash and then, in a second wave, Buck Owens, Bonnie Owens, Ferlin Husky, Doyle Holly, and Del Reeves. Most had something in common besides musical talent: they realized quickly that climbing onto a stage every night beat the heck out of almost anything else.[1]

The club scene paid the bills. In the 1950s and '60s, upward of twenty Bakersfield clubs were offering live music (especially country music) at any given time. Strikingly, the kinship among the performers far outweighed their competitiveness. They rooted for one another. In those days, a person could visit the Blackboard on a Wednesday night and hear artists such as Patsy Cline, Connie Smith, or Roger Miller sing—for five dollars. Once in a while, the *Grand Ole Opry* show would come to what was then called the Civic, featuring Roy Acuff and a whole package of Nashville stars. But then times changed. The clubs almost all disappeared. And one by one, the musicians followed. The legacy of that time need not die with them, but to a great extent it has.

Admirers are often disappointed to learn that the city has little in the way of a music scene today, at least as far as country and related genres are concerned. Other flash points of music and culture elsewhere in America have rooted deeper and endured longer, in every case because the community outside of that artistic core has embraced the phenomenon, whether the scene in question suits every taste or not. (It never does and can't.) The weight of community enthusiasm has been enough for artistic movements to grow legs. Saloons (or art galleries) beget restaurants, which beget jobs, which beget hotels, which beget apartments and markets and home improvement stores. That infrastructure never developed in Bakersfield, at least not around music.

How to kindle creative sparks into an economic bonfire that warms all hearths: that's a conversation every city that aspires to become the capital of something needs to have with itself. It's a conversation Bakersfield should have initiated decades ago—and not just for the sake of tourism. Much bigger things are at stake in resurrecting and celebrating the legacy of the Bakersfield Sound: civic pride, but also a greater understanding of the city's place in history—musical, economic, and cultural. It's good to remember who you were because it says a lot about what you'll become.

Every American city, whether it prides itself on its public sculptures or deep-dish pizza, on hot-air balloons or woolen jackets, on abundant trout streams or Greek architecture, needs to develop that identity or, if it has been allowed to escape, remember what it once was.

Bakersfield's identity, once upon a time, just happened to be genre-shaping American music. Its residents should never forget that.

APPENDIX A

The Founders

Every movement has its pioneers, and every cultural breakthrough has its architects: the lone individuals who were there at the beginning and who, though they might not have grasped the broader implications of their endeavors, displayed a tenacity and sense of purpose that others recognized and were drawn to.

The Bakersfield Sound story has several such characters. Chief among them are Bill Woods, Fuzzy Owen, and Ferlin Husky, none of whom thought they were doing anything more remarkable than making a living in a way that did not subject them to the brutal heat of a central California harvest.

Bills Woods: Piped Piper

He never had a big hit record and never became a bona fide star, but it's hard to imagine what the Bakersfield music phenomenon of the 1950s and '60s might have been without Bill Woods. Almost every prominent Bakersfield musician of that era seems to have crossed paths with Woods, a versatile entertainer and disc jockey who came to be a trusted and influential mentor—and a seminal shaper of the music's evolution. He gave Buck Owens his first big job as a performer and encouraged both Ferlin Husky and Herb Henson—two other vital recruiters of talent—to relocate to Bakersfield, where they became important figures in the early development of the scene.

Woods once sat down and tallied the names of performers whose lives he had changed in some significant way, whether because he had advised them, hired them to play with his Orange Blossom Playboys, or found them a job elsewhere. He came up with forty-seven names.[1]

"Bill Woods started a whole bunch of talent in this town," singer-guitarist Tommy Hays once explained.

> *He could play keyboard, guitar, fiddle, darn near anything. And man, could he talk. That was his real talent. He could sell an Eskimo an icebox. He got me a recording session with Smiley Maxedon, who had a radio show. He said, "Smiley, this fella plays guitar." Smiley said, "Well, Bill, we're in pretty good shape right now as far as guitar players go." Bill said, "Well, I know you can find something for one as good as Tommy." Smiley says, "Well, uh, okay, Bill."*

There was just no saying no to Bill Woods.

The son of a Pentecostal preacher, Woods was born in 1924 in Denison, Texas, a town along the Red River, which separates Texas from Oklahoma. Dwight Eisenhower was born there too, back in 1890, and Buck Owens was born just down the road in nearby Sherman. Woods got his first guitar, a Regal, at age twelve, not long after his family followed a late-1930s oil boom to Longview, Texas. He didn't show much interest in playing at first, but things changed at the tent camp where the Woods family settled. "A Mexican family lived next door, and they played trumpets and guitars most every night out in front of their tent," Woods said. "One day I asked if I could take my guitar and sit out there and watch them, and maybe play along. They said, 'Sure,' and it grew from there."

In August 1940, the Rev. L. F. Woods brought his family to Arvin, California, a farm town twenty miles south of Bakersfield. Bill, sixteen, took a job driving a grape-hauling truck for a local winery. The winery was really just a hole in the ground manned by a couple of workers with boots and pitchforks who stomped on the freshly harvested grapes until they were reduced to pulverized skins. "After seeing them stomp on those grapes, spitting their tobacco juice and Lord knows what else, I decided I would never drink wine," Woods recalled. "But I have drank enough coffee to kill me."

Bill Woods, on the fiddle, with an early version of his Orange Blossom Playboys, circa 1954: Red Simpson's older brother Buster Simpson on stand-up bass, far left, and Jack Trent on piano. The unidentified guitar player, Roy, was blind.
(Photo courtesy of the Kern County Museum.)

After a year, the family moved a hundred miles north to Woodlake, near Visalia, and Bill played his guitar in church. When World War II broke out, Woods moved farther north to Richmond, where he worked as a boilermaker in the Kaiser Shipyards, building Liberty and Victory ships. The managers allowed workers with the talent and inclination to head out to different shipyards and entertain workers during the lunch hour, and as a matter of course, Woods was tagged for this detail. "They'd bring in movie stars—Lana Turner, Victor Mature. Then on Saturday night we'd play at the Moose halls and other places," Woods said. He played upright bass with the Arizona Wranglers, a group fronted by Fresno bandleader Elwin Cross. "It was really swinging back, then," Woods recalled.

BILL WOODS
WESTERN BAND LEADER · DISK JOCKEY · RADIO SALESMAN
KBIS BAKERSFIELD, CALIFORNIA

Bill Woods, then a KBIS disc jockey, reads his fan mail into an outsized
RCA BX44 microphone.
(Photo courtesy of the Kern County Museum.)

After the war, Woods played a little in Bakersfield, then in Las Vegas, and then, returning again to Bakersfield, at the Clover Club. What followed that experience was the most important gig of his career to that point: playing piano and fiddle for Tommy Duncan, the vocalist who had become famous as the front man for the biggest western swing band of the era, Bob Wills and the Texas Playboys.

It was while on the road with Duncan in 1949 that Woods met Ferlin Husky, then a budding singer-guitarist trying to find his way in the music business. Woods eventually suggested Husky move to Bakersfield, where he said the club scene was rapidly becoming something special. Husky—who by then had adopted the short-lived stage name Terry Preston—took that advice. Woods likewise invited Henson, then a little-known musician living in Modesto, to try his luck in Bakersfield, and by 1953, Henson had his own daily program on KERO-TV.

Bill Woods was one of the top names on the Bakersfield Records label.
(Robert E. Price collection.)

In 1950, Woods began what would be a fourteen-year run at the Blackboard, and his lead guitarist for much of that time was Buck Owens; over the years, several performers claimed to have given Owens his first job on a honky-tonk stage, but it was indisputably Woods who encouraged him to shed his reticence, step up to the microphone, and sing. Woods and his band played eight times a week—seven days a week and twice on Sunday. On top of that, Woods worked as a disc jockey for KPMC, later known as KNZR. It was an exhausting schedule. "I must have been crazy," Woods recalled.

As if all that weren't enough, Woods had a decade-long run as a stock-car racer of some note. He retired from that side gig in the early 1960s to again concentrate on music: trucker songs had become a popular emerging genre on country radio, and Woods jumped into the fray in 1963 with his version of the oft-recorded Terry Fell song "Truck Drivin' Man."

But when Woods retired as a racer, he didn't retire all the way. He should have. One night, he was in Oildale at the Bakersfield Speedway hosting a remote broadcast for KWAC radio when he was approached by a man who needed a driver for the evening's "destruction derby." The guy he'd arranged to have drive the car hadn't shown up. "Hell, I'll drive it," Wood volunteered. As the event began, Woods could sense that something wasn't right with the car, and he turned toward the pit area, intending to take a look. But before he could escape the melee of shredding sheet metal, his car was hit almost simultaneously in the front and back. Two vertebrae in Woods's back popped loose. It was the beginning of a lifetime of back pain. Woods reinjured his back three years later and was never quite the same. After two years of couches, beds, and television sets, he took a job as assistant manager of a Mojave radio station and then came back to Bakersfield and started playing in the clubs yet again. "But my fingers were messed up, [and] my nerves were shot, from that wreck," Woods said. That was not enough to stop him though. Woods improved well enough to land a job playing piano on tour with Merle Haggard in 1972–73, and he helped record several songs, including "It Ain't Love but It Ain't Bad."

In 1971, as a tribute to their long friendship, Haggard recorded a Red Simpson song titled "Bill Woods from Bakersfield." Woods returned the salute. The fourth of his seven children arrived in 1971, but the baby, born prematurely, was so undersized that the Woodses put off naming him for fear he wouldn't survive. Once the danger had passed, Woods, figuring the infant had endured a trial as serious as anything his singing ex-con friend had ever braved, finally named the boy Merle Haggard Woods.

In the last decade of his life, Woods played the role of elder statesman, mentor, and living relic of music history. But his health was precarious. He underwent a hip replacement and then triple bypass surgery, and shortly afterward, he suffered a stroke. He died in April 2000 at age seventy-five, with seven of his nine children gathered around him at his hospital bedside.

Woods died knowing that among local musicians and those who had lived through the era, he was widely recognized as the man who had made it all happen. "He was a guy who figured, 'If I don't make it myself, at least I can help others make it,'" said Cousin Rich Allison, a disc jockey. "He is the father of the Bakersfield Sound."

Fuzzy Owen: The Businessman

An abandoned ruin of a building stands alone, ringed with weeds, on a neglected lot in east Bakersfield. The faded lettering on an exterior wall identifies the empty building as an old auto-upholstery shop, but Charles "Fuzzy" Owen remembers it as something else, something grander. It was here, in 1956, inside this comically tiny building a half block off East Truxtun Avenue, that Owen's cousin, Lewis Talley, undertook one of the first stirrings of his professional ambitions: the Tally Records recording studio. Owen joined him a month later.[2]

Among their first customers was twenty-six-year-old Buck Owens, who came in to record an original rockabilly tune, a little ditty called "Hot Dog." It was a foot-stompin' number that reflected Owens's zeal for singers such as Elvis Presley and Little Richard. Owens, using the pseudonym Corky Jones, apparently managed to play guitar during his session without bumping his elbows against the walls of 601 East Eighteenth Street, but it must have been a close call. "That little old building," Fuzzy once said, "ain't much bigger than a bathroom." He and Talley stayed just two or three months, recording a few records that went nowhere. Then they moved.

Fuzzy Owen's place in Bakersfield music history is secure, given his long tenure as Merle Haggard's manager, his status as a longtime regular on the *Trading Post* show, and his early connection with clubs such as the Blackboard, the Lucky Spot, and the Clover Club. But the long-defunct Tally recording studio remains one of Fuzzy's most memorable associations.

Born in Conway, Arkansas, in April 1929, Owen came west to Bakersfield to stay with relatives in 1949. During the day, he picked cotton; at night, he played at the Blackboard, then just a hole-in-the-wall tavern. His band's Ernest Tubb–inspired sound featured Fuzzy on steel guitar, Talley on rhythm guitar and vocals, and George French on accordion. Later, Fuzzy worked in the Sierra Nevada foothill village of Springville, east of Porterville, playing a three-month gig with the Sons of the Ryaneers. A two-year stint in the US Army followed, and Owen returned to Bakersfield in 1952.

Fuzzy Owen, right, and Lewis Talley, center, watch disc jockey Red Butler introduce their band for a live KPMC broadcast before a studio audience, circa 1960. Butler, who spoke literally when he referred to Cousin Herb Henson as "cousin," later organized a contest to name Merle Haggard's band. The choices were the Strangers and the Sam Hill Band. Listeners chose wisely.
(Photo courtesy of the Kern County Museum.)

In 1953, he and Bonnie Owens, who had recently separated from Buck, recorded "A Dear John Letter," written by John Grimes, who went by the name Hillbilly Barton. "But this little Mar-Vel Records we put it on didn't have no distribution," Fuzzy said. "They printed up a hundred copies, maybe." Lewis and Fuzzy still liked the song though—so much so that they concocted a barter with Barton: they would trade him Talley's 1947 Kaiser automobile for ownership of the song. A car for a going-nowhere song? Barton was ecstatic, figuring he had just pulled off a scam for the ages, and he boasted about it far and wide. The car-for-a-song transaction paid off for the buyers, however, when Ferlin Husky and Jean Shepard recorded the song later that year for Capitol Records: it went to number one on the national country charts. "We were happy for them," said Bonnie Owens. "It told us we were on the right track." Barton wasn't though—now he was enraged at having been taken. His name hadn't even been included on the songwriting credits. Complicating matters was the fact that Barton hadn't possessed the right to sell the song in the first place—his publishing company in Los Angeles should have had some say in the matter. In the end, Barton's name was added to the credits along with Talley's and Owen's, so he salvaged a small measure of redemption. More importantly, Talley and Owen had established themselves as players—small players, but players just the same.

By 1955, Talley and Owen had started up Tally Records, Lu-Tal Publishing (owned by Talley), Owen Publishing (owned by Owen), and their laughably cramped recording studio. After a few months, they moved the studio to Baker Street, next door to Saba's Men's Store, whose owner was their landlord. "We built the studio inside a little room there," Owen said. "We put a bunch of thick blankets against the walls and put in acoustic tile. We had a used, monaural one-track Stencil Hoffman [tape machine]. That's the first time I ever heard of that brand, and the last time. You can't get no smaller than one track." It was in that studio, in early 1956, that Owen and Talley recorded a Bakersfield rock 'n' roller named Wally Lewis. His song "Kathleen" was leased for production and distribution to another company and reached number fifteen a few months later.

Owen, Talley, and Cliff Crofford were determined to get the Tally Records name into the industry's sphere of awareness, so in 1956 they traveled to Nashville to attend the yearly country disc jockeys' convention. Elvis Presley had just transformed the pop-music world with a succession of number one hits, starting with "Heartbreak Hotel," and word was out that he would be at the convention. Owen, young, slender, upright, and sporting the same black pompadour and snazzy red blazer fans might have expected on Elvis, found himself engulfed by young female fans who weren't yet sure just what their idol looked like at close range. Owen and friends, mobbed from all sides, beat a hasty retreat.[3]

Back in Bakersfield a few months later, the studio moved for the third and final time—to Talley's house on Hazel Street. Talley and his wife lived in the front, and the men built their studio in the back, using the same pathetic old Stencil Hoffman tape machine and three-channel mixing board they'd been carting around for three years. The entire studio wasn't much bigger than twenty feet by thirty feet. "We built a horseshoe-shaped echo chamber, and the bathroom was in the echo chamber," Fuzzy said. "While the tape was running, no one could go to the bathroom." The studio was open for about three years, until Talley got a divorce—his wife had had an affair with Wally Lewis—and sold the house.

Despite those humble beginnings, Tally Records was poised for a break; it came in the form of a quiet, slightly self-conscious newcomer: Haggard, a few short months removed from a two-year, nine-month stay at San Quentin State Prison. It was 1961, and Haggard had landed a job sharing the stage with Fuzzy as the Lucky Spot's backup band. Tally Records' first, and last, big signing soon followed.

Owen sold Haggard's Tally Records catalog to Capitol in 1964, and in January 1965, Haggard had his first top-ten release, "(All My Friends Are Gonna Be) Strangers," which had been a minor hit on Tally Records the year before. Haggard and his band, dubbed the Strangers in honor of that first hit song, were on their way.

Talley, Haggard's bus driver and close confidant, died of a heart attack in 1986 at age fifty-eight. Owen remained an active member of Haggard's managerial entourage for years, spending half his time on the road until he reached his eighties.

Bill Woods fostered an atmosphere of camaraderie and mutual support that turned Bakersfield into a West Coast music mecca, but Fuzzy Owen and Lewis Talley were vital players too. Their ability to spot talent (especially Haggard), their consistent presence in the clubs where the Sound was developing, their Tally Records label, and their recording studios—low-tech and laughable though they may have been—were milestones. Without cousins Fuzzy and Lewis, the Bakersfield phenomenon wouldn't have been the same.

Ferlin Husky: Just Passing Through

Ferlin Husky was just a wiry twenty-five-year-old with a guitar and a pencil-thin mustache when he moved to Bakersfield in 1950. He stayed less than four years, but they were four productive years, both for Husky and for the talented performers he found, fostered, and befriended.[4]

Husky, a Mississippi native, was calling himself Terry Preston when, in 1950, at Bill Woods's suggestion, he moved from Salinas to Bakersfield to take a job as a disc jockey with KBIS. The show was broadcast live from the Rainbow Gardens. Husky, also a budding recording artist, gradually worked himself from behind the turntable to the front of the stage. His band, the Termites, became the star of the show, held before an all-ages crowd every Friday and Saturday night.

Going out to dance was a special occasion. No matter how poor they were or how dirty their jobs—farm laborers and oil-field workers were the primary customers—people washed up and donned clean Levi's and western shirts and perhaps cowboy hats. Some wore suits. It was a special occasion, the highlight of their week, and ticket prices reflected it: for many of the dancers, two dollars was a steep charge. But the dance hall was nothing special to see. It had the acoustics of an airplane hangar and the intimacy of a school cafeteria. Of course, it wasn't any worse than the competing dance halls of the day: the Beardsley Ballroom, the tiny

Rhythm Roundup, and Cousin Ebb's Pumpkin Center Barn Dance. "The stage was three feet off the floor, and there were no tables, just benches all the way around the hall," Husky said. "There was no liquor or nothing, just a place outside, so many feet from the building, where you could get wine and beer."

With his sharp eye for talent, Husky spotted Tommy Collins, a twenty-one-year-old singer from Oklahoma who was visiting Bakersfield in 1951 with his girlfriend. Collins saw the star-making potential of the burgeoning club scene and decided to stick around, although his girlfriend, sixteen-year-old Wanda Jackson, chose to go home—and eventually become America's rockabilly queen of the 1950s.

Ferlin Husky, circa 1956: he called himself Terry Preston in those days, but the man who gave other singers their stage names eventually went back to using his own. *(Photo courtesy of the Kern County Museum.)*

Collins lived in a room on the top floor of the home on Monterey Street that Husky and his wife rented, but he got more from Husky than just lodging: his memorable stage name as well as vital professional direction and even some assistance developing his singing style. Husky also showed Collins how to handle rowdy crowds, something the Rainbow Gardens had in abundance. "There were some tough old boys there, and they liked to fight," Collins once explained. "And fights would break out. I mean bad ones. There've been killings. I have watched Ferlin more than once … come down off the bandstand and put an arm around each one of them's waist and walk outside with them. And how he kept them from fighting, I don't know."

A year after Collins moved in, the Huskys took in Dallas Frazier, a twelve-year-old songwriting prodigy from a ranch near the Pumpkin Center labor camp, who'd won a talent contest at the Rainbow Gardens. Frazier, who roomed with Collins, went on to make regular television appearances on *Trading Post* over the next seven years and, after moving to Tennessee, penned the 1980s hit "Elvira" and another three hundred tunes.

In 1948, Husky signed with 4 Star Records, partly because the Maddox Brothers and Rose, one of the dominant West Coast country groups of the 1940s, were signed to that label. But by 1952, he had moved to Capitol Records. And while he waited for his big break, he played guitar in the local clubs, first with Bill Woods's Orange Blossom Playboys and then in Tommy Collins's band.

In 1953, that big break arrived: "A Dear John Letter," a duet with Jean Shepard of Visalia, became a national hit. Husky shaved off his Clark Gable mustache and hit the road to trade on his new fame. By the end of that year, he was gone for good, but in the short interval during which he lived in Bakersfield, he had helped launch the career of or create three new young stars: Collins, Frazier, and Shepard. Not bad for four years' work.

Collins, looking for a replacement for Husky, eventually hooked up with Alvis Edgar "Buck" Owens Jr., who, Husky claimed, benefited from the influence of his predecessor. Owens, in Husky's view, succeeded thanks in part to "the tone of his voice, a trebly, penetrating sound that I set for him ... That real whangy-dangy, penetrating nasal sound: that's Buck."

Advertisement for a show starring Terry Preston, a.k.a. Ferlin Husky, at the Rainbow Gardens in about 1952. The venue's name often turned up as *Garden* rather than *Gardens*, as was the case here.
(Image courtesy of the Bakersfield Californian.*)*

In 1953, Husky forever parted with Terry Preston, the stage name he had used in his earliest professional recordings and stage

195

appearances. Husky's father, abetted by Capitol Records producer Ken Nelson, had finally convinced Ferlin that his given name had as good a "country" ring as any he might invent. The record-buying public liked this more authentic version of Husky. Again with Shepard, Husky recorded another hit, "Forgive Me, John," a sequel to their breakthrough song, and he then won acclaim for "Hank's Song," a tribute to Hank Williams, who had died in 1953. Husky and his comic alter ego, Simon Crum, were now big-name performers.

In 1956, he rerecorded a song he had cut five years before on the West Coast as Terry Preston. The difference between the two versions of "Gone," Husky said, aptly exemplifies the difference between the Bakersfield and Nashville sounds. "When I rerecorded it in Nashville in 1957 as Ferlin Husky, I used an echo chamber and a choir, a group of singers. The first time, it was just me, a drummer, and a couple of guitars." "Gone" became the first country single of the Nashville Sound era to cross over to the pop top ten.

In 1957, Husky demonstrated his versatility by playing a featured acting role in a Kraft TV Theater play, and in 1958 he made his movie debut in a film starring Zsa Zsa Gabor and singer Faron Young, titled *Country Music Holiday*. He had few hits in the years that followed, but in 1967 he reached the top ten with "Once." And in 1974, he made the charts with two singles: "Freckles and Polliwog Days" and "Champagne Ladies and Blue Ribbon Babies," both written or cowritten by his old friend and protégé Dallas Frazier. In 1990, at age sixty-four, Husky moved to Branson, Missouri, and started a lengthy run at assorted theaters, appearing regularly with his old sidekick, the ubiquitous Mr. Crum.

When Husky died in March 2011 at the age of eighty-five, he was eulogized as a leading proponent of the lush orchestral sound that became the hallmark of the Nashville Sound of the late 1950s and early '60s—the antithesis of the teen-oriented rock 'n' roll of Elvis Presley that so dramatically cut into mainstream country record sales. That was the irony of Ferlin Husky's career: "Dear John Letter" is widely regarded as the song that put the Bakersfield Sound on the map, and "Gone" is widely regarded as one of the songs that helped restore Nashville. That's some musical epitaph.

And a Cast of Thousands

T he performers who scattered the first discernible seeds of the Bakersfield Sound were many and diverse, and there is plenty of room for argument about their worthiness. One could easily make a case for the omissions from this list, such as Jimmie Rodgers, the Carter Family, and Ernest Tubb, all of whom profoundly advanced American music. These are one man's nominees, selected because of the time and the place they made their marks, the contributing subgenres they represented, and the influences they had on the Bakersfield-area performers who brought the Sound toward its next incarnation. Let the debate begin.

Woody Guthrie: The Dust Bowl Troubadour

Woody Guthrie's role in the development of West Coast country wasn't so much as an innovator of musical style—although he was that too—as it was as a shaper of audience. Guthrie, born in Okemah, Oklahoma, was on his own by the age of fourteen, or nearly so: his mother was institutionalized with Huntington's disease, and his father was forced to take work in Texas. He married at nineteen but left his wife behind to go to California with the Dust Bowl Okies. He soon rose to regional fame as the radio partner of Maxine "Lefty Lou" Crissman; their program, which featured hillbilly and "traditional" country music, earned him the first reliable, living-wage paychecks of his life. At about that time Guthrie began to write and perform the politically charged protest songs he became best known for. Some of them would later turn up on his first commercial recording, the 1940 album *Dust Bowl Ballads*.

Guthrie's fan base was huge—among established Californians and particularly among Okie migrants, who heard in his words the stories of their struggles and in his music a simplicity that they could replicate on their front-porch stoops and around their campfires. The "Dust Bowl Troubadour" became the hero of many an impoverished Okie farm laborer.

Guthrie's unapologetically direct communist inclinations became a liability when, at the outset of World War II, Nazi Germany signed a nonaggression pact with the Soviet Union. The owners of the radio station that employed Guthrie, sensing political (and sponsor) blowback, ended the show. Guthrie moved back to Texas for a time, which made his wife happy, but wanderlust soon gripped him again, and he headed to New York. In 1940, driven in part by his distaste for Irving Berlin's "God Bless America," he wrote "This Land Is Your Land," and his enduring fame was assured.

Ultimately, Guthrie became much more closely associated with folk music than with country—Bob Dylan, Pete Seeger, Billy Bragg, Bruce Springsteen, and John Mellencamp are among the many who cite him as an influence. But in Bakersfield and the San Joaquin Valley, before there were honky-tonks, before there were weekday-afternoon country music television shows, there was Woody Guthrie, the man who made the poorest of the poor feel like they mattered.[1]

Bob Wills: The Original Playboy

Bob Wills, a fiddle player, songwriter, and leader of the Texas Playboys, fronted what was probably the most famous of western swing bands. Wills, born in Hall County, Texas, in 1905, is widely acknowledged as the direct inspiration for an entire generation of country musicians, including every important performer to come out of Bakersfield in the 1950s and '60s.[2]

He lived in Texas migrant camps as a child and picked cotton from an early age. Like so many others, music was his way out: he made his first solo appearance as a fiddler at the age of ten and in 1931, at age twenty-six, landed a job on a Fort Worth radio program. Three years later, following a successful stint with the Light Crust Doughboys, Wills formed the Texas Playboys, featuring lead singer Tommy Duncan. By the early 1940s, Wills's trademark high-pitched yowl—"Ah-haaaah! San Antone!"—had become a national catchphrase.

The band played up and down the West Coast during World War II, popularizing western swing for a generation of young men and women from across the country who had come to work in the shipyards and factories. Wills stayed put in California after the war and organized a new version of the Playboys that performed throughout the San Joaquin Valley, at clubs such as Oildale's Beardsley Ballroom, well into the late 1950s.

Merle Haggard cut an album of Wills songs in 1970, *A Tribute to the Best Damn Fiddle Player in the World*, which featured many of the original Playboys—and forever sealed Wills's status as a demigod in the eyes of the Bakersfield singer-songwriter. Wills's last recording session took place in December 1973 at Haggard's Kern River estate east of Bakersfield. He died in 1975 at the age of seventy.

Several of Wills's bandmates had noteworthy careers fronting their own western swing combos. The best known was Duncan, but Milton Brown was probably the most historically significant—not for his hit records (as a bandleader, he had none) but for his stylistic contributions. In 1927, he and guitarist Herman Arnspiger joined the Wills Fiddle Band, which by 1930 had changed its name and landed a regular slot on WBAP in Dallas as the Aladdin Laddies. Most famously, he and Wills were paired in the Light Crust Doughboys, a.k.a. the Fort Worth Doughboys; their RCA Victor recordings of "Nancy Jane" and "Sunbonnet Sue" eventually came to be considered the first examples of western swing music. In September 1932, Brown split from Wills and formed his Musical Brownies with brother Derwood. They produced a substantial catalog over the next three years before Brown, in the company of a sixteen-year-old girl, suffered fatal injuries while driving home from a show one night in March 1936. Nationwide fame largely eluded him, but Brown came to be accepted, along with Wills, as an originator of western swing.

Spade Cooley: The King of Santa Monica

Jimmy Thomason and Spade Cooley, circa 1948.
(Photo courtesy of the Kern County Museum.)

Spade Cooley, a Los Angeles–based singer, fiddler, and bandleader, was one of the West Coast's biggest wartime stars. Born Donnell Clyde Cooley in 1910 in Pack Saddle Creek, Oklahoma, to an impoverished family, he moved to Oregon when he was four and then in 1930 to the San Joaquin Valley city of Modesto. By that time, Cooley, trained classically as a violinist and cellist, was playing dances. He earned his nickname Spade from his prowess at poker.[3]

In 1934, Cooley established himself as a movie stand-in for Roy Rogers; their resemblance was striking. Not long after that, Cooley started his own band, quickly became a star at the Venice Pier Ballroom near Los Angeles, and landed a recording contract. His first hit, "Shame, Shame on You," recorded in 1944, became his theme song. By the time he had risen to headliner status at the prestigious Santa Monica Ballroom, Cooley had come to rival Wills as a top star of western swing.

With his good looks and engaging personality, Cooley was a natural for the big screen. He appeared in several movies, including *Chatterbox*, *The Singing Bandit*, *The Singing Sheriff*, *Outlaws of the Rockies*, and *Texas Panhandle*. In 1947, he landed his own television show on KTLA, *The Hoffman Hayride*, named for a sponsoring TV manufacturer. The show attracted 75 percent of the viewing audience throughout the late 1940s. Ratings eventually dwindled, and the show went off the air in the early 1950s, but Cooley was still a popular live performer. He toured extensively throughout the mid- and late 1950s and played at the Blackboard on a regular basis.

When he hit fifty, Cooley bought a ranch near Mojave and went into semiretirement; it was there in July 1961 that his life took a dark turn. Cooley attacked his estranged wife, beating and kicking her to death while their fourteen-year-old daughter watched. In a sensational trial at the Kern County Courthouse in Bakersfield, he was convicted of murder and sentenced to life in prison. His prospects for parole looked favorable when, in November 1969, thanks to a record of good behavior, he was granted leave from the Vacaville prison to participate in a benefit concert in Oakland. After a well-received performance, Cooley, fifty-nine, walked backstage and suffered a fatal heart attack.

Rose Maddox: Queen of the Hillbillies

America's premier hillbilly band: the Maddox Brothers and Rose.
(Publicity shot/public domain.)

Rose Maddox was the lead singer and undisputed star of the Maddox Brothers and Rose, a hilarious, screwball quintet from Alabama. The Maddoxes weren't just hillbilly vaudeville though—they were a proto-rockabilly band of such leading-edge influence that some music historians consider them the world's first rock 'n' roll band. (Listen to 1949's "George's Playhouse Boogie" and judge for yourself.) Born in Boaz, Alabama, in 1926, Rose left her early-childhood home in 1933 with her family and traveled to California by freight car—a trip chronicled in her 1996 album *$35 and a Dream*. The family settled in Modesto but traveled throughout the San Joaquin Valley picking fruit and cotton.[4]

The Maddox Brothers made their professional debut in 1937 with a fifteen-minute program on Modesto's KTRB. The show's sponsor had laid down one stipulation: the band must have a "girl singer." So Rose, just eleven, joined brothers Cal, Henry, Fred, and Don. Rose's primary qualifications: her availability and, according to Fred, they "knew she could sing loud."

The Maddoxes' legendarily wild stage antics translated well to vinyl. They recorded more than one hundred records for the 4 Star label and then switched to Columbia Records in the early 1950s, releasing thirty singles, including the gold record "Philadelphia Lawyer." They toured the San Joaquin Valley extensively in the 1950s and '60s, playing Bakersfield's Blackboard more than twenty times by Rose's estimate. In 1960, they disbanded, and Rose launched a successful solo career that included three singles with Buck Owens.

She died in 1998 at age seventy-two. Bonnie Owens, Loretta Lynn, Barbara Mandrell, Dolly Parton, and Janis Joplin have cited her as a major influence in their music.

Lefty Frizzell: Honky-Tonk Man

Lefty Frizzell, a singer, guitarist, and songwriter, had a style perhaps most recognizable among these early contributors as something we might hear today. Born William Orville Frizzell, in Corsicana, Texas, in 1928, son of a Texas oil driller, Frizzell got his nickname in the boxing ring. He participated in Golden Gloves and developed a wicked left hook.[5]

LEFTY FRIZZELL
Personal Manager   P. O. Box 1689
Jack Starnes, Jr.   Beaumont, Texas

Lefty Frizzell portrays his kicked-back style in this publicity shot.
(Publicity shot/public domain.)

Frizzell, weaned on the music of Jimmie Rodgers (he later cut a memorable tribute album of Rodgers's standards), earned regional notice in the early 1940s playing the Texas dance hall and club circuit. He broke into the top ten with two singles, both released in 1950: "I Love You a Thousand Ways" and "If You Got the Money, Honey, I've Got the Time." Frizzell had four songs in the national top ten simultaneously in 1952, about the same time he became a regular member of the *Grand Ole Opry.*

He played at Bakersfield venues from the early 1950s, and at one point his band featured Bakersfield's Roy Nichols—who'd broken in with the Maddox Brothers—on lead guitar. Frizzell, who also played occasionally at the Blackboard, had thirteen career top-ten songs, including three number one hits. He died in Nashville following a stroke at the age of forty-seven. In his too-short life, Frizzell introduced a vital ingredient to the Bakersfield Sound stew: honky-tonk.

•••

The preceding performers set the stage, musically and otherwise, for what was to follow. But from 1951 forward, in the oil and farming burg of Bakersfield, perceptible signs of a unique and distinct culture began to emerge. What follows is an incomplete list of some of the most prominent and striking voices.

Road-Warrior Romeo: Billy Mize

When contemporaries speak of Billy Mize, they always seem to start with his matinee-idol looks: in the vernacular of the 1950s, Billy was a dreamboat. "He sang like a bird," guitarist Roy Nichols once said of him. "Looked good too. You didn't have a chance with girls when Billy was around."[6]

Apart from his looks, though, Mize's credentials as singer, songwriter, and progenitor of the emerging genre were as legitimate as those of anyone on the scene, and his sweet tenor voice, which was infused with 1950s mainstream pop as much as rollicking honky-tonk, was distinctive.

In the immediate years after World War II, Mize was performing alongside Bill Woods for Okie migrants in and around farm labor camps, and when television came to the Central Valley, Mize was one of the top-billed musicians.

He got his start on TV in 1953 with Herb Henson, as so many did, and when Henson's chief rival, Jimmy Thomason, quit to enter politics, Mize switched from KERO to KBAK and took the

204

host's seat. He teamed with Cliff Crofford for a year and a half on KBAK's *Chuck Wagon Gang*. Among the guests was sixteen-year-old Merle Haggard, in what is thought to have been his first television appearance.

After the Thomasons returned to Bakersfield in 1956, picking up where they had left off with a third incarnation of what was by now known as simply *The Jimmy Thomason Show*, Mize rejoined the *Cousin Herb's Trading Post* gang, becoming the show's host in 1962 after Cousin Herb was forced to scale back following a heart attack. After Henson died in September 1963, the show moved to KBAK, and Mize became the show's host for its final years.

In a two-year display of astounding road-warrior grit, Mize racked up three thousand miles a week driving his pink 1959 Cadillac back and forth between Bakersfield and Los Angeles, hosting two live, daily TV music shows: *Trading Post* and *Gene Autry's Melody Ranch*, on KTLA.

All told, Mize performed on several Los Angeles–area shows, including more than one at a time at several junctures: *The Hank Penny Show*, *Town Hall Party*, *The Cal Worthington Show*, and *Country Music Time*. He eventually sold his heroic, well-traveled Caddy to Buddy Mize, his songwriting brother.

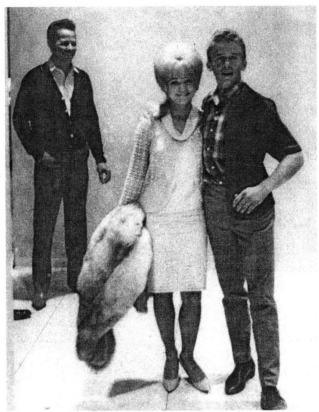

Billy Mize, left, seems to be getting a kick out of seeing Ronnie Sessions
sidle up next to Barbara Mandrell, circa 1967.
(Photo courtesy of Kern County Museum.)

Before the Academy of Country Music gave its TV Personality of the Year award to Glen Campbell in 1968, Mize owned the trophy, winning three years in a row.

Mize, a native of Arkansas City, Kansas, who came to Bakersfield in 1935 by way of Riverside, recorded for Columbia, Decca, United Artists, Zodiac, and others, but his finest moment in the studio was probably the day in June 1966 that Dean Martin recorded three of his songs, including "Terrible Tangled Web."

A female fan casts her gaze at three Bakersfield stars sporting identical pompadours—Merle Haggard, Billy Mize, and Bobby Durham—circa 1968. *(Robert E. Price collection.)*

Mize suffered a stroke on Christmas Eve 1991 that cost him his smooth, rich singing voice, but he recovered well enough to play guitar again, and for another ten years, girlfriend in tow, he became a fixture in the crowd most Monday nights at Trout's Cocktail Lounge in Oildale.

The Chicken Picker: Roy Nichols

Sometimes, right in the middle of a performance, Merle Haggard would turn around onstage and call out, "Roy Nichols!" This was not just a simple bandstand courtesy, but a signal to the audience: here comes a guitar solo, folks, so pay attention. And often, after one of Nichols's unpredictable journeys up and down the neck of his Fender Telecaster, Haggard would burst out laughing in utter amazement. Nichols's solos, as often as not, were unrehearsed, ad-libbed escapades whose outcome no one—perhaps not even Nichols himself—could predict.[7]

Nichols, twenty-two years a Stranger, was legendary for such live musical explorations. There was always a little jazz—no, a lot of jazz—in Nichols's style, and his talent for edge-of-the-moment, stream-of-consciousness ruminations gave Haggard's music a distinctive vibe.

Of course, Nichols himself had a talent for showing up in some unlikely places. Haggard was not alone in his astonishment at finding Roy Nichols onstage seemingly everywhere he went. In his long and remarkable career, Nichols was something of a musical Kilroy, the guitar-playing version of the mystical GI who scrawled his name on World War II battle sites all across Europe. Name most any prominent band in West Coast country music from the 1940s, '50s, '60s, or '70s, and you could say, "Nichols was here." The ubiquitous guitarist was a sideman with the Maddox Brothers and Rose, Lefty Frizzell, Herb Henson, Wynn Stewart, and starting around 1965 or so, Haggard and the Strangers.

Born in 1932 in Chandler, Arizona, and raised in Fresno, California, Nichols was two weeks shy of his sixteenth birthday when he met Fred Maddox, bass player and resident smart aleck of the Maddox Brothers. Maddox, whose band was already a hillbilly icon in the country music world of 1949, had heard Nichols playing guitar on Barney Lee's Saturday-morning radio program in Fresno. Nichols and Maddox had barely been introduced when Maddox hustled the teenager out into the parking lot and explained the rules of employment. Just like that, Nichols became a member of the Maddox Brothers band. During his eighteen-month association with the Maddoxes, the young prodigy earned ninety dollars a week, a staggering fortune for a sixteen-year-old.

"He could play anything," Rose Maddox said. "He was good at all of it. Every guitar picker in the country wanted to play like him, but none of them ever compared. He was one of a kind. But the music aside, he was like any sixteen-year-old kid—feisty, causing us trouble. But my mother brought him under."

One night in Mesa, Arizona, at a Maddox Brothers and Rose show at the local high school gymnasium, a teenage couple worked their way up to the very front of the crowd. Their elbows and chins resting on the front edge of the stage, Buck Owens and Bonnie Campbell studied the show with intensity, noting every riff and wiggle. "I never took my eyes off Rose Maddox," Bonnie said years later. "Buck never took his eyes off Roy Nichols."

Because the band's touring schedule took them out of town for weeks at a time, Fred had to go to Roy's school superintendent and initiate a series of meticulous legal steps: he became not only Roy's legal guardian but also his officially sanctioned tutor. It was Henry, Fred's brother, who would actually serve as Roy's academic tutor. What Fred had to teach young Roy was of a more practical nature: the art of sneaking out of their hotel rooms without being caught by Lula Maddox, the family's colorful but domineering matriarch and band manager.

Nichols proved an apt pupil. During intermissions he would canvass the dance hall crowd, line up dates with pretty girls, and then hustle back to the stage. By all accounts, he did pretty well for himself. But a gig in Las Vegas marked the beginning of the end. "I'd sneak out at night, playing the slots," Nichols explained. "Lula caught me one night and told me never to do it again. But I did it anyway, the next night. So she fired me."

During his brief stay with the Maddoxes' band, Nichols recorded more than one hundred songs while performing seven nights a week almost year-round. But he already had another job waiting for him back in the valley, with Roy "Smiley" Maxedon, whose daily one-hour radio show was broadcast live on Hanford's KNGS. Nichols also played dances three nights a week, staying up all night until it was time for the 7:00 a.m. radio program.

In 1953, Nichols went to work for Frizzell. His first encounter with Haggard occurred soon afterward, at the Rainbow Gardens. Haggard and Nichols could not know it at the time, but their meeting that night marked the beginning of a friendship that would span four decades.

In 1954, after making several recordings with Frizzell, Nichols returned to work for another year with Maxedon. He then joined *Trading Post* and stayed with the show, off and on, until Henson's death in November 1963. During that time he also played at the Foothill Club in Long Beach with Billy Mize and Cliff Crofford and toured and recorded with Johnny Cash.

In 1960, Nichols joined Wynn Stewart's band in Las Vegas. Eventually, he became reacquainted with the young man hired to play bass—Haggard, who'd grown up some since their meeting a few years back. The two worked as sidemen together until Nichols, his wife, and his one-year-old daughter moved back to Bakersfield in 1965. Nichols was working at Tex's Barrel House when he met up again with Haggard, whose monetary disasters in the Sin City card rooms had hastened his departure from Nevada. In August 1966, when Haggard formed the first incarnation of the Strangers, Nichols was his first hire.

By this time, Bakersfield's core of first-rate performers was starting to regard its collective contribution to country music as the equal of Nashville. "Yeah, finally, we started to feel that way," Nichols said. "We had so many talented musicians. We were doing okay with Merle, and Buck and Don Rich were getting hot then too. I got to listening a lot to Don. He had a technique."

Once his guitar playing found its way onto the national airwaves, Nichols began to exert a profound influence on guitarists everywhere. His innovative approach to the guitar would be embraced by three generations of rock and country guitarists. Like Buck Owens, Don Rich, James Burton, and other members of the West Coast Telecaster school, Nichols emphasized the instrument's brilliant high register and explored finger-picking techniques that mixed bent notes up the neck against the instrument's open strings—not too different in principle from the approach of Django Reinhardt, Nichols's earliest guitar hero. But it was a wholly new type of sound. The bright, percussive effects these techniques drew out of the Telecaster eventually became known as "chicken-picking." He also worked out a distinctive descending-note move that Lula Maddox once likened to the sound of "a horsey fartin'." But whereas Nichols's aggressive earlier work foretold the advent of rockabilly by at least a half decade, his mature style was something more spare and leisurely. Between 1966 and 1987, Haggard and the

Strangers were a formidable combo that featured Nichols, Burton, and Farmersville-bred steel guitarist Norm Hamlet. It was Roy Nichols's golden era.

But the long bus trips and countless appearances over the years took their toll. In March 1987, Nichols quit the road and retired from the band. The following year he was inducted into the Western Swing Society Hall of Fame in Sacramento. He died in 2001.

Guitars in Their Genes: Gene Moles

Bakersfield country and 1960s surf rock might seem like two completely different musical genres, but Gene Moles made a convincing case to the contrary. Denver Eugene "Gene" Moles certainly had his Bakersfield Sound bona fides. He played on Jimmy Thomason's Bakersfield television show when it first went on the air in 1953, picked on Buck Owens's first session for Capitol Records in 1959, and performed at the Lucky Spot for nine years.[8]

He made a flesh-and-blood contribution to country music too: his son, guitar virtuoso Denver Eugene Moles Jr., is a well-known and respected session player in Nashville. Moles Jr., who goes by Eugene, made a name for himself in the 1990s as lead guitarist for Del Reeves at the *Grand Ole Opry*. He also formed a band with two other homegrown musicians—singer-guitarist Dennis Payne and drummer Alvis Barnett—in a band called Bakersfield.

His father got his first real indication that Eugene had the right stuff, hereditarily speaking, when Mark Yeary, then Merle Haggard's piano player, got to hear him up close in 1976. Eugene, then eighteen, was asked to fill in for ailing Roy Nichols on a six-week tour with the Strangers. "Mark told me, 'My God, Gene, your boy's a monster,'" Gene Moles recalled. "He had his own crowd on his side of the stage, mostly girls."

Eugene had an eventful apprenticeship, handling lead guitar duties for Crazy Creek, a Bakersfield country-rock act in the mid-1970s. He performed on *Hee Haw* in 1982, but even then he hadn't quite worked all the rock 'n' roll out of his system. In 1985, he swung the axe for a rock band called Street Legal.

But then, as so many young men do, he began turning into his father, and his father was a country picker. When Eugene headed to Nashville in December 1989, the move was probably inevitable. "When I was five years old, I used to go to the Cousin Herb Henson show and the Jimmy Thomason show and watch my father," Eugene said. "I always played guitar too. I knew what I was going to do with my life all those years."

To be a true Bakersfield country musician, a guitar player has to have a little Okie in him. Eugene qualifies. His father, the second-youngest of seven children, was born in June 1928 in Wetumka, Oklahoma, sixteen miles from Henryetta. His grandparents moved to Selma, California, just south of Fresno, in 1936, and Eugene's father got his first guitar seven years later, at age fifteen.

Gene's first job was in 1946 at the Paris Gardens in Selma, where he made three dollars a night working for a matronly boss-lady known only as Texas Mom. He moved to Bakersfield in September 1949 to play in Tex Butler's band at the Blackboard, alongside pianist George French, for ten dollars a night.

The Louise and Jimmy Thomason Show made him a regional star of sorts in 1953. It also earned him the reputation that in 1959 got him into Capitol Records' Hollywood studios, where—"shaking in my boots," Gene admitted—Moles helped Owens cut "Sweet Thing" and other tracks.

Then came the surf-rock twist in Gene's career. In 1961, he met Nokie Edwards of the Ventures, and the two of them, performing as the Marksmen, cranked out one of their cocompositions one Saturday on *American Bandstand*.

Eugene was born in June 1958 and was playing guitar, a Mosrite Junior Ventures model, at age twelve. "By the time he was about fourteen, Eugene was shreddin'," remembered Chuck Seaton, a Bakersfield guitarist who has played with Big House and the Buckaroos.

In 1991, Eugene joined Alvis Barnett, a bull-riding drummer who'd grown up playing in a family gospel-music quartet at the *Grand Ole Opry*. For more than a decade, they played behind Del Reeves, whose hits such as "Girl on the Billboard" and "Women Do Funny Things to Me" made him a star in the early 1960s. In

January 1996, Moles and Barnett drafted Dennis Payne, a cowriter on Red Simpson's 1967 song "The Highway Patrol" and nephew of hall-of-fame songwriter Leon Payne, to form their own band, which knocked around in Nashville for several years.

Gene Sr. spent his last years running his own small guitar-repair shop on Niles Street; he had been calling himself the Doctor of Guitars ever since his days on the assembly line as an inspector for Mosrite guitars. Moles opened his repair shop in 1991, twenty-two years after Mosrite's demise, and he stayed there until April 2002, when he died from pulmonary fibrosis, a progressive lung disease, at his home in Bakersfield. His son Eugene plays on.

Lost in Vegas: Bobby Durham

Somewhere, at some point in his forty-some-year career in country music, Bobby Durham came to a fork in the road. Somehow, he didn't notice. Maybe he was having too much fun or making too much money. Maybe his life as a Las Vegas nightclub performer was such a whirlwind of parties and people and music that he couldn't shake loose from it. Durham kept right on going down that neon-lined strip, and after a while, the turn-offs got fewer and farther between.[9]

The Bakersfield-born singer-guitarist might have been a recording star. Lord knows he had the pedigree. When Durham, the son of a Dust Bowl dirt farmer, was just eleven, he would hop rides with singer Billy Mize, who drove to Los Angeles five days a week for his daily TV show. Tommy Collins took Durham under his wing. Joe Maphis showed him a few guitar licks.

But there came a time when Durham might have—perhaps should have—left Vegas for Nashville. But he didn't. "Your goal in the music business is records," Durham explained. "I made so much money in Vegas that I lost sight of it. Between Vegas and everything else, a twenty-year chunk of my life went by in a weekend."

Durham certainly had the motivation to succeed. His father, Virgil Durham, was a farmer in Childress, Texas, who migrated to California in the mid-1930s. Twenty-seven family members were crammed into a single Model A Ford: the babies and small children got to ride, and the rest took turns walking. Yes, walking.

Bobby was born in Bakersfield in 1942; his brother Wayne, in 1948. It was a musical family: their older brother Ray was Lefty Frizzell's road manager, and the younger boys performed almost from the time they could walk in a pair of boots.

Bobby, sometimes paired with Wayne, performed on Jay Stewart's *Town Hall Party*, Cliffie Stone's *Hometown Jamboree*, *Cousin Herb's Trading Post*, and a slew of other Bakersfield and Los Angeles TV shows. "I made more money in forty-five minutes doing Cousin Herb's TV show than my daddy made in a whole day," Durham said. "I knew music was the way to go for me."

Durham became a member of Cousin Ebb Pilling's Squirrel Shooters, the house band at the Pumpkin Center Barn Dance, starting in 1954, when he was still a preteen. By the time he entered high school, Durham was a veteran playing four nights a week with Jolly Jody and the Go-Daddies, the city's preeminent rockabilly band in the late 1950s and early '60s. By 1962, he was a member of Gene Davis's Palomino Riders, the house band at North Hollywood's Palomino Club, where the regular patrons included Glen Campbell, James Burton, and Roger Miller.

That same year Durham signed with Capitol Records, setting to vinyl songs written by Buck Owens, Red Simpson, and Wynn Stewart, among others. He recorded Haggard's "My Past Is Present," which Durham believes is the first Haggard-written song ever recorded by anyone. Three years later, just before Haggard hit it big, Durham did Merle another favor and loaned him his fifteen-hundred-dollar gold Nudie Cohen suit for a big show.

In 1968, Durham recorded an album for RCA and producer Chet Atkins—the last serious work he would do in the studio, at least as the featured performer, for fifteen years. That same year he began a five-year run with the post–Buddy Holly Crickets, touring the United States, Canada, and Europe. Then in 1972, he began an eleven-year run in Las Vegas. That gig turned out to be one big all-night jam session.

"One night in 1975, Waylon Jennings and his band came to

see us, and he brought his steel guitar player, Ralph Mooney, who had played on my records," Durham said.

> *Afterward we all went over to Alan Mead's house—he was my steel guitar player—and we had a big party. After a couple hours, I went home. The next evening I went over to see Waylon's show. The curtain opens, and here's Waylon kinda looking out into the crowd. I'm way in the back, on the other side of the bar. Waylon says, right into the microphone, 'Okay, Durham, what'd you do with my steel guitar player?' I ran out and hopped in my car and drove over to Alan's house, and there's Ralph in bed, still asleep, eight o'clock at night. I rousted him up and brought him back to the club.*

Starting in 1975, Durham spent three years as the owner of a nightclub in Colorado Springs, Colorado. In 1983, with his mother ill, he returned to Bakersfield and began performing in town, with his brother Wayne, as the Durham Brothers. In 1984, the brothers took their mom to Nashville for a show at the *Grand Ole Opry*: they were on the bill. "That was the thrill of my lifetime," Durham said. "I just wish my daddy had been around to see it."

The band recorded for Sugarfoot Records and managed to place a song, "Do You Still Drink Margaritas," at the top of the country chart in Australia. Unfortunately, Durham was still drinking margaritas himself, a fact that created a major snag in his three-year marriage to Bakersfield singer Theresa Spanke. There was something about Bobby ramming her Corvette into the back of a California Highway Patrol cruiser. In 1988, they divorced but almost immediately reconciled, remaining together for a few more years as man and ex-wife—and bandmates in the Tex Pistols, which played regularly at Trout's for years. Conveniently, they lived across the street from the club and down a few houses—so if Durham was going to rear-end any more CHP cruisers, he'd be on foot.

Durham hasn't done any serious recording since he made an album for Hightone Records, an Oakland-based indie, in 1985.

Wayne Durham moved to Los Angeles, where he became an executive with an international investment company. He still plays bass guitar. In 1995, Bobby gave up alcohol and switched to iced tea and Dr Pepper. "I was as bad as Wynn Stewart and those guys," he said "drinking and everything. I just happened to survive it."

Wynn Stewart: A Lasting Embodiment

Wynn Stewart was an influential figure in the early development of the Bakersfield Sound—even though he was essentially based in Los Angeles and Las Vegas—and he remains something of a defining embodiment of the era forty years after the peak of his career and thirty years after his death.[10]

Winford Lindsey Stewart, born in Morrisville, Missouri, in 1934, was a singer, guitarist, songwriter, bandleader, and nightclub owner who worked with, and gave significant help to, a number of important California performers.

At the age of thirteen, Stewart landed a regular spot performing on a live radio show in Springfield, Missouri. When his family moved to Los Angeles in 1949, Stewart brought his musical ambitions with him. He signed his first record deal at sixteen and in 1954 formed a band that featured mostly Bakersfield musicians, including guitarist Roy Nichols and piano player George French.

With the help of Skeets McDonald, one of his heroes, Stewart signed with Capitol in 1956, and his first single on the label, "Waltz of the Angels," went to number fourteen on the country chart. He appeared often at Bakersfield clubs, including the Blackboard, where in 1956 he introduced Buck Owens to Harlan Howard, the man who would become Owens's longtime songwriting collaborator.

In 1960, on a bit of a cold streak, Stewart turned his attention from making records to running (and co-owning) a nightclub—the Nashville Nevada. His most noteworthy hire was Merle Haggard, who played bass for him briefly in 1961.

Stewart moved back to Bakersfield in 1965 and re-signed with Capitol. His first several singles bombed, but then he nailed one with "It's Such a Pretty World Today," released in 1967. The song, the biggest hit of his career, went to number one on the country chart and won the Academy of Country Music's Song of the Year award. All told, Stewart had six top-ten hits, including the follow-up to "Pretty World," "'Cause I Have You."

WYNN STEWART

Wynn Stewart gave Merle Haggard the most high-profile job of his career to that point: as bass player for the Stewart-led house band at the star's Las Vegas club. *(Capitol Records publicity shot/public domain.)*

Stewart, who suffered a fatal heart attack in 1985, at age fifty-one, wrote or cowrote songs that played important roles in two significant careers: one for Merle Haggard ("Sing a Sad Song") and one for Buck Owens ("Above and Beyond"); Rodney Crowell's version of the latter hit number one in 1989. The wider public heard from Stewart again in 2010 when Volkswagen used his song "Another Day, Another Dollar" in a television commercial for its Jetta. For Wynn Stewart fans of all ages, and there are a surprising number, it was a nice, unexpected tribute. Most of those fans would agree: Stewart was a brighter light than history acknowledges.

"Wynn Stewart," announced singer Dave Alvin, holding court one night in 2014 before a Bakersfield show, "was the guy. People need to appreciate what he did."

The Farmer Boys: Two Boys and a Jukebox

Producer Ken Nelson was most closely associated with Merle Haggard and Buck Owens, but his ties to California country, especially the Bakersfield Sound, ran deep. One of his earliest forays into the San Joaquin Valley brought to the fore a two-man hillbilly act out of the Tulare County town of Farmersville, the Farmer Boys.[11]

Musical twins born of separate mothers, Bobby Adamson and Woody Wayne Murray both came into the world in September 1933 in rural Arkansas. They met in 1951 in a Farmersville café when Adamson began harmonizing to a song on the jukebox, and Murray, sitting across the room, joined in. A few months later Henson heard them singing at Tulare's Happy-Go-Lucky Club, dubbed them the Farmer Boys, and made them regulars on his Bakersfield TV show.

Henson introduced them to Nelson, who signed them to a three-year deal. Their first recording session, in January 1955, was as Bakersfield as it could be: with Roy Nichols on lead guitar, the session included "You're a Humdinger," written by Tommy Collins. They went on to tour the Lower Forty-Eight with Webb Pierce, Red Sovine, and then Elvis Presley.

By their third recording session, in May 1956, the Elvis influence had become apparent: they were moving toward rockabilly. Their final session, in February 1957, produced the minor hit "Someone to Love," cowritten by Buck Owens and Red Simpson. Owens played lead guitar—and made a deep impression on Nelson in the process. Six months later, Nelson signed him to Capitol.

Kay Adams: Little Pink Mack

Ken Nelson's stable of Bakersfield musicians included a half-dozen "girl singers." Among the most talented was Kay Adams, a native of Knox City, Texas, who moved to Bakersfield in 1965 and became a regular on two TV shows, *Buck Owens' Ranch Show* and *The Dave Stogner Show.*[12]

She initially recorded for Tower Records, a Capitol Records subsidiary that in 1965 sold her masters to the main label. Her first sessions for Capitol took place that December. By that time she had already made an impression at the inaugural Academy of Country Music (ACM) Awards and had been named Top New Female Vocalist, completing a near-sweep for Bakersfield-based acts. Adams then promptly strung together a succession of follow-up hits such as "Six Days a Waiting," "Old Heart Get Ready," "Anymore," "Don't Talk Trouble to Me," "Trapped," "Roll Out the Red Carpet," "I Cried at Your Wedding," "Honky Tonk Heartache," and "She Didn't Color Daddy." The following year, she was nominated for the ACM's Top Female Vocalist award.

But Adams became best known for her breakthrough hit in the country music subgenre of truck-driving songs. "Little Pink Mack," driven by a Fender Telecaster, gave the public a woman driver's point of view. At the time the song was regarded as something of a gender stereotype–buster thanks to such lyrics as "It's got polka dot curtains hangin' on a sleeper of pink."

Adams refined her truck-driving credentials with the 1966 album *A Devil Like Me Needs an Angel Like You* with a master of the style, Dick Curless. She also sang on the sound-track album of the western movie *Killers Three* (1968), which featured Merle Haggard and Bonnie Owens as well. She was still at it well into her golden years, recording "Mama Was a Rock (Daddy Was a Rolling Stone)" with BR5-49 for a 1996 truck-driving-themed compilation CD, *Rig Rock Deluxe: A Musical Salute to the American Truck Driver*, and at age sixty-eight, recording "Trixie's Diesel-Stop Cafe" with the bluegrass Dixie Bee-Liners on their 2009 album *Susanville*.

Susan Raye: The Girl from Oregon

The "girl singer" most closely associated with Buck Owens was Susan Raye, a native of Eugene, Oregon. At age seventeen Raye

219

was hired as deejay and live performer for Portland's KWAY Radio. At age nineteen, Raye met Owens's manager, Jack McFadden, in a Portland nightclub where, fully nine months pregnant, she performed. Within a few weeks she was touring the Pacific Northwest with the Buckaroos.

Her first appearances on *Hee Haw* began in 1969, and she moved to Bakersfield the following year and signed with Capitol Records. Her debut single, "Maybe If I Close My Eyes," got some airplay in 1969, and her first major hit, "One Night Stand," followed soon after.[13]

Her biggest hit, "L.A. International Airport," released in 1971, became a crossover hit that reached number nine on the country chart and number fifty-four on the pop chart. "I've Got a Happy Heart," which peaked at number three, followed. That October she married Buckaroo drummer Jerry Wiggins—and eventually raised six children.

Raye was best known, though, for her duets with Owens, the biggest selling of which was "The Great White Horse," released in 1972. Her last charted solo hit—"Whatcha Gonna Do with a Dog Like That?"—was released in 1975. At age forty, after recording twenty-five albums, including five duet albums with Owens, and with two gold records, she quit the music business and returned to college. Raye became a marriage, family, and child counselor; she and husband Jerry remained in Bakersfield.

Buddy Alan: The Apple Doesn't Fall Far

At about the same time Susan Raye was dipping her toe in entertainment fame, another Buck Owens protégé was getting started—his eldest son. Buddy Owens, a.k.a. Alvis Alan Owens, a.k.a. Buddy Alan, started out a rocker, forming his first band, the Chosen Few, at the age of fourteen. He had switched to country by his late teens, and in 1965, he moved to Arizona with his mother Bonnie Owens and new stepfather, Merle Haggard. But his father's pull never diminished, and in 1965, he performed in Bakersfield at his father's Christmas concert.[14]

Three years later, he joined the Capitol lineup and recorded his first single, a duet with his father. "Let the World Keep on a Turnin'" hit the top ten. That same year he recorded his first solo single, "When I Turn Twenty-One," written by Haggard. In late 1970, he and Don Rich recorded "Cowboy Convention," and Alan was named Most Promising Male Artist by the ACM. He followed with a string of modest successes but never quite got that breakthrough song that might have secured a career.

He continued to make records until 1975 but left the music business in 1978 to attend college in Arizona. After graduation he embarked on a new career with brother Michael as a radio mogul. As Buddy Alan Owens, he became the music director—and eventually part of the ownership team—at two stations in Tempe, Arizona. For four years in a row, starting in the late 1980s, he was voted *Billboard*'s Music Director of the Year.

But his performing career really never ended. When his father died in 2006, Buddy Owens recommitted himself to Bakersfield, to Buck Owens's Crystal Palace, and in particular to his father's legacy. He accepted the President's Medal at California State University–Bakersfield, awarded posthumously, for his father in 2012, a symbolic fulfillment of one of Buck's few public shortcomings: academic achievement. He picked up where his father left off onstage as well, fronting the Buckaroos two weekends per month, commuting from Arizona. Those appearances have tailed off in recent years, but Buddy Owens was still hitting the stage in Bakersfield with some regularity well into his sixties.

Freddie Hart: Easy Lovin'

The Capitol Records/Bakersfield galaxy of performers was greatly enhanced and stabilized by one of Buck Owens's side businesses: music publishing. In 1970, Blue Book Music, Owens's enterprise with Harlan Howard, signed a songwriter named Frederick Segres, known professionally as Freddie Hart. Hart's best-known song was his number one hit "Easy Loving," which won the Country Music Association

Song of the Year award in 1971 and 1972. But Hart had a successful performing career too, charting singles from 1953 until 1987.[15]

Born to a sharecropper family in Loachapoka, Alabama, Hart quit school at age twelve and at age fifteen lied about his age to join the US Marine Corps during World War II. He moved to California after the war and in 1951 joined Lefty Frizzell's band. He stayed only a year, but Frizzell helped Hart land his first recording contract with Capitol Records in 1953. Nothing clicked with the record-buying public, however, not even the song "Loose Talk." Carl Smith liked it enough to record it in 1955, and it finally became a hit. In the years that followed, Hart's songs were recorded by Nashville royalty such as Patsy Cline ("Lovin' in Vain"), George Jones ("My Tears Are Overdue"), and Porter Wagoner ("Skid Row Joe").

Hart switched to Columbia Records in 1958, had some success, moved to Kapp Records, and then, in 1969, re-signed with Capitol. It was at that point he came to be identified with the Bakersfield Sound. He signed with Owens's songwriting and management company and soon scored a top-thirty hit with "The Whole World's Holdin' Hands." His song "Togetherness," which had sold well in 1968, became a top-fifteen hit for Buck Owens and Susan Raye that summer.

"Easy Loving," recorded in 1969 for his album *California Grapevine*, was released as a single in 1970. It eventually hit number one on the country charts and number seventeen on the pop charts, cracked adult contemporary radio, sold a million copies, and won a slew of awards, including a Grammy and best-song trophies from both the Academy of Country Music and the Country Music Association. A succession of top-five hits followed, and Hart started his own songwriting enterprise—but not before he'd made a lot of money for Buck Owens.

Hart was a regular presence on the country charts through 1981; his last single, "The Best Love I Ever Had," managed to reach number seventy-seven in 1987. A few years later he reemerged as a gospel singer.

Bobby Austin: Paycheck's Partner

That early Bakersfield-dominated band of Wynn Stewart's included another bassist—not Merle Haggard—who made a noteworthy contribution to the city's musical heritage. Bobby Austin, born in Wisconsin, moved to Los Angeles in 1955 and joined Stewart's band alongside Nichols and French. He did some session work with Buck Owens and Tommy Collins before Capitol Records signed him in 1962. Austin penned his first hit single with cowriter Johnny Paycheck in 1966. "Apartment No. 9" was named the Academy of Country Music's Song of the Year in 1966—and then it traversed the country and found its way into Tammy Wynette's repertoire, becoming her first hit the following year. Paycheck later recorded his own version, and in 1998, Melissa Etheridge recorded it for a Wynette tribute album.[16]

Austin's other big success was "Try a Little Kindness"—not for himself but for fellow Capitol recording artist Glen Campbell. "Try a Little Kindness" reached number four on the country chart and number twelve on the pop chart and was certified gold—Austin's only visit to that altitude. The last Austin song to make the charts was "Knoxville Station," recorded in 1972. He died in 2002.

The Insurance Man: Tommy Hays

It must seem to Tommy Hays like everyone he played music with in the 1950s got a recording contract of some sort and a shot at the big time. Few made it all the way, of course, but they still got their chance. Hays, who was born in Hartshorne, Oklahoma, in 1929, chose instead the security of a day job and built a solid business selling insurance. But along with his golden-throated younger brother Kenny Hays, Tommy Hays was never far from a stage, and he bore firsthand witness to much of Bakersfield's music history. He was, as Chris Shiflett of Foo Fighters has called him, "the classic unsung hero of that scene" in Bakersfield.[17]

Hays, like so many other musicians, started performing in church, playing guitar in services from the age of ten. As a young man, he went on to perform on Billy Mize's *Chuck Wagon Gang* and Henson's *Trading Post* shows, played in the house bands at the

Lucky Spot, Clover Club, and Blackboard, and had his own radio show on KMPC, which served as a warm-up set and advertisement for his band's evening shows at Oildale's Beardsley Ballroom.

Hays was a sideman much in demand. He was a member of Cousin Ebb's Squirrel Shooters, even fronting the band for a memorable two-week run in the late 1950s. He recorded in Hollywood with "Smiley" Maxedon and toured with Bob Smith and the Bluebonnet Playboys, a band that promoted its concerts by hopping up onstage during movie intermissions and playing a fifteen-minute set between the two films of the double feature. Hays had his own Western Swingsters too, a western swing band that, with ever-changing lineups over a period of several decades, was still playing with band members in their eighties.

Hays came west in 1947, from Oklahoma by way of Mississippi, and spent many hours harvesting cotton, paying his Okie dues. At the end of a long day's work, there was no television and few records. "We didn't have any other entertainment," Hays said. "If you wanted entertainment, you did it yourself." He met Mize as a teenager in the late 1940s, and their affection and admiration for each other never faded. In 2006, they held a dual CD-release party at the Crystal Palace—not the kind of thing eighty-year-olds often do—to a packed house, a testament to their staying power. Long after Hays's original Western Swingsters departed or retired, he was still in fine form on guitar. He was also one of the last, great repositories of Bakersfield Sound anecdotes and tall tales—some of which were actually true.[18]

The Argyle Chameleon: Gary S. Paxton

In the competition for the quirkiest recording artist ever to pass through Bakersfield during its country music heyday, there is no competition. In fact, with apologies to Red Simpson, there is really only one candidate: Gary S. Paxton.[19]

Paxton might be best known for the 1960 number one pop hit "Alley Oop," written by Bakersfield's Dallas Frazier and recorded by a thrown-together band Paxton called the Hollywood Argyles. Paxton followed that up with another hastily assembled group, the Cryptkickers, whose "Monster Mash" also went to number one. He soon became a successful and sought-after rock 'n' roll record producer, with credits that included Tommy Roe's 1965 hit "Sweet Pea" and 1966's "Hooray for Hazel" and both of the Association's 1966 hits, "Along Comes Mary" (which won Paxton an engineering Grammy) and "Cherish."

Later in the 1960s, Paxton became interested in the burgeoning Bakersfield Sound, and in 1967, having just produced his first country hit, "Hangin' On" by the Gosdin Brothers, he relocated to Nashville West. Always a manic entrepreneur, he created several businesses and founded four record labels, including Bakersfield International.

Along the way, Paxton was shot three times by hit men hired by an unhappy country singer he was producing; he was romantically linked to televangelist Tammy Faye Bakker, whose infatuation with Paxton was cited in the press as a possible cause of then-husband Jim Bakker's career-ending dalliance with church secretary Jennifer Hahn (whom Jim Bakker then allegedly tried to hush with a payoff from ministry funds); and he transformed himself into a Dove- and Grammy Award–winning songwriter and Christian recording artist.

Paxton was inducted into the Country Gospel Music Hall of Fame in 1999 and, still a sight to behold with shoulder-length auburn-red hair, remained active well into the twenty-first century's second decade.

Most of these performers, among a great many others, owed much of their success to Capitol Records in Hollywood and to the producer who knew when to doodle and when to interrupt, when to interject his opinion and when to let the tape roll. Ken Nelson built and cultivated a stable of creative, independent artists by guiding their direction with his trademark light touch.

APPENDIX C

The Landmarks

There's something about physical proximity to history. Whether it's the poignant calm of the battlefield at Gettysburg or the bustle of the Manhattan sidewalk outside John Lennon's Dakota building, there's something curiously magnetic about places where fame, and infamy, once passed. People have always seemed willing to spend time and money to walk where celebrities, variously defined, have walked before—even if, in some cases, the celebrity only walked there in his bathrobe to pick up the morning newspaper.

Got your camera? You can tour movie stars' homes in and around Hollywood, Malibu, Beverly Hills, Newport Beach, and Palm Springs. You can take Chicago's Untouchables Tour and visit scenes of assorted mob hits. You can touch the hallowed Harlem asphalt where hip-hop music was born. Just wash your hands afterward. With a little initiative, you can also visit the spots where the Bakersfield Sound, that trebly, concrete-floored strain of distinctly American music, was born more than half a century ago.

With a Kern County map or your GPS-equipped smartphone, along with this book, you can cruise down the Oildale street where Merle Haggard grew up, tough and wild; drive by the broom closet–sized building near Baker Street where a third-tier country star named Buck Owens recorded rockabilly records under a pseudonym; even pass near the long-defunct dance club where performers like Lefty Frizzell inspired a generation of young, poor Oklahoma transplants—including some who sang and played guitar pretty well themselves.

This is the Bakersfield Sound Tour, a self-guided, distinctly unglamorous excursion through central Kern County. Create a playlist of relevant songs from back in the day (recommendations follow), and you'll have yourself a living, breathing documentary. This is not a hypothetical exercise: fans whose obsessions are sufficiently extreme have been known to actually put such tours together, on their own or with local expertise. Certain country music stars, faced with hours of downtime before a Bakersfield show, still occasionally arrange return-to-mecca pilgrimages to the Sunset Federal Labor Camp or the patch of grass that was once the Blackboard.[1]

Here, on the pages that follow, is my comprehensive Bakersfield Sound Tour. Just to make sure I wasn't overplaying anything or leaving out a worthy spot altogether, I ran my list past music historian Bob Mitchell, for whom the aura of place is so mesmerizing that he bought Buck Owens's house on Panorama Drive overlooking the Saudi Arabia–like vista of the vast Kern River oil field; Mitchell bought the place in 1996 and lived in it for four years. Here in no particular order are some of my tour highlights, along with suggestions for matching musical accompaniment. It might take some doing to locate the more obscure gems, but I can't do everything for you.

The Sunset Labor Camp, 8301 Sunset Boulevard, just east of Lamont's Sunset and Vineland schools. Just three of the original buildings remain from the defining Okie migrant camp of the late 1930s. Parts of the humble housing project, also known as the Arvin federal labor camp and the Weedpatch camp, were used as a location for the 1940 film *The Grapes of Wrath*. The more historic buildings aren't much to look at today, but the camp still brings out powerful emotions in many of the people who grew up here. Homely or not, it is the scene of an annual Dust Bowl Festival every fall. Mitchell has personally chauffeured several film industry people out to the camp for tours. "They practically have a religious experience when they see those buildings," Mitchell told me. Accompanying song: "They're Tearin' the Labor Camps Down" by Merle Haggard.

Hag's boxcar, 1303 Yosemite Drive and 3801 Chester Avenue. This small, exceedingly modest house is the holy grail of any Bakersfield Sound tour. It's the place all songwriters want to visit. Hag mentions it as the influence for many of his classic songs. His long-suffering mother Flossie lived here for years after he left home for trouble and fame. The house originally sat about 250 feet from the Southern Pacific Railroad tracks and a mile from the Kern County Sheriff's Office, appropriately enough, but as of 2015, preservationists were raising funds to move it to the Kern County Museum on Chester Avenue, about two and a half miles away.

One of Haggard's favorite themes is the railroad; in "Oil Tanker Train" he remembers his mother awakening him as a boy and telling him to hurry outside their boxcar home to watch a passing train. Haggard mourns the deteriorating condition of the old house in his 1999 autobiography, *My House of Memories*, expressing relief that his parents didn't live to see their "wood and stucco jewel box" reach its present condition. Accompanying song: "Oil Tanker Train" by Merle Haggard.

The Blackboard, 3801 Chester Avenue. At least that would be the address if the most famous honky-tonk in Bakersfield history were still standing. The building (in its later years a shooting range, pizza parlor, and sports bar, among other things) was knocked down the week of September 7, 2001, to make way for eventual expansion by the Kern County Museum and its parent agency, the Kern County Superintendent of Schools office. Let's run that by one more time: the Blackboard building, a museum piece in and of itself, was knocked down by its landlord—the Kern County Museum—which also happens to run a country music museum with considerably less street visibility. Whatever. The good news: there's been talk of building a freestanding country music exhibit on the museum grounds that would essentially be a re-creation of the Blackboard, right down to its distinctive sign. The empty lot where the Blackboard stood, about two hundred yards south of 3801 Chester Avenue, is now part of a large, grassy field that will eventually be home to a new, unrelated exhibit.

As long as you're here, though, park and check out the nearby museum, which has a number of intriguing rarities, including one of Merle Haggard's more tastefully sequined stage jackets and Joe Maphis's double-necked, built-in-Bakersfield Mosrite guitar. But call first to make sure that stuff is on display; some of it was loaned to the Country Music Hall of Fame and Museum in Nashville. Mitchell's song selection for this tour stop was written and recorded by Maphis, who was inspired by a gig at the low-ceilinged, poorly ventilated honky-tonk. Accompanying song: "Dim Lights, Thick Smoke (and Loud, Loud Music)" by Joe and Rose Lee Maphis.

The Bakersfield sign, 2800 Buck Owens Boulevard. The original sign, actually a footbridge, spanned Union Avenue just south of California Avenue from the late 1940s. It was torn down in 1999, but Buck Owens preserved the blue porcelain letters and had them attached to his own re-creation outside his Crystal Palace dinner club and museum.

While you're here, go inside the Crystal Palace for a plate of Okie fries. The place is a full-scale museum of Buck Owens memorabilia, complete with a stunning collection of larger-than-life bronze statues of country music giants, including Owens, Haggard, and Johnny Cash. Owens performed here live most Friday and Saturday nights literally right up until the night he died in 2006. The music still flows.

In its original location, the Bakersfield sign was the unofficial entrance to the city—Highway 99, before that state route was turned into a freeway and rerouted west of the downtown area. Ask any of the Dust Bowl folk what that sign meant to them, and you'll get the picture. Accompanying song: "Streets of Bakersfield"—but Owens's original 1972 version, not the overplayed (and considerably more successful) remake with Dwight Yoakam.

Tally Records, 601 East Eighteenth Street, at the corner of

Truxtun Avenue and Kern Street. When Lewis Talley and Charles "Fuzzy" Owen launched their own record label, Tally Records, in 1954, this was their first recording studio. They stayed here only about three months, but that was long enough to get Buck Owens on vinyl singing a couple of rockabilly songs. Owens, fearing he'd be blackballed for straying outside Nashville's accepted parameters, used a pseudonym: Corky Jones. The old studio, vacant for at least twenty years, was most recently an upholstery shop, a very small upholstery shop. Accompanying song: "Rhythm and Booze" by Buck Owens/Corky Jones.

Tally Records, versions two (911 Baker Street) **and three** (419 Hazel Street). Talley and Owen moved their recording studio to Baker Street, next door to Saba's Men's Store, in 1955. It was there in early 1956 that Owen and Talley recorded a rock 'n' roller named Wally Lewis. His song "Kathleen," leased for production and distribution to another company, reached number fifteen on the charts in 1957. A few months later, Talley built a new recording studio in the backyard of his house on Hazel Street, alongside the garage. That would have been convenient for both Talley and Owen, since they lived next door to each other. Whether the other neighbors found it convenient is a matter lost to history. (Don't bother the present occupants.) Merle Haggard, Tally Records' first and biggest signing, recorded "Skid Row" for them in 1962. It was his first recording. Accompanying song: "Skid Row" by Merle Haggard.

Rainbow Gardens, 2301 South Union Avenue. It's now the Basque Club, but back in the early 1950s, the Rainbow Gardens was an all-ages dance hall. It's where Buck Owens and Merle Haggard first saw their idols, Bob Wills and Lefty Frizzell, the two spiritual grandfathers of the Bakersfield Sound. That legendary hillbilly outfit from Alabama (by way of Modesto), the Maddox Brothers and Rose, played here too, as did Ferlin Husky, who in many ways got the whole scene started. Haggard, still just a teen, had an impromptu audition with Frizzell here prior to a show. Frizzell was so impressed that he allowed Haggard to go onstage

230

first as his opening act. Accompanying song: "If You've Got the Money" by Lefty Frizzell.

The Lucky Spot, 2303 Edison Highway. Now they call it the Empty Spot. Well, they ought to. The old honky-tonk where Bonnie Owens once sang lustily has been torn down. It's the only building on the block that's gone, replaced by an asphalt lot and, fifty feet back from the road, Lucky Spot Auto Body.

The Lucky Spot, according to Mitchell, is "one of the two spots, along with the Blackboard, where the Bakersfield Sound was forged. When the Blackboard and the Lucky Spot were torn down within a few years of each other, I gave up agitating that Bakersfield Sound sites be preserved. It was clear that no one gave a shit." Accompanying song: "A Bar in Bakersfield" by Merle Haggard.

The Clover Club, 2611 Edison Highway, just down the street from the Lucky Spot. Bonnie Owens was among the local stars who worked here. For the cast of Henson's *Trading Post*, this was home base. But use your imagination; it's a dirt lot now. Accompanying song: "Why Don't Daddy Live Here Anymore" by Bonnie Owens.

Tex's Barrel House, 1524 Golden State Highway. It's now the Deja Vu strip club, but in the 1950s and '60s, it was a lively country juke joint with an oil field–themed name and advantageous proximity to the Blackboard, less than a mile north. Accompanying song: "If The World Ran Out of Diesel" by Red Simpson.

Bakersfield Civic Auditorium, 1001 Truxtun Avenue. It's now called Rabobank Theater, but this is the same place where in September 1963 Capitol Records recorded the *Country Music Hootenanny* live album featuring Collins, Owens, Haggard, Henson, Glen Campbell, and many other popular Bakersfield Sound artists. It was here, at that show, that Capitol A&R man Ken Nelson "discovered" Haggard. On the recording, Tommy Collins has this great cornball line: "It's great being here with you tonight … Of course, I only live over yonder a couple of blocks. I'm from Maine. The main part of Oklahoma." Accompanying song: "I Got Mine" by Tommy Collins (live version from the *Country Music Hootenanny* album).

Tommy Collins's house, a white-with-green-trim two-story at the northwest corner of Twenty-First and Pine Streets. Don't bother the occupants—just park across the street and imagine Collins, the great tragic figure of the Bakersfield Sound era, strumming on the veranda. Collins, whose real name was Leonard Sipes, had a solid run as a recording artist and a great career as a songwriter. Merle Haggard recorded more than thirty of his songs, and Owens another dozen. His most noteworthy songwriting credit, "If You Ain't Lovin' (You Ain't Livin')," recorded by George Strait and dozens of others, made him a small fortune. But Collins was tortured by the fact that he never hit it as big as his protégés, Owens and Haggard—his lovely mini-estate just west of downtown Bakersfield notwithstanding. Accompanying song: "You Better Not Do That" by Tommy Collins.

Buck's house, 309 Panorama Drive. Buck Owens lived in this large, ranch-style house overlooking the Panorama Bluffs during his *Hee Haw* years, 1968–74. It was also where Owens was living when he had his final number one hit, "Made in Japan," prior to his comeback hit with Dwight Yoakam in 1989, "Streets of Bakersfield." Don't bother the occupants. Accompanying song: "Made in Japan" by Buck Owens.

Buck's other old houses. Back when Owens was sufficiently unknown and could safely list his home address in the phone book, he listed 206 Harding Avenue and 204 Jones Street at various times. Accompanying song: "The House Down the Block" by Buck Owens.

Buck's North Chester studio, 1213 North Chester Avenue. This remodeled 1930s movie theater in the heart of Oildale was Buck's headquarters back in the heyday, a place where Buck and Hag laid down many of their recordings. In 1971, twelve of the top one hundred country singles were recorded there. Goldie Hawn's 1972 country album *Goldie*, recorded in part in Bakersfield, was one of the studio's more amusing asterisks. The building later became Fat Tracks, a recording studio with an odd link to Bakersfield music: for years Rick Davis, father of Korn lead singer Jonathan Davis, ran the place. Accompanying song: "If We Make It through December" by Merle Haggard, who recorded the song in that studio.

Gary S. Paxton Sound Services Inc., 1201 North Chester Avenue. The quirky songwriter-producer lived in Bakersfield for four years and made his mark. His Oildale studio, created out of an abandoned bank just a few doors down from Buck's studio, brought in artists of three general types: acts that had signed on with one of Paxton's four record labels (Bakersfield International, Countrypolitan, GSP, and Garpax) or had production deals with Paxton; western Canadian rock bands, delivered by a Paxton associate (there were about thirty such bands); and local country and rock acts, including Bobby Durham and Chicano rocker Augie Moreno. Among the studio's more unique features: an underground bank vault that was repurposed as an echo chamber and a control room that was built into a converted Greyhound bus, giving Paxton a mobile studio. Paxton Sound Services, perhaps the most musically eclectic studio of its time, produced at least one hit: the Gosdin Brothers' "Hangin' On," which hung on to *Billboard*'s country charts for eleven weeks. The studio closed when Paxton, battling substance abuse problems, bad investments, and marital woes, moved to Nashville. Accompanying song: "Hangin' On" by the Gosdin Brothers.

Buck Owens's grave, Greenlawn Southwest Cemetery, 2739 Panama Lane. Buck is buried in the Buck Owens Family mausoleum, an elaborate, above-ground structure that is the largest building in the graveyard except for the Georgian mansion that serves as the office and mortuary. Buck is interred with his mother and the ashes of his first wife, Bonnie Campbell Owens. The image of an acoustic guitar adorns each of the heavy, rust-metal doors leading in to the mausoleum, and over the entrance are the words "The Buck Owens Family" and "Buck's Place." Accompanying song: "Dust on Mother's Bible" by Buck Owens.

Don Rich's grave, Hillcrest Cemetery, 9101 Kern Canyon Road. Rich, who sang high harmony on so many of Buck Owens's hits, died in a 1974 motorcycle accident, marking the end of the Buckaroos' most productive years. Rich is buried here in a modest grave. "Buck will tell you this: Don was as seminal a part of Buck's sound as Buck," according to Mitchell. "Don was extraordinary." Bill Woods, a musician, deejay, and entrepreneur who gave Owens one of his first jobs at the Blackboard playing guitar, is buried nearby. Accompanying song: "Soft Rain" by Don Rich (from a live recording on KUZZ).

Pumpkin Center Barn Dance, eight miles south of Bakersfield on Taft Highway. This old Quonset hut, once the stomping ground of the Ozark Squirrel Shooters, is well disguised amid the borderline blight of this old farmers' supply town, but you can pick it out if you look closely. Accompanying song: "Punkin Center Barn Dance" by David Allan Coe. (I doubt this song was written about Cousin Ebb's place because the United States has at least seven places on the map called Pumpkin Center or Punkin Center—three in Texas alone, as well as Arizona, Kansas, Louisiana, and Missouri—but for this musical tour we just can't ignore a song with such a name.)

Trout's, 805 North Chester Avenue. This is perhaps the last authentic Bakersfield Sound–era honky-tonk. It was originally a bar/café, but according to Vern Hoover, who bought Trout's in 1956, the fiddle player, guitarist, and TV host Jelly Sanders, one of the great sidemen of the era, started playing here regularly around 1970. Keyboardist-songwriter Red Simpson also had a decade-long Monday-night run at Trout's—and he still shows up now and then. Ask him, and he'll probably play some of the greatest Bakersfield

Sound songs of the period—Simpson-penned tunes such as "You Don't Have Very Far to Go," recorded by Haggard, and "Close Up the Honky Tonks," recorded by Owens. Simpson had a dozen hits of his own too, many in the truck-driving subgenre popular in the late 1950s to mid-1960s. Accompanying song: "(Hello) I'm a Truck" by Red Simpson.

Louie Talley Cafe, 2111 Edison Highway. The music entrepreneur was also in the coffee shop business, and he made a go of it at several locations, including this spot just down the street from those two famous Edison Highway honky-tonks. A few years later he ran a café in the Padre Hotel, back in that landmark's pre-pre-pre-renovation era, when Milton "Spartacus" Miller was the benevolent if slightly off-kilter landlord. Accompanying song: "Arkie's Got Her Shoes On" by Fuzzy Owen with Lewis Talley.

KUZZ Studios, 910 Chester Avenue. The original office of Bakersfield's most famous radio station is just a block down the street from the Big Shoe, a clog-shaped shoe repair shop and landmark from what some have called the Disneyland school of architecture. In 1960, Valley Radio Corp. bought KIKK radio, switched its format to country music, and hired Henson as president and general manager. The station's call letters were changed to KUZZ to play on Henson's celebrity, and Cousin Herb, whose TV show continued to make him a fixture in living rooms throughout the Central Valley, became "Kuzzin Herb." Accompanying song: "Y'all Come" by Cousin Herb.

Beer Can Hill, 5001 North Chester Avenue. Actually, that's the address of Bakersfield Speedway, the dirt-racing track north in Oildale. Beer Can Hill, a cultural touchstone for many Bakersfield Sound–era participants (translation: a good place to loll about and drink beer), is just north. The hangout was the inspiration for the only recording to ever feature Haggard and Owens together. Accompanying song: "Beer Can Hill" by Merle Haggard, Buck Owens, and Dwight Yoakam.

Merle Haggard's mansion, 18200 Highway 178. Hag's expansive home along the Kern River, near the mouth of the Kern Canyon, was the scene of more than a few wild parties attended by country music royalty. It later became a private medical facility after its celebrity owner moved to Northern California, and then it fell into abandoned disrepair. Tours are decidedly discouraged, but you can get a feel for the surroundings where Haggard lived throughout most of the 1970s. This is the place he called home during his heyday. Accompanying song: "Kern River" by Merle Haggard.

Tommy's hilltop, 3000 China Grade Loop. The top of the China Grade Loop coming east from Oildale was a point of inspiration for Tommy Collins, who sat in a car parked alongside the road here and wrote "High on a Hilltop," which became a hit for his friend Haggard. Accompanying song: "High on a Hilltop" by Merle Haggard.

Fred & Gene's Cafe, 3317 State Road. This is the café that rowdy teen Merle Haggard tried to burglarize late one night, stone drunk, in December 1957—despite the fact that it was still open for business. His conviction following that arrest, along with his previous record of incorrigibility, led to his incarceration at San Quentin State Prison. Accompanying song: "I'm a Lonesome Fugitive" by Merle Haggard.

There. Feel the giddy chill of proximity to greatness? Try rolling up the windows. If that doesn't work, wrap yourself up in a Buck Owens replica bolero-style suede fringe jacket, available at the Bakersfield Sound Tour gift shop, which, in my more fanciful moments, I envision opening one day. A splash of cold water in the face usually fixes that though.

ACKNOWLEDGMENTS

This book would not have been possible without Buck Owens. I don't mean without his fame or his incredible succession of hits or his disarming public persona, although this book would have had little reason to exist absent those factors. What I mean is, the book wouldn't have existed without Buck's support and enthusiasm for this undertaking. In June 1997, out of the clear blue sky, Buck called me on the phone to tell me how much my recent newspaper articles about the Bakersfield Sound had meant to him, how I'd gotten it right, how I'd preserved a piece of something that seemed to be slipping away. At that point we evolved from casual acquaintances to something, at least in my mind, that approached friendship. If Mr. Bakersfield believed me capable of competently characterizing the music of the historic migration that became the Bakersfield Sound, I believed it too.

Neither would this book have been possible without Logan Molen, chief operating officer of TBC Media and the one guy who believed in this project perhaps even more than I did. Logan has a keen grasp of the evolving dynamics of publishing in a rapidly changing era for journalism. He also happens to know and appreciate a multitude of American musical genres and their interrelation. And he is the calmest man I know, which doesn't hurt.

Richard Chon lent his graceful pen to the editing process and made several useful content suggestions. Richard, who happens to be a fiddle player of some renown, contributed valuable elements that only a trained, practicing musician could have brought to this endeavor. His observations about the vocal characteristics and/or guitar techniques of Merle Haggard, Buck Owens, Roy Nichols, and Don Rich are spot on.

And finally, Richard Collins pored meticulously through the entire second draft. His writer's eye for detail left no semicolon unturned. Richard, who is the dean of the School of Arts and Humanities at California State University–Bakersfield, has an erudite way about him—he may even own a tweed blazer with elbow patches—but he is as authentically qualified to evaluate a book about the Dust Bowl as anyone I know. His parents came to California from Missouri and Oklahoma in 1937, living in tent camps and working the fields until they got on their financial feet. Having lived the experience themselves, Richard says, they treated John Steinbeck's *The Grapes of Wrath* as if it were a documentary.

Without this team and the unique perspectives they brought to the project, this book would have forever remained a daydream.

I also need to thank Jim Shaw of Buck Owens Productions, Lori Wear of the Kern County Museum, writer-historian Gerald Haslam, and three colleagues at the *Bakersfield Californian*: Felix Adamo, who curated the photos (and snapped a few of them himself); Glenn Hammett, who designed the front and back covers (and the newspaper rack card, on which they were loosely based, back in 1997); and Jennifer Self, a masterful writer and music historian herself who, whether she knows it or not, is one of the great champions of the Bakersfield Sound's legacy. And finally, Katie Price didn't merely present me with two clever, musically gifted children, Jill and Ben. She also introduced me, on memorable, separate occasions, to Buck Owens and Merle Haggard. Impressive work for an avowed Shaun Cassidy fan.

NOTES

Introduction

1. The first half of the introduction is taken almost verbatim from the author's concert review/vignette from a 2014 Merle Haggard show in Bakersfield. Robert E. Price's "A Lion in Winter, but He Still Has One Hell of a Roar" was published in the *Bakersfield Californian* on March 16, 2014.

2. Merle Haggard's sister, Lillian Haggard Rea, told this story to the author on August 14, 2012.

3. This section on the stylistic and thematic migrations, the instrumentation, and the costuming of country music is generally informed by Richard Peterson's *Creating Country Music: Fabricating Authenticity*; D. K. Wilgus's "Country-Western Music and the Urban Hillbilly" from the *Journal of American Folklore*; and especially Colin Escott's *Lost Highway: The True Story of Country Music*, which presents a succinct description of movie-cowboy influences (32–33); and Gerald Haslam's *Workin' Man Blues: Country Music in California*, which introduces us to Roy Rogers and Tex Ritter (56–62) and the music industry's most influential tailor, "Nudie" Cohen (94–95).

4. Paired with the discs themselves, Scott Bomar's liner notes for Bear Family Records' *The Other Side of Bakersfield*, vols. 1 and 2, is as convincing a testament to the rock 'n' roll influences of mid-1950s Bakersfield music as any document or recording available.

5. Chapters 5 and 8, in particular, of James N. Gregory's seminal *American Exodus: The Dust Bowl Migration and Okie Culture in California* inform this brief overview of the impact of Okie migration on the Bakersfield area.

Chapter 1: The Great Convergence

1. The heart of this chapter comes from the author's introduction to the *Bakersfield Californian*'s series on this music, "The Bakersfield Sound: Raw, Real and Not Nashville," published on page A1 on June 22, 1997.
2. This description of the simple majesty of the Fender Telecaster guitar owes much to Gretchen Wenner's 2003 article for the *Bakersfield Californian*, "Twang to Bang: Leo Fender's Telecaster Rocketed the Electric Guitar into the Stratosphere, and Bakersfield Was a Key Launch Pad"; to Dave Hunter's 2012 "The Music Man HD-130 Reverb," from *Vintage Guitar* (64–66); and consulting editor Richard Chon's personal observations and cranked-up-to-eleven prose.
3. Price, "The Bakersfield Sound: Raw, Real and Not Nashville."
4. Gregory, *American Exodus*, chapter 1.
5. Chris Shiflett, "Episode 12—Steve Earle," *Walking the Floor*, podcast audio, April 2014, https://soundcloud.com/chrisshiflettdeadpeasants/walking-the-floor-episode-12-steve-earle.
6. Substantial portions of this chapter reflect not only Price's "Raw, Real" article but also *The Bakersfield Sound: Buck Owens, Merle Haggard, and California Country*, the companion book to the Country Music Hall of Fame's 2013–14 Bakersfield Sound exhibit, written by Scott B. Bomar, Randy Poe, and Robert E. Price, particularly pages 13–25.

Chapter 2: Toward Eden

1. The author's overview of the Dust Bowl migration and its direct effect on the formulation of a vibrant music scene in the Bakersfield area, "From Dust Bowl Labor Camp to Bakersfield Sound Honky-Tonk," is reproduced nearly in its entirety in this chapter. The article was originally written as a 2005 academic paper for the California State University–Bakersfield master's program in history and was accessed

on the author's blog From the Vault (http://rpricearchive.blogspot.com/2009/04/bsound.html).

2. James Gregory's *American Exodus* is the backbone of this chapter. These are his observations about the causes and geographic dimensions of the Dust Bowl (chapter 2, especially pp. 4–7) and the population growth impact (chapter 3).

3. Gregory, *American Exodus*, 41, 72, 83, 119.

4. James Gregory discusses how Americans of Scotch-Irish ancestry came to be regarded as ethnic "others" in his PBS interview for *The First Measured Century*, aired in December 2000 (http://www.pbs.org/fmc/interviews/gregory.htm).

5. Haslam's *Workin' Man Blues* discusses some of the early stars of the emerging genre in chapter 5, "The 1930s."

6. Price, "From Dust Bowl Labor Camp."

7. Arvin camp director Tom Collins, an employee of the US Resettlement Administration, kept an informal journal whose entries, though never formally published, were collected as the Kern Migratory Labor Camp Reports. Many entries, including this one, discussed the residents' entertainment habits. Accessed from the Doris M. Weddell collection.

8. Gregory, *American Exodus*, 228.

9. Haslam, *Workin' Man Blues*, 94.

10. The author's interview with Faith Petric on August 5, 2005, was incorporated into "From Dust Bowl Labor Camp."

11. The murder ballad that held such fascination for Petric is explored in John Q. Anderson's 1960 article for Western Folklore, "The Waco Girl: Another Variant of a British Broadside Ballad."

12. Charles L. Todd and Robert Sonkin, both of the City College of New York, took disc-recording equipment supplied by the Archive of American Folk Song to Arvin, Bakersfield, El Rio, Firebaugh, Porterville, Shafter, Thornton, Visalia, Westley, and Yuba City, California, and recorded the music of Dust Bowl refugees throughout the late 1930s and early 1940s. Todd wrote an article for the *New York Times* that captured the spirit of some of those occasions. His article,

"Music and Dances of Migratory Workers in California Day-Long Fete," published on September 21, 1941, is cited here.

13. Price, "From Dust Bowl Labor Camp."
14. Haslam, *Workin' Man Blues*, 88–89.
15. Ibid., 90–91.
16. Price, "From Dust Bowl Labor Camp."
17. Ibid.
18. Gregory, *American Exodus*, 246–47.
19. Price, "From Dust Bowl Labor Camp."

Snapshot: Otherness

1. Substantial portions of this essay first appeared as a column by Robert E. Price, "This Crisis Parallels Another from 1930s," published in the *Bakersfield Californian* on April 30, 2006, on page B1. The column was informed by two books in particular: Gregory's *American Exodus* and Neil Foley's *The White Scourge: Mexicans, Blacks, and Poor Whites in Texas Cotton Culture* (Berkeley: University of California Press, 1999).

Chapter 3: Honky-Tonk Paradise

1. The author's 1997 article on the Blackboard saloon and other Bakersfield adult, live-music venues of the era, "The Blackboard: The Honky-Tonk, Bar None," published in the *Bakersfield Californian*, is the primary source for this chapter. The opening vignette is based on the author's 1997 interview with Rose Maddox.
2. Chris Shiflett, "Episode 6—Dwight Yoakam, Pt. 1," *Walking the Floor*, podcast audio, November 2013, https://soundcloud.com/chrisshiflettdeadpeasants/walking-the-floor-episode-6-dwight-yoakam-pt-1.
3. Michael Quinion's blog *World Wide Words* outlines this etymological debate at http://www.worldwidewords.org/qa/qa-hon2.htm.

4. Kitty Wells finally performed the once-banned "It Wasn't God Who Made Honky-Tonk Angels," her response to Hank Thompson's opening volley, at the Grand Ole Opry a few years later ("Flashback: Kitty Wells Sings Controversial Song on the Opry," http://www.rollingstone.com/music/videos/flashback-kitty-wells-sings-controversial-song-on-the-opry-20140722).

5. Price, "The Blackboard."

6. Ibid.

7. Los Angeles Times columnist Jack Smith returned to his old hometown of Bakersfield to write about the city's emerging profile as a center of musical innovation. His essay "The Country Music Capital of the West" appeared in the April–May 1973 issue of *Travel & Leisure*.

8. Price, "The Blackboard."

9. Ibid.

10. From the author's interview with Fuzzy Owen, Haggard's longtime manager and confidant, April, 19, 2015.

11. Bonnie Owens, the singing cocktail waitress, told the author her story for his 1997 article for the *Bakersfield Californian*, "Talk about Spousal Support."

12. The author's short biographical column on Johnny Barnett, the former bandleader at Bob's Lucky Spot, appeared in the *Bakersfield Californian* in 2001 as "Singer Not Yet Ready to Throw in the Towel."

13. Price, "The Blackboard."

14. In 1969–70, the Kern County Grand Jury investigated the activities of the two Bakersfield Police Department chiefs mentioned, Horace Grayson (1946–66) and Jack Towle (1966–73), and their top assistant, who were suspected of cooperating with certain local elements involved in prostitution and gambling. Those suspicions had compelled a national law enforcement organization to rescind Bakersfield's membership. Despite damning testimony, no indictments were forthcoming. The report, unpublished and never made public, was given to the author by a high-ranking,

long-retired member of the Bakersfield Police Department in 2003.
15. Price, "The Blackboard."
16. Ibid.
17. Bryce Martin, a former music writer for the *Bakersfield Californian*, reminisced about his final, early-1980s visits to Tex's Barrel House and the Blackboard in a June 2007 essay, "Two Bakersfield Bars," for his blog *The Brycian Chronicles*.

Snapshot: It's That Kid!

1. Louise Thomason, widow of fiddle player and longtime television host Jimmy Thomason, told the author this story about the couple's first meeting with Elvis Presley for Price's 1997 article, "Elvis Might Have Come to Bakersfield (Really)," published in the *Bakersfield Californian*.

Chapter 4: Vegas of the Valley

1. The first three-quarters of this chapter is from the author's 2000 article in the *Bakersfield Californian*, "Once a Road Well-Traveled," on Bakersfield's Union Avenue and its place in the cultural landscape of California's Great Central Valley from the postwar years into the 1980s.
2. Chris Page looked at the heyday of nightlife in the city's African American district of Cottonwood for his 2001 article for the *Bakersfield Californian*, "Hip Strip: Mayflower District's Lakeview Avenue Was Where the Elite Soul and Blues Artists Came to Groove."

Chapter 5: What's on TV?

1. The *Journal of Country Music* explored the legacy and personalities of Bakersfield's country music television in 2002 with the author's "Bakersfield Bandstand: Cousin Herb and the Pioneers of Early Country Television in California's Central Valley." The journal article was

based substantially on four of Price's 1997 articles for the *Bakersfield Californian*: "Ya'll Come—and for Herb, Ya'll Did"; "The Other Cousins on Country Television"; "From Boy Wonder to Burnout: Don't Count Out Frazier"; and "King of His Own Country: The Joyous Din Buck Created Was Like Nothing Nashville's Tender Ears Had Ever Heard."

2. Dave Stogner tells his personal and professional story in the lengthy biographical article "Only a Memory Away: The Dave and Vi Stogner Story." It resides on the *Corralitos California History* blog, dated August 2000 (http://www.corralitoshistory.com/daveStogner).

3. Price, "Bakersfield Bandstand," 22–23.

4. Ibid., 24–26.

5. Ibid., 26.

Snapshot: The Mosrite

1. This section comes from two of the author's 1997 articles in the *Bakersfield Californian*: "When Mosrite Was Lead Guitar," focusing on Semie Moseley's efforts to make the Mosrite a valued name in the worlds of rock and country music, and "It's in the Genes," which tells the story of Gene Moles, who worked closely with Moseley and helped him land the Ventures as the company's most prominent customers, and the story of Gene's guitar-shredding son Eugene.

Chapter 6: Buck Owens

1. The author's 1997 article for the *Bakersfield Californian*, "King of His Own Country," is the single most important source here, but this chapter is also informed generally by Gerald Haslam's book, *Workin' Man Blues: Country Music in California*, specifically pages 184–85 and 190–92, and by 2013's *Buck 'Em! The Autobiography of Buck Owens*, with Randy Poe.

2. Chris Shiflett, "Episode 6—Dwight Yoakam, Pt. 1, *Walking the Floor,* podcast audio, November 2013, https://soundcloud.com/chrisshiflettdeadpeasants/walking-the-floor-episode-6-dwight-yoakam-pt-1.

3. Price, "King of His Own Country."

4. Ibid.

5. Owens and Poe, *Buck 'Em,* 106.

6. Billy Gibbons of ZZ Top stated his admiration of Don Rich to Matt Munoz of the *Bakersfield Californian,* who used the quotation in his August 8, 2012, article, "Cool BuZZ for Tres Hombres from Texas."

7. Price, "King of His Own Country."

8. Ibid.

9. Owens and Poe, *Buck 'Em,* 168–71.

10. Ibid., 255.

11. Ibid., 257.

12. Ibid., 261.

13. Price, "King of His Own Country."

14. Nicholas Dawidoff was touring the country, interviewing country music celebrities, in 1997, at about the same time the author was writing his newspaper series on the Bakersfield Sound. Dawidoff devotes a chapter to Buck Owens in his book *In the Country of Country: People and Places in American Music.* Owens's comments about the Crystal Palace are on page 246.

15. Price, "King of His Own Country."

Chapter 7: Merle Haggard

1. This chapter is from the author's liner notes written in 2007 for *Merle Haggard: The Original Outlaw,* Time-Life Music's Legends of American Music compact disc set.

2. Alex Halberstadt captured Haggard's admiration for Lefty Frizzell in an article for *Salon* titled simply "Merle Haggard," published November 14, 2000.

3. Price, liner notes, *Merle Haggard: The Original Outlaw.* Haggard's longtime bus driver and confidant, Ray McDonald, reported decades later that Haggard was convinced the teacher, a Republican, was deeply unhappy with President Harry Truman's dismissal of General Douglas MacArthur as commander in chief of US forces in Korea, and she knew Haggard was from a family of Democrats.

4. Chris Heath's profile of Haggard, "The Last Outlaw," was published in *GQ* in November 2005.

5. Price, *Merle Haggard.*

6. Merle Haggard delves into his agony as a San Quentin prisoner in his second autobiography, this one with Tom Carter, published in 1999, *My House of Memories: For the Record.* His rejection by the prison parole board is described on page 135.

7. Price, *Merle Haggard.*

8. Elizabeth Bukowski's profile, "Merle Haggard: For 35 Years the Country Legend's Been Kickin' Ass and Making God Laugh—He Don't Need No Stinkin' Sound Check," was published by *Salon* on November 15, 1999.

9. Price, *Merle Haggard.*

10. Halberstadt, "Merle Haggard."

11. Author's interview with Fuzzy Owen.

12. Price, *Merle Haggard.*

13. Chris Shiflett, "Episode 6—Dwight Yoakam, Pt. 1," *Walking the Floor*, podcast audio, November 2013, https://soundcloud.com/chrisshiflettdeadpeasants/ walking-the-floor-episode-6-dwight-yoakam-pt-1.

14. Halberstadt, "Merle Haggard."

15. Price, *Merle Haggard.*

16. "The Merle Haggard Bio," *Merle Haggard: Home of the Hag*, http://merlehaggard.com/bio/.

17. Price, *Merle Haggard.*

18. Peter La Chapelle, a reporter for the *Bakersfield Californian* turned university history professor, wrote one of the defining documents on country music's role in southern conservative

politics, 2007's *Proud to Be an Okie: Cultural Politics, Country Music, and Migration to Southern California*. One of La Chapelle's characterizations of Haggard's Okie and blue-collar pride is on pages 74–75.

19. Price, *Merle Haggard*.
20. Haggard with Carter, *My House of Memories*, 221.
21. Ibid., 218.
22. Ibid., 227.
23. Price, *Merle Haggard*.
24. David Gates's profile of Haggard, "The Lion in Winter," was published in *Newsweek* on April 14, 1996.
25. Heath, "The Last Outlaw."
26. The author compared Haggard's stature in his hometown, among those who knew of his unsavory past, to that of Fresno writer William Saroyan, who was also given to episodes of wild living, in a 2006 column. Price's "Haggard Not Civic Icon, but He's Still Our Legend" appeared in the *Bakersfield Californian* on July 19, 2006. The author discovered the "raincoat" quote in Brian Darwent's essay on the Armenian American novelist and playwright, "Sayoran's Life and Work: An Overview," from *William Saroyan: The Man and Writer Remembered*, edited by Leo Hamalian, page 33.
27. Shellie Branco covered the unveiling of Merle Haggard Drive in "Merle Haggard: King of the Road," published in the *Bakersfield Californian* on February 14, 2008.
28. The author contributed to a no-byline article on Haggard's honorary doctorate presentation in "CSUB Awards Haggard, Owens Top Honors," published in the *Bakersfield Californian* on June 14, 2013.

Snapshot: The Man in Black Needs Cash

1. This snippet of real life from Johnny Cash's sometimes-tortured middle age is taken wholly from the author's September 19, 2003, column in the *Bakersfield Californian*,

"Dirty, Hungry and in Need of Some Cash." Follow-up information, incorporated here, is from Price's column of September 26, 2003, "There's an Election in November?"

2. Johnny Cash with Patrick Carr, Cash: *The Autobiography* (New York: Harper Collins, 1997), 58–59.

Chapter 8: The Two Defining Songs

1. The story of "Streets of Bakersfield" is from the author's article in the *Bakersfield Californian* of July 3, 2005, "Two Men, Two Recollections of How Buck's Hit Was Born."

2. Chris Shiflett, "Episode 6—Dwight Yoakam, Pt. 1, *Walking the Floor*, podcast audio, November 2013, https://soundcloud.com/chrisshiflettdeadpeasants/walking-the-floor-episode-6-dwight-yoakam-pt-1.

3. Merle Haggard's "Okie from Muskogee" and its unanticipated impact were the subjects of the author's column in the *Bakersfield Californian* of November 29, 2009, "The Song That Once Roiled America Is 40 Years Old."

4. La Chapelle devotes most of chapter 6 in his seminal *Proud to Be an Okie* to Haggard and, in particular, "Okie from Muskogee." Especially insightful are pages 186–91.

5. Robert Hillburn's review, "Haggard Acclaimed in Anaheim," was published in the *Los Angeles Times* on March 22, 1971.

6. La Chapelle, *Proud to Be an Okie*, 186.

7. John Grissim listed several of the "Okie" knockoffs in "I'm Still Not Sure It Wasn't Planned," which he wrote for *Rolling Stone* in 1970.

8. Charlie Burton, in a 1971 piece for *Rolling Stone*, "We Don't Smoke Marijuana in Muskogee—We Steal," helpfully tallied the score on the ideologically diverse musical covers of "Okie."

9. Musician Deke Dickerson wrote the liner notes for *Hag: The Capitol Recordings, 1968–1976* and republished them

in his *Musings of a Muleskinner* blog on November 2, 2010, from which Haggard's comments about political protest are excerpted (http://muleskinner.blogspot.com/2010/11/from-hag-capitol-recordings-1968-1976.html).

10. The author interviewed Merle Haggard and Marty Stuart before a live audience of three hundred at the Oildale and Beyond symposium at California State University–Bakersfield on November 7, 2009.

11. Peter Cooper retells the story of Haggard's left-leaning, latter-day response to his own conservative anthem in "Immeasurable Merle Haggard Is Singer, Songwriter, Survivor," published in the *Nashville Tennessean* on April 7, 2012.

Chapter 9: The A&R Man

1. Robert E. Price's profile "Ken Nelson: Bakersfield Bonanza," *Journal of Country Music* 19, no. 3 (1998): 32–35, is the basis of this chapter.

2. Bill Friskics-Warren wrote Nelson's obituary for the *New York Times*: "Ken Nelson, Record Producer behind Bakersfield Sound, Dies at 96," published January 10, 1998.

3. Price, "Ken Nelson: Bakersfield Bonanza."

Chapter 10: The Mentor, the Muse, and the Protégé

1. The first third of this chapter is from Robert E. Price's profile of Tommy Collins, "The Man Who Could've Been," *Bakersfield Californian*, June 22, 1997, E7.

2. The Collins quote about guitarist Fred Carter comes from Dale Vinicur's liner notes for the 1992 Bear Family Records compact disc set *Tommy Collins: Leonard.*

3. The middle section of this chapter is from Robert E. Price's profile of Bonnie Owens, "Talk about Spousal Support," *Bakersfield Californian*, June 29, 1997, E12.

4. The final section of this chapter draws substantially from Robert E. Price's profile of Red Simpson, "The Truck-Drivin' Man Who Wasn't, or the Ballad of the Green Boots," *Bakersfield Californian*, July 6, 1997, E1.
5. Scott B. Bomar's extensive liner notes for the Bear Family Records compact disc set *Hello, I'm Red Simpson* is the definitive biography of the Bakersfield singer-songwriter. Bomar devotes pages 55–61 to the story of the unlikely success of "I'm a Truck."
6. Price, "The Truck-Drivin' Man Who Wasn't."

Snapshot: Millennium Eve

1. This snapshot comes from the author's April 2001 conversation with Yoakam, published as the November 2001 cover story for the *Journal of Country Music*, "Dwight Yoakam: Route 23 Came West, Too," in which Yoakam describes the memorable setting for his first significant collaboration with Buck Owens.

Chapter 11: The Next Wave

1. Price, "Dwight Yoakam: Route 23 Came West, Too."
2. The author explored newer manifestations of the California (and Bakersfield) sound in the *Bakersfield Californian*'s July 13, 1997, edition. "Country Music Departs Tradition" provides the best overview and opens with Buck Owens's joke.
3. Chris Shiflett, "Episode 12—Steve Earle," *Walking the Floor*, audio podcast, April 2014, https://soundcloud.com/chrisshiflettdeadpeasants/walking-the-floor-episode-12-steve-earle.
4. Gerald W. Haslam's pioneering *Workin' Man Blues: Country Music in California* engagingly describes the advent of the California country-rock sound. The genesis of that sound is covered primarily in chapters 13 and 15, and the Eagles are discussed on pages 234–36.

5. The author's interview with the Mavericks' Robert Reynolds is from "Buck Owens' Shuffle Influenced Mavericks Music," *Bakersfield Californian*, July 13, 1997.
6. Chris Shiflett, "Episode 24—Brad Paisley, Pt. 2," *Walking the Floor*, podcast audio, April 2015, https://soundcloud.com/chrisshiflettdeadpeasants/walking-the-floor-episode-24-brad-paisley-pt-2.
7. Ibid.
8. Shiflett, "Episode 12—Steve Earle."
9. Three of the author's articles from the *Bakersfield Californian* of July 13, 1997, discuss artists based in Austin, Texas, who owe much to Owens and/or Haggard: "Bakersfield Sound Is Alive, Well—in Texas"; "Just Saying No to Cowboy-Pop"; and "Fiddlin' around the Country."
10. Price, "Bakersfield Sound Is Alive, Well—in Texas."
11. Shiflett, "Episode 6—Dwight Yoakam, Pt. 1," *Walking the Floor*, podcast audio, November 2013, https://soundcloud.com/chrisshiflettdeadpeasants/walking-the-floor-episode-6-dwight-yoakam-pt-1.
12. Ibid.
13. Pete Knapp meticulously lists artists who have been welcomed under the umbrella of Americana, including many who regard themselves as rock or country artists, in his Peteknapp.com blog entry "What Is Americana Music?" The article, dated October 6, 2008, is here: http://www.peteknapp.com/what_is_americana_music.html.
14. The Tweedy–Cousin Herb connection has been repeated often, with many sources citing an unspecified interview of Tweedy the author was unable to locate. But Cousin Herb's sons, Mike and Rick, confirm that the familial link is factual. See the October 13, 2009, entry on Robert E. Price's Stubblebuzz blog, "Cousin Herb's Widow" (http://stubblebuzz.blogspot.com/2009/10/cousinherb.html).
15. Shiflett, *Walking the Floor*. Also, Shiflett discusses his affection for the Fender Telecaster and the guitar's place in rock and country music culture in a video prepared

by the Fender Musical Instruments Corp.: https://vimeo.com/116387684.

16. In addition to their on-air duties, Amanda Eichstaedt and Mike Varley write the Bakersfield and Beyond blog, a companion to their KWMR radio program. The author's October 24, 2014, in-studio visit is here: https://bakersfieldandbeyond.wordpress.com/2014/10/.

Afterword

1. This closing essay is based in part on the author's February 10, 2006, column in the *Bakersfield Californian*, "Bakersfield Sound Grows Ever More Faint." The column was inspired by a family member's request that the author write an obituary of Tommy Ash, a drummer who had played with many prominent Bakersfield musicians of the era.

Appendix A: The Founders

1. The author's profile of Bill Woods, "It All Comes Back to Bill," published in the *Bakersfield Californian* on June 22, 1997, is the backbone of the first portion of this appendix.

2. The author's profile of Charles "Fuzzy" Owen, "'Fuzzy' Recollections," published in the *Bakersfield Californian* on June 29, 1997, constitutes the middle portion of this appendix.

3. Scott B. Bomar, from the liner notes for *The Other Side of Bakersfield*, vols. 1 and 2, Bear Family Records B00IMF140A and B00IMF150O, 2014, compact discs.

4. The author's profile of Ferlin Husky, "Back When Ferlin Was Terry and Terry Was It," published in the *Bakersfield Californian* on June 22, 1997, is the basis on the third portion of this appendix.

Appendix B: And a Cast of Thousands

1. Ed Cray's exhaustive biography of Woody Guthrie, *Ramblin' Man: The Life and Times of Woody Guthrie*,

brings life to Guthrie's time in Southern California and the San Joaquin Valley (104–07, 117–24).

2. Bob Wills is a recurring character in Haslam's *Workin' Man Blues*. He references Wills's contributions throughout, but especially on pages 77–82.

3. Rich Kienzle's 1977 article for *Country Music*, "When a Country Star Turns Murderer: The Strange Tragic Case of Spade Cooley" (34–38), lays out the elements of the Cooley tragedy.

4. The author draws on Johnny Whiteside's entertaining *Ramblin' Rose: The Life and Career of Rose Maddox* (3–13, 37–44, 159–60, 220–22).

5. Haslam's *Workin' Man Blues* (134, 149–50, 251).

6. Mize is a central character in Price's "The Other Cousins on Country Television," *Bakersfield Californian*, June 29, 1997.

7. Price's "Fender-Bender: Roy Made Telecaster Ring," published in the *Bakersfield Californian* on July 6, 1997, profiles guitar player Roy Nichols. Substantial portions are republished here.

8. Gene Moles, Eugene Moles, and the elder Moles's affiliation with Mosrite guitars and the Ventures are the subjects of Price's "It's in the Genes," *Bakersfield Californian*, July 13, 1997. Substantial portions are republished here.

9. Bobby Durham's lifelong flirtation with elusive stardom is the subject of Price's "Viva Las Vegas: 20 Years Went By 'in a Weekend' for Durham." This article, published in the *Bakersfield Californian* on July 18, 1997, is the basis of substantial portions of this section.

10. Haslam's *Workin' Man Blues* summarizes the importance of Wynn Stewart (159–60, 177–78).

11. Richard Weize's liner notes to Bear Family Records' 1991 compact disc *The Farmer Boys: Flash, Crash and Thunder* is the author's key source material.

12. Bill Friskics-Warren profiled Kay Adams for the November 21, 1996, edition of *Nashville Scene* with "Mother Trucker:

Adams Keeps On Rollin'" (http://www.nashvillescene.com/nashville/mother-trucker/Content?oid=1180913).

13. Chris Page's profile of Susan Raye, "Suddenly Susan," *Bakersfield Californian*, August 30, 1998, provides some of the key source material here.

14. The author's June 1997 interview with Buddy Alan Owens is the source material here. It appeared in Price's series of articles for the *Bakersfield Californian*, published over four consecutive Sundays, June 22–July 13, 1997, as one of several short profiles of Bakersfield Sound–associated artists, among them Bob Wills, Rose Maddox, Wynn Stewart, Lefty Frizzell, Susan Raye, and Spade Cooley.

15. Information about Freddie Hart's life and career is from his biography at the CMT website (http://www.cmt.com/artists/freddie-hart/biography/).

16. Information about Bobby Austin's life and career is from the website Rockabilly Hall of Fame (http://www.rockabillyhall.com/BobbyAustin.html).

17. From Matt Munoz's interview with the Foo Fighters guitarist, "Get Up Close and Personal with Chris Shiflett," *Bakersfield Californian*, April 17, 2014.

18. Tommy Hays wrote a three-page autobiographical article titled "This Is My Story and I'm Sticking to It: Tommy Hays," upon which this section is based. His unpublished article is dated May 6, 2009.

19. Tony Cummings's biographical sketch of the artist, "Gary S. Paxton: From 'Monster Mash' to 'He's Alive': An Incredible Journey," appears on the website Cross Rhythms and is dated September 2011 (http://www.crossrhythms.co.uk/articles/music/Gary_S_Paxton_From_Monster_Mash_to_Hes_Alive_an_incredible_journey/44188/p1/).

Appendix C: The Landmarks

1. The Bakersfield Sound Tour was probably first conceived by disc jockey and A&R man Bob Mitchell, who was known to

take country music artists who'd come to Bakersfield for a show on afternoon drives throughout the area to see places of interest, such as the Arvin federal labor camp. The author seized on that concept and expanded on it in his October 9, 2005, article in the *Bakersfield Californian*, "To Know This Sound You Must First Know This Town," which is the basis of this appendix. Los Angeles–based music writer Scott B. Bomar took it yet a step further—or tried—when in October 2006 he went to the Bakersfield Convention and Visitors Bureau and proposed a formal tour, accompanied, as Mitchell and Price had suggested, by a soundtrack of appropriate songs. The visitors bureau didn't take him up on it, primarily because the chief executive who liked the idea abruptly moved out of state. Bomar's "Bakersfield Sound Driving Tour Script," an unpublished draft document, was nevertheless incorporated in this book's revised tour.

Interviews by the Author

Because most of the interviews in this book were originally conducted for and included in newspaper, magazine, journal, or liner-note articles that embedded attribution and other citations into the body of the article, rather than in bibliographical form, some details of those interviews are not available. However, here, by chapter, are the names of those who were interviewed. Where no location is noted, interviews were conducted by telephone.

Chapter 1: Marty Stuart, Herb Pedersen, Tommy Collins, Ferlin Husky, Cary Ginell, Paul Wells, Fred Carter, Jim Shaw (in his office at Buck Owens Productions, Bakersfield, California), Dallas Frazier.

Chapter 2: Faith Petric, Bill Woods (in his living room in Bakersfield), Jimmy Phillips (at a Denny's restaurant in Bakersfield).

Chapter 3: Fuzzy Owen (at his home in Bakersfield), Adolf Limi (at his home in Bakersfield), Rosa Dykes (at Trout's Saloon in Oildale), Greg Limi, Al Cordero, Wanda Markham (at Trout's Saloon in

Oildale), Jeannie Robbins (at her home in Oildale), Bonnie Owens (at an outdoor concert venue in Tulare, California), Johnny Barnett (at his home in Lamont, California), Hershel Dykes (at Trout's Saloon in Oildale), Sammy Hambaroff.

Chapter 4: Gary Jaussaud, Ben Sacco, Gene Moles (at his guitar repair shop in Bakersfield).

Chapter 5: Bill Woods (at his home in Bakersfield), Red Simpson (at his home in Bakersfield), Louise Thomason (at her home in Bakersfield), Al Brumley Jr., Dallas Frazier, Rick Henson, Daryl Stogner, Jim Shaw (in his office at Buck Owens Productions, Bakersfield, California), Katherine Henson Dopler.

Chapter 6: Buck Owens (in his office at Buck Owens Productions, Bakersfield).

Chapter 7: Lillian Haggard (at her home in Bakersfield), Fuzzy Owen (at his home), Bonnie Owens (at Fat Tracks Recording Studio in Oildale), Merle Haggard (at California State University–Bakersfield).

Chapter 8: Buck Owens (in his office/den at the Crystal Palace dinner club and museum in Bakersfield), Homer Joy, Merle Haggard.

Chapter 9: Ken Nelson (at his home in Somis, California), Buck Owens (in his office/den at the Crystal Palace), Bonnie Owens, Jean Shepard.

Chapter 10: Tommy Collins, Bonnie Owens, Red Simpson (at his home in Bakersfield).

Chapter 11: Buck Owens (in his office at Buck Owens Productions), Tommy Collins, Dwight Yoakam (in an interview room at the offices of his management company in Glendale, California), Robert Reynolds, Casper Rawls, Tony Villanueva, Monty Byrom (at the author's home in Bakersfield).

Appendix A: Bill Woods (at his home), Cousin Rich Allison, Fuzzy Owen (at his home), Bonnie Owens (at Fat Tracks Studio), Ferlin Husky, Tommy Collins.

Appendix B: Roy Nichols (at his home in Bakersfield), Billy Mize (at Trout's Saloon), Rose Maddox, Bonnie Owens, Gene Moles (at his home in Bakersfield), Eugene Moles Jr., Chuck Seaton (at the Crystal Palace), Bobby Durham (at his home in Oildale), Dave Alvin (at the Bakersfield Fox Theater), Buddy Alan Owens (at the Crystal Palace), Tommy Hays (at his home in Bakersfield).

Appendix C: Bob Mitchell, Mitch Styles, Scott B. Bomar (at the offices of the Bakersfield Convention and Visitors Bureau), Fuzzy Owen (at his home).

SELECTED BIBLIOGRAPHY

This book is substantially based on a series of newspaper articles written for the *Bakersfield Californian* in June–July 1997. Consequently, as is the practice in newspaper journalism, the sources—in many cases, the author's personal interviews and direct observations—are identified within the body of the original articles. The passage of time since the publication of those articles makes the extrication of the original sources cited therein difficult and in some cases unreliable. Therefore, source articles from that 1997 series are listed here in the same style and manner as other secondary sources.

Anderson, John Q. "The Waco Girl: Another Variant of a British Broadside Ballad." *Western Folklore* 19 (1960): 107–18.

Bomar, Scott B. "Bakersfield Sound Driving Tour Script." Unpublished draft document. May 2006.

———. Liner notes. *Hello, I'm Red Simpson.* Bear Family Records B0068DU7V0, 2011, compact discs.

———. Liner notes. *The Other Side of Bakersfield*, vols. 1 and 2. Bear Family Records B00IMF140A and B00IMF150O, 2014, compact discs.

Bomar, Scott B., Randy Poe, and Robert E. Price. *The Bakersfield Sound: Buck Owens, Merle Haggard, and California Country.* Nashville: Country Music Hall of Fame, 2012.

Branco, Shellie. "Merle Haggard: King of the Road." *Bakersfield Californian*, February 14, 2008: A1.

Bukowski, Elizabeth. "Merle Haggard: For 35 Years the Country Legend's Been Kickin' Ass and Making God Laugh—He Don't Need No Stinkin' Sound Check." *Salon*, November 15, 1999. http://www.salon.com/1999/11/15/haggard/.

Burton, Charlie. "We Don't Smoke Marijuana in Muskogee. We Steal." *Rolling Stone*, March 18, 1971: 48.

Cash, Johnny, with Patrick Carr. *Cash: The Autobiography*. New York: Harper Collins, 1997.

Collins, Tom. Kern Migratory Labor Camp Reports, US Resettlement Administration, 1936. Unpublished journals loaned from Doris M. Weddell collection.

Cooper, Peter. "Immeasurable Merle Haggard Is Singer, Songwriter, Survivor." *Nashville Tennessean*, April 7, 2012: E1.

Cray, Ed. *Ramblin' Man: The Life and Times of Woody Guthrie*. New York: Norton, 2006.

Cummings, Tony. "Gary S. Paxton: From 'Monster Mash' to 'He's Alive': An Incredible Journey." *Cross Rhythms*, September 2011. http://www.crossrhythms.co.uk/articles/music/Gary_S_Paxton_From_Monster_Mash_to_Hes_Alive_an_incredible_journey/44188/p1/.

Dawidoff, Nicholas. *In the Country of Country: People and Places in American Music*. New York: Pantheon Books, 1997.

Escott, Colin. *Lost Highway: The True Story of Country Music*. Washington, DC: Smithsonian, 2003.

Friskics-Warren, Bill. "Ken Nelson, Record Producer Behind Bakersfield Sound, Dies at 96." *New York Times*, January 10, 1998. Accessed March 3, 2014. http://www.nytimes.com/2008/01/10/arts/10nelson.html?_r=0.

———. "Mother Trucker: Adams Keeps On Rollin'." *Nashville Scene*, November 21, 1996. http://www.nashvillescene.com/nashville/mother-trucker/Content?oid=1180913.

Gates, David. "The Lion in Winter." *Newsweek*, April 14, 1996. http://www.newsweek.com/lion-winter-176802.

Gregory, James N. *American Exodus: The Dust Bowl Migration and Okie Culture in California*. New York: Oxford University Press, 1989.

Grissim, John. "I'm Still Not Sure It Wasn't Planned." *Rolling Stone 59* (1970): 14.

Haggard, Lillian Rea. Interview with author. August 14, 2012.

Haggard, Merle, with Tom Carter. *My House of Memories: For the Record*. New York: Harper Entertainment, 1999.

Haggard, Merle, with Peggy Russell. *Sing Me Back Home: My Story*. New York: Times Books, 1981.

Haggard, Merle, Marty Stuart, and Robert E. Price. "Oildale and Beyond." Presentation at CSU–Bakersfield. Author's live public interview. November 7, 2009.

Halberstadt, Alex. "Merle Haggard." *Salon*, November 14, 2000. http://www.salon.com/2000/11/14/haggard_3/.

Haslam, Gerald W. *Workin' Man Blues: Country Music in California.* Berkeley: University of California Press, 1999.

Heath, Chris. "The Last Outlaw." *GQ*, November 2005. http://www.gq.com/entertainment/music/200511/merle-haggard-profile-chris-heath.

Hillburn, Robert. "Haggard Acclaimed in Anaheim." *Los Angeles Times*, March 22, 1971: D-1.

Hunter, Dave. "The Music Man HD-130 Reverb." *Vintage Guitar*, January 2012: 64–66.

Kern County Grand Jury. Untitled, unpublished investigation into the Bakersfield Police Department, 1970.

Kienzle, Rich. "When a Country Star Turns Murderer: The Strange Tragic Case of Spade Cooley." *Country Music* 5 (1977): 34–38.

Kingsbury, Paul, ed. *The Country Reader: Twenty-Five Years of the Journal of Country Music.* Nashville: Country Music Foundation Press and Vanderbilt University Press, 1996.

Kingsbury, Paul, Michael McCall, and John W. Rumble, eds. *The Encyclopedia of Country Music.* 2nd ed. New York: Oxford University Press, 2012.

Knapp, Pete. "What Is Americana Music?" *Peteknapp.com* (blog), October 6, 2008. http://www.peteknapp.com/what_is_americana_music.htm.

La Chapelle, Peter. *Proud to Be an Okie: Cultural Politics, Country Music, and Migration to Southern California.* Berkeley: University of California Press, 2007.

Martin, Bryce. "Two Bakersfield Bars." *The Brycian Chronicles* (blog), June 28, 2007. http://bryceisright.blogspot.com/2007/06/two-bakersfield-bars-by-bryce-martin.html.

Mayer, Steven. "Architects of a Sound." *Bakersfield Californian*, February 23, 2006: A1.

"The Merle Haggard Bio." *Merle Haggard: Home of the Hag.* http://merlehaggard.com/bio/.

Meyer, Carson. "Flashback: Kitty Wells Sings Controversial Song on the Opry." *Rolling Stone*, July 22, 2014. http://www.rollingstone.com/music/videos/flashback-kitty-wells-sings-controversial-song-on-the-opry-20140722#ixzz3Y9uKjhS3.

Munoz, Matt. "Cool BuZZ for Tres Hombres from Texas." *Bakersfield Californian*, August 8, 2012: E6.

———. "Get Up Close and Personal with Chris Shiflett." *Bakersfield Californian*, April 17, 2014: 24.

Owens, Buck, and Randy Poe. *Buck 'Em! The Autobiography of Buck Owens*. Milwaukee: Backbeat Books, 2013.

Page, Chris. "Hip Strip: Mayflower District's Lakeview Avenue Was Where the Elite Soul and Blues Artists Came to Groove." *Bakersfield Californian*, February 25, 2001: F1.

———. "Suddenly Susan." *Bakersfield Californian*, August 30, 1998: E1.

Peterson, Richard A. *Creating Country Music: Fabricating Authenticity*. Chicago: University of Chicago Press, 1997.

Price, Robert. "Back When Ferlin Was Terry and Terry Was it." *Bakersfield Californian*, June 22, 1997: A8.

———. "Bakersfield Bandstand: Cousin Herb and the Pioneers of Early Country Television in California's Central Valley." *Journal of Country Music* 23, no. 1 (2002): 18–26.

———. "Bakersfield Born, Memphis Bred." *Bakersfield Californian*, July 13, 1997: F1.

———. "Bakersfield Sound Grows Ever More Faint." *Bakersfield Californian*, February 10, 2006: B1.

———. "Bakersfield Sound Is Alive, Well—in Texas." *Bakersfield Californian*, July 13, 1997: F10.

———. Bakersfield Sound profiles: Bob Wills, Rose Maddox, Wynn Stewart, Lefty Frizzell, Susan Raye, Spade Cooley. *Bakersfield Californian*, June 29–July 13, 1997.

———. "The Bakersfield Sound: Raw, Real and Not Nashville." *Bakersfield Californian*, June 22, 1997: A1, A8.

———. "The Blackboard: The Honky-Tonk, Bar None." *Bakersfield Californian*, June 29, 1997: E1.

———. "From Boy Wonder to Burnout: Don't Count Out Frazier." *Bakersfield Californian*, June 29, 1997: E1.

———. "Buck Owens' Shuffle Influenced Mavericks Music." *Bakersfield Californian*, July 13, 1997: F11.

———. "Crofford Made His Mark in Movies, Bakersfield Clubs." *Bakersfield Californian*, November 25, 2009: 17.

———. "Country Music Departs Tradition." *Bakersfield Californian*, July 13, 1997: A1.

———. "Dirty, Hungry and in Need of Some Cash." *Bakersfield Californian*, September 19, 2003: B1.

———. "Dwight Yoakam: Route 23 Came West, Too." *Journal of Country Music* 22 (2001): 8–11.

———. "Elvis Might Have Come to Bakersfield (Really)." *Bakersfield Californian*, August 16, 1997: D1.

———. "Fiddlin' around the Country." *Bakersfield Californian*, July 18, 1997: F11.

———. "Fender-Bender: Roy Made Telecaster Ring." *Bakersfield Californian*, July 6, 1997: E6.

———. "From Dust Bowl Labor Camp to Bakersfield Sound Honky-Tonk." *From The Vault*, April 28, 2009. http://rpricearchive.blogspot.com/2009/04/bsound.html.

———. "'Fuzzy' Recollections." *Bakersfield Californian*, June 29, 1997: E10.

———. "Haggard Not Civic Icon, but He's Still Our Legend." *Bakersfield Californian*, July 19, 2006: B1.

———. "It All Comes Back to Bill." *Bakersfield Californian*, June 22, 1997: A8.

———. "It's in the Genes." *Bakersfield Californian*, July 13, 1997: F1.

———. "Just Saying No to Cowboy-Pop." *Bakersfield Californian*, July 13, 1997: F10.

———. "Ken Nelson: Bakersfield Bonanza." *Journal of Country Music* 19, no. 3 (1998): 32–35.

———. "King of His Own Country: The Joyous Din Buck Created Was Like Nothing Nashville's Tender Ears Had Ever Heard." *Bakersfield Californian*, July 13, 1997: F1.

———. "Like a Country Song, Nashville and Bakersfield Kiss, Make Up." *Bakersfield Californian*, March 22, 2012: E1.

———. Liner notes. *Merle Haggard: The Original Outlaw*. Time-Life Music's Legends of American Music B000W1USL8, 2007, compact discs.

———. "A Lion in Winter, but He Still Has One Hell of a Roar." *Bakersfield Californian*, March 16, 2014: D1.

———. "The Man Who Could've Been." *Bakersfield Californian*, June 22, 1997: A7.

———. "Merle Finally Gets That High School Diploma." *Bakersfield Californian*, April 26, 2015: A1.

———. "Merle Haggard 'Blown Away' by His Music's Revival." *Bakersfield Californian*, April 19, 2015: D1.

———. "Once a Road Well-Traveled." *Bakersfield Californian*, October 8, 2000: A1.

———. "The Other Cousins on Country Television." *Bakersfield Californian*, June 29, 1997: E11.

———. "The Song That Once Roiled America Is 40 Years Old." *Bakersfield Californian*, November 29, 2009: B9.

———. "Singer Not Yet Ready to Throw in the Towel." *Bakersfield Californian*, July 25, 2001: B1.

———. "Talk about Spousal Support." *Bakersfield Californian*, June 29, 1997: E12.

———. "There's an Election in November?" *Bakersfield Californian*, September 26, 2003: B1.

———. "This Crisis Parallels Another from 1930s." *Bakersfield Californian*, April 30, 2006: B1.

———. "To Know This Sound You Must First Know This Town." *Bakersfield Californian*, October 9, 2005: D1.

———. "The Truck-Drivin' Man Who Wasn't, or the Ballad of the Green Boots." *Bakersfield Californian*, July 6, 1997: E1.

———. "Two Men, Two Recollections of How Buck's Hit Was Born." *Bakersfield Californian*, July 3, 2005: A1.

———. "Viva Las Vegas: 20 Years Went By 'in a Weekend' for Durham." *Bakersfield Californian*, July 18, 1997: F10.

———. "When Mosrite Was Lead Guitar." *Bakersfield Californian*, July 6, 1997: p. E1.

———. "Ya'll Come—and for Herb, Ya'll Did." *Bakersfield Californian*, June 29, 1997: E11.

Price, Robert, and staff. "CSUB Awards Haggard, Owens Top Honors." *Bakersfield Californian*, June 14, 2013: A1.

Ryan, John. *The Production of Culture in the Music Industry*. Lanham, MD: University Press of America, 1985.

Saroyan, William, and James H. Tashjian. *My Name Is Saroyan*. New York: Harcourt, 1984.

Shiflett, Chris. Interviews of Brad Paisley, Dwight Yoakam, and Steve Earle. *Walking the Floor* (blog), 2014–15. http://chrisshiflettmusic.com/walkingthefloor/.

Smith, Jack. "The Country Music Capital of the West." *Travel & Leisure*, April–May 1973: W2–W3.

Stogner, Dave. "Only a Memory Away: The Dave and Vi Stogner Story." *Corralitos California History* (blog), August 2000. http://www.corralitoshistory.com/daveStogner.

Todd, Charles L. "Music and Dances of Migratory Workers in California Day-Long Fete." *New York Times*, September 21, 1941: X7.

Vinicur, Dale. Liner notes. *Tommy Collins: Leonard*. Bear Family Records BCD 15577 EI, 1992, compact discs.

———. Liner notes. *Untamed Hawk: The Early Recordings of Merle Haggard*. Bear Family Records 4000127157447, 1995, compact discs.

Weize, Richard. Liner notes. *The Farmer Boys: Flash, Crash and Thunder*. Bear Family Records B000001AYN, 1991, compact disc.

Wenner, Gretchen. "Twang to Bang: Leo Fender's Telecaster Rocketed the Electric Guitar into the Stratosphere, and Bakersfield Was a Key Launch Pad." *Bakersfield Californian*, December 20, 2003: A1.

Whiteside, Jonny. *Ramblin' Rose: The Life and Career of Rose Maddox*. Nashville: Country Music Foundation Press and Vanderbilt University Press, 1997.

Wilgus, D. K. "Country-Western Music and the Urban Hillbilly." *Journal of American Folklore* 78 (1970): 157–79.

Wilson, Charles R., and William Ferris, eds. *Encyclopedia of Southern Culture*. Chapel Hill: University of North Carolina Press, 1989.

INDEX

A

Academy of Country Music 122, 134, 139, 141, 172, 206, 217, 219, 222, 223
Al Brumley 65, 71, 72, 257
Al Cordero 39, 256
Allan Sherman 90
Americana 172, 178, 179, 252, 261
Andy Griffith 152
Andy Moseley 73, 85
Arkies 8, 19, 22, 235
Arlo Guthrie 139
Arvin Federal Labor Camp 26, 227, 256
Automobiles 1, 57, 104, 123, 190

B

Bakersfield Inn 55, 56, 58
Bakersfield Records 10, 186
Bakersfield sign 56, 229
The Band ix, 7, 32, 41, 43, 44, 45, 83, 91, 92, 93, 96, 97, 98, 112, 116, 133, 159, 161, 171, 178, 179, 199, 202, 209, 211, 215, 224
Barbara Mandrell 72, 73, 81, 123, 202, 206
Barney Lee 208
Beardsley Ballroom 41, 50, 161, 192, 199, 224
The Beatles 5, 79
Beer Can Hill 235

Ben Haggard xi, 121
Benny Goodman 25
Ben Sacco 57, 257
Betty Campbell 43
Billboard 14, 125, 151, 212, 221, 233
Bill Haley and The Comets 10
Bill Monroe 10
Bill Rea 72
Bill Woods x, 7, 10, 24, 32, 36, 38, 39, 41, 42, 43, 46, 49, 58, 64, 77, 89, 151, 157, 161, 182, 183, 184, 185, 186, 187, 192, 194, 204, 234, 253, 256, 257, 258
Bill Woods Roundup 58
Billy Bragg 198
Billy Gibbons 94, 246
Billy Mize 10, 24, 36, 42, 44, 47, 49, 67, 68, 73, 76, 79, 84, 112, 161, 165, 204, 206, 207, 210, 213, 223, 258
Black blizzards 17
Blackboard x, 7, 10, 26, 31, 32, 33, 34, 35, 36, 37, 38, 39, 40, 41, 42, 43, 44, 45, 46, 47, 48, 49, 50, 53, 62, 86, 112, 129, 151, 162, 181, 186, 189, 201, 202, 204, 212, 216, 224, 227, 228, 229, 231, 234, 242, 243, 244, 262
Bobby Austin 116, 223, 255
Bobby Durham 207, 213, 233, 254, 258

Bob Dylan 12, 126, 198

Bob & Earl 61

Bob Hope 59

Bob Nolan and the Sons of the Pioneers 25

Bob Teague 110

Bob Warner 44

Bob Wills xiii, 21, 25, 29, 41, 49, 50, 58, 69, 72, 87, 89, 108, 120, 124, 185, 198, 230, 254, 255, 262

Bonnie Campbell 156, 209, 234

Bonnie Campbell Owens 234

Bonnie Owens 36, 43, 45, 65, 68, 72, 111, 116, 120, 141, 145, 156, 158, 165, 180, 190, 202, 219, 220, 231, 243, 250, 257, 258

BR5-49 219

Brad Paisley 5, 176, 252, 265

Bruce Springsteen 198

Bryce Martin 51, 244

Buck v, vii, x, xi, xiii, 3, 5, 11, 12, 13, 15, 16, 26, 31, 32, 38, 39, 42, 43, 45, 53, 68, 75, 76, 78, 79, 80, 86, 88, 89, 90, 91, 92, 93, 94, 95, 96, 97, 98, 99, 100, 101, 102, 117, 118, 119, 120, 123, 128, 131, 132, 134, 135, 136, 137, 141, 142, 144, 145, 148, 149, 150, 153, 154, 156, 157, 159, 162, 163, 164, 165, 167, 168, 169, 170, 171, 172, 173, 174, 175, 176, 177, 179, 180, 182, 183, 186, 188, 190, 194, 195, 202, 209, 210, 211, 214, 216, 217, 218, 219, 220, 221, 222, 223, 226, 227, 229, 230, 232, 233, 234, 235, 236, 237, 238, 240, 245, 246, 249, 251, 252, 256, 257, 259, 262, 263, 264

The Buckaroos xiii, 4, 11, 72, 81, 90, 92, 93, 94, 96, 98, 99, 100, 121, 133, 134, 212, 220, 221, 234

Buck Owens v, vii, x, xi, xiii, 3, 5, 12, 13, 16, 26, 31, 32, 38, 39, 42, 45, 53, 68, 75, 76, 78, 79, 80, 86, 88, 91, 92, 93, 95, 96, 97, 98, 99, 100, 101, 102, 117, 118, 119, 123, 128, 131, 132, 134, 136, 137, 141, 142, 144, 145, 148, 149, 150, 153, 156, 157, 159, 162, 163, 164, 165, 167, 168, 169, 171, 173, 175, 176, 179, 180, 182, 183, 186, 188, 202, 209, 210, 211, 214, 216, 217, 218, 219, 220, 221, 222, 223, 226, 227, 229, 230, 232, 233, 234, 235, 236, 237, 238, 240, 245, 246, 251, 252, 256, 257, 259, 262, 263

Buck Owens' Ranch 68, 80, 96, 97, 99, 164, 219

Buddy Alan 96, 220, 221, 255, 258

Buddy Holly xiv, 10, 141, 214

Buddy Owens 96, 220, 221

Buster Simpson 160, 184

C

Cactus Jack 25

California State University-Bakersfield 79

Cal Worthington 205

Capitol Records 13, 64, 73, 79, 89, 91, 115, 120, 124, 141, 143, 145, 149, 151, 152, 160, 163, 164, 190, 194, 196, 211,

212, 214, 217, 219, 220, 221, 222, 223, 225, 231

Carl Perkins 26

Carl Smith 222

Carnegie Hall xiii, 93, 164

Carol Channing 60

The Carter Family 7, 197

Cary Ginell 9, 256

Charles L. Todd 23, 241

Charlton Heston 59

Checotah, Oklahoma 7, 106

Chet Atkins 9, 12, 214

Chuck Berry xiv, 5, 87, 95

Clarence "Leo" Fender 2

Cliff Crofford 10, 44, 67, 112, 191, 205, 210

Cliffie Stone 73, 143, 149, 214

Clover Club 10, 41, 43, 44, 45, 46, 47, 48, 66, 112, 157, 161, 162, 185, 189, 224, 231

Colonel Tom Parker 10

Columbia Records 9, 11, 129, 144, 153, 202, 222

Commander Cody and His Lost Planet Airmen 139

Connie Smith 41, 165, 181

Corky Jones 87, 188, 230

Costuming xiii, 239

Cotton Club 61, 62

Country Music Association 123, 134, 139, 147, 221, 222

Country Music Hootenanny 144, 231, 232

Cousin Herb Henson 63, 66, 153, 179, 189, 212

Cousin Rich Allison 188, 258

Crazy Creek 211

The Crocketts 19

Crystal Palace 101, 102, 133, 135, 167, 176, 221, 224, 229, 246, 257, 258

D

Dale Evans 144

Dallas Frazier 8, 14, 41, 73, 74, 155, 194, 196, 224, 256, 257

Dan Keel 130

Dave Alvin 179, 218, 258

Dave Stogner 25, 67, 77, 78, 219, 245

David Allan Coe 234

David Gilmour 4

Decca Records 146

Deke Dickerson 249

Dellwood Club 61, 62

Del Reeves 180, 211, 212

Denison, Texas 7, 183

Dennis Payne 78, 211, 213

Desert Rose Band 8, 178

Dick Clark 59, 95

Dick Curless 164, 219

Dixie Bee-Liners 219

Dolly Parton 97, 159, 202

Don Law 9, 11, 146, 153

Don Markham 40

Don Rich 3, 4, 11, 81, 91, 92, 93, 94, 120, 134, 177, 210, 221, 234, 237, 246

Dorothy Dandridge 60

Doyle Holly 92, 93, 180

Dude Martin 25

Dust Bowl xiii, xiv, xv, 6, 7, 8, 16, 17, 18, 20, 27, 28, 29, 30, 54, 106, 180, 197, 198, 213, 227, 229, 238, 239, 240, 241, 242, 260, 263

"Dust Bowl Ballads" 7, 198

Dusty Rhodes 83, 156, 180

Dwight Yoakam 15, 32, 89, 101, 119, 134, 137, 167, 168, 169, 171, 178, 229, 232, 235, 242, 246, 247, 249, 251, 252, 257, 263, 265

E

Ebb Pilling 214
Eddie Cochran 10
Eddy Arnold 5
Ed Sullivan 95
Edward Stanley 17
Elvis Presley 10, 13, 26, 52, 58, 84, 151, 188, 191, 196, 218, 244
Elwin Cross 25, 77, 185
Emmylou Harris 170, 171, 175, 178
Ernest Tubb xii, 72, 139, 189, 197
Eugene Moles 211, 254, 258
Everly Brothers 13, 42, 126
Exene Cervenka 179

F

Faith Petric 22, 241, 256
Farmer Boys 64, 89, 144, 163, 218, 254, 265
Farm Security Administration 22
Faron Young 143, 196
Fender Telecaster xiv, 2, 3, 4, 81, 86, 94, 141, 149, 153, 179, 207, 219, 240, 252
Ferlin Husky 8, 26, 41, 73, 74, 142, 147, 149, 155, 180, 182, 185, 190, 192, 193, 195, 196, 230, 253, 256, 258
Flossie Haggard 103, 108
The Fort Worth Doughboys 199
Fox Theater ix, 258
Frankie Avalon 13
Frank Zabaleta x, 33, 35, 49
Fred Carter Jr. 12
Freddie Hart 41, 84, 221, 255
Fred & Gene's Café 112
Fred Ross 23
Fuzzrite 82

Fuzzy Owen 10, 35, 36, 44, 45, 46, 64, 65, 72, 115, 120, 144, 145, 146, 151, 162, 182, 188, 189, 192, 235, 243, 247, 256, 257, 258

G

Gary Jaussaud 57, 59, 257
Gary S. Paxton 224, 233, 255, 260
Gary S. Paxton Sound Services Inc. 233
Gene Autry 19, 29, 72, 205
Gene Davis 214
Gene Moles 44, 59, 70, 81, 83, 180, 211, 245, 254, 257, 258
Gene Torigiani 129
George Jones 41, 124, 222
George Wallace 139
Glen Campbell 41, 68, 75, 79, 81, 89, 119, 123, 131, 142, 146, 153, 206, 214, 223, 231
Gold Rush 16
The Gosdin Brothers 225, 233
Grady Martin 12, 153
Gram Parsons 171, 178
The Grapes of Wrath 6, 227, 238

H

Hank Penny 205
Hank Snow 10
Hank Thompson 33, 243
Hank Williams xiii, 96, 133, 155, 196
Harlan Howard 42, 216, 221
Harry James 25
Hee Haw 68, 80, 97, 98, 99, 100, 101, 134, 154, 211, 220, 232
Helen "Peaches" Price 157
Henry Sharp 89

Herb Henson 26, 36, 63, 64, 65, 66, 68, 74, 96, 131, 153, 179, 182, 189, 204, 208, 212
Herb Pedersen 8, 178, 256
Herman Arnspiger 199
Hershel Dykes 36, 48, 257
High Pockets Club 45
Hillbilly Barton 190
The Hollywood Argyles 224
Homer Joy 132, 133, 257
Honky-tonk v, x, xiii, xiv, xv, 5, 7, 8, 26, 27, 31, 32, 33, 34, 41, 44, 48, 49, 50, 51, 54, 62, 65, 67, 71, 87, 89, 102, 142, 146, 156, 172, 180, 186, 198, 202, 204, 228, 229, 231, 234, 235, 240, 242, 243, 262, 263
Horace Grayson 48, 243

I

The Ink Spots 60
Irving Berlin 198

J

Jack McFadden 157, 220
Jack Towle 48, 243
James Brown 61
James Burton 4, 13, 119, 146, 178, 210, 214
James Haggard 106, 107, 108
James N. Gregory 17, 239
Jane Russell 60
Janis Joplin 202
Jay Farrar 178
Jeannie Robbins 43, 257
Jeannie Seely 165
Jean Shepard 36, 49, 142, 147, 190, 194, 257
Jelly Sanders 42, 44, 47, 58, 64, 73, 79, 86, 89, 91, 115, 234

Jerry Ward 120, 157, 180
Jerry Wiggins 220
Jesse Colin Young and the Youngbloods 139
Jim Bakker 225
Jimi Hendrix 81
Jimmie Davis 69
Jimmie Icardo 60
Jimmie Rodgers xiii, 7, 20, 41, 111, 197, 203
Jimmy Bryant 144
Jimmy Phillips 26, 256
Jimmy Thomason 26, 45, 52, 53, 66, 69, 70, 200, 204, 205, 211, 212, 244
Jimmy Wright 44
Jim Shaw 13, 97, 101, 238, 256, 257
Joe D. Gulli 57
Joe Limi x, 33, 35, 49
Joe Maphis 32, 213, 229
John Mellencamp 198
Johnny Barnett 44, 115, 243, 257
Johnny Cash 66, 72, 79, 121, 122, 123, 129, 131, 178, 210, 229, 248, 249
Johnny Cuviello 39, 49, 71
Johnny "Guitar" Watson 61
Johnny Paycheck 223
John Steinbeck 6, 18, 238
John S. "Tudy" McDaniels 61
Jolly Jody and the Go-Daddies 26, 214
Jonathan Davis 233
June Carter 131
June Carter Cash 131
Junior Brown 165

K

Kaiser Shipyards 16, 184
Kapp Records 222

Katherine Henson Dopler 80, 257
Kay Adams 78, 141, 164, 218, 254
KBAK 52, 66, 75, 76, 79, 112,
      204, 205
Keith Richard 4
Ken Maynard 19
Ken Nelson 13, 115, 117, 141, 145,
      147, 149, 152, 160, 164, 196,
      218, 225, 231, 250, 257,
      260, 263
Kenny Hays 40, 223
Kern River x, 7, 47, 106, 123, 125,
      199, 227, 236
KERO 66, 71, 75, 76, 79, 186, 204
Kinky Friedman and the Texas
      Jewboys 139
Kitty Wells 33, 243, 262
KMPH 65
KNZR 187
Korn 135, 233
K-Tel Records 133
KTLA 201, 205
KUZZ 75, 76, 80, 101, 176,
      234, 235
KWAC 187
KWMR 179, 253

L

Lana Turner 184
Lawrence Welk 72
Lee Gillette 143
Lefty Frizzell 41, 72, 109, 111,
      202, 203, 208, 214, 222,
      226, 230, 231, 246, 255, 262
Lemon Pipers 81
The Lennon Sisters 72
Leon Payne 213
Les Paul 143
Lewis Talley 3, 10, 36, 46, 65, 71,
      115, 125, 151, 164, 188, 189,
      192, 230, 235

Light Crust Doughboys 69, 199
Lillian Haggard 239, 257
Little Jimmie Dickens 41
Little Jimmy Dickens 81
Little Richard xiv, 9, 13, 26,
      89, 188
Loretta Lynn 202
Louise Thomason 52, 53, 71,
      244, 257
Louisiana Hayride 12, 52
Lucky Spot 10, 41, 44, 45, 47, 48,
      112, 115, 162, 189, 191, 211,
      224, 231, 243
Lu-Tal Publishing 190
Lyle Lovett 178

M

Mac MacAtee and the Skillet
      Lickers 156
The Maddox Brothers 31, 111,
      194, 201, 202, 204, 208, 230
Maison Jaussaud 55, 57, 59
Mark Hopkins Hotel 25
Mark Yeary 211
Marty Robbins 79, 139
Marty Stuart 4, 6, 9, 127, 155,
      250, 256, 261
Mar-Vel Records 190
Marx Brothers 60
Mary Chapin Carpenter 178
The Mavericks 176, 252
Melissa Etheridge 223
Mel Owens 101
Merle v, vii, ix, x, xi, 4, 7, 10, 11,
      16, 41, 43, 44, 45, 51, 61,
      72, 79, 92, 96, 99, 103, 105,
      106, 107, 108, 109, 110, 111,
      112, 113, 115, 116, 117, 118,
      119, 120, 127, 128, 131, 134,
      137, 138, 141, 142, 144, 145,
      148, 155, 156, 157, 158, 159,

160, 170, 173, 175, 179, 187, 188, 189, 199, 205, 207, 210, 211, 214, 216, 217, 218, 219, 220, 223, 226, 228, 229, 230, 231, 232, 233, 235, 236, 237, 238, 239, 240, 246, 247, 248, 249, 250, 257, 259, 260, 261, 263, 264, 265

Merle Haggard v, vii, ix, x, xi, 4, 7, 10, 16, 41, 44, 51, 61, 72, 79, 92, 96, 99, 103, 105, 113, 117, 118, 120, 127, 128, 131, 134, 137, 141, 142, 144, 148, 156, 160, 175, 179, 187, 188, 189, 199, 205, 207, 211, 216, 217, 218, 219, 220, 223, 226, 228, 229, 230, 231, 232, 233, 235, 236, 237, 238, 239, 240, 246, 247, 248, 249, 250, 257, 259, 260, 261, 263, 264, 265

Merle Travis 72

Milton Brown 69, 76, 199

Milton "Spartacus" Miller 235

Mitch Styles 258

Mosrite Guitar 73, 81, 82, 213, 229, 254

Myra Pipkin 24

N

Nashville Sound 9, 11, 196

Nashville West 5, 225

National Songwriters Hall of Fame 14

Nat King Cole 61

Nelson Riddle 9

Nokie Edwards 82, 83, 212

O

Okie From Muskogee 120, 122, 137, 138, 139, 249

Old Dominion Barn Dance 32

Oscar Whittington 36, 38, 40, 89

Owen Bradley 9, 146

Owen Publishing 190

P

Padre Hotel 235

Pat Boone 9, 13

Patsy Cline 41, 181, 222

Patsy Montana 19

Pete Seeger 198

Pink Floyd 4

Pinky's 58

Porterville Camp 24

R

Rainbow Gardens 8, 41, 42, 50, 59, 111, 153, 161, 165, 192, 194, 195, 209, 230

Ralph Mooney 119, 215

Ramones 82

Ranch Show 68, 80, 96, 97, 99, 164, 219

Raul Malo 176

Ray Stevens 144

Red River 7, 18, 183

Red Simpson x, 8, 13, 36, 45, 47, 66, 78, 122, 142, 160, 163, 173, 179, 184, 187, 213, 214, 218, 224, 231, 234, 235, 251, 257, 259

Rhythm Ranch 41, 161

Rhythm Rancho 161, 166

Richard Nixon 123, 139

Rickenbacker Guitar 83

Ringo Starr 101

Robbie Fulks 178

Robert E. Geiger 17

Robert Reynolds 252, 257

Robert Sonkin 23, 241

Rodney Crowell 178, 217

Roger Miller 41, 78, 125, 181, 214
Rolling Stone magazine 139
The Rolling Stones 5, 14, 33,
    89, 126
Ronald Reagan 139
Ronnie Sessions 73, 81, 206
Rosa Dykes 36, 256
Rosanne Cash 165
Rose Lee Maphis 68, 229
Rose Maddox 8, 31, 142, 153,
    201, 202, 208, 209, 242,
    254, 255, 258, 262, 265
Roy Acuff 144, 181
Roy Clark 75, 96, 97, 165
Roy Nichols 4, 10, 36, 47, 65, 72,
    111, 116, 119, 120, 123, 146,
    157, 180, 204, 207, 208, 209,
    211, 216, 218, 237, 254, 258
Roy Rogers xiii, 19, 31, 144,
    200, 239
Rudy Vallee 72

S

San Quentin State Prison 45, 139,
    191, 236
Santa Fe Railroad 7, 107
Semie Moseley 81, 82, 83, 245
Sherman, Texas 7, 136
Simon Crum 196
Simon & Garfunkel 89
Skeets McDonald 13, 216
Smiley Maxedon 183
Solomon Burke 178
Sonny James 144
Sons of the Ryaneers 189
Son Volt 178
Spade Cooley 21, 22, 58, 72, 200,
    254, 255, 261, 262
Speedy West 144
Stencil Hoffman 190, 191

Steve Earle 9, 174, 177, 240, 251,
    252, 265
Steve Sholes 9, 146
The Strangers x, 4, 63, 72, 79, 117,
    119, 120, 121, 146, 157, 159,
    189, 191, 208, 210, 211
Strawberry Alarm Clock 89
Street Legal 211
Streets of Bakersfield 15, 101, 132,
    133, 134, 135, 137, 168, 176,
    229, 232, 249
Stuart Hamblen 19, 108
Sugarfoot Records 215
Sunset Labor Camp 24, 227
Susan Raye vii, 219, 220, 222,
    255, 262

T

Tally Records 11, 45, 46, 115, 144,
    164, 188, 190, 191, 192,
    229, 230
Tammy Faye Bakker 225
Ted Mitchell 91
Tennessee Ernie Ford 72, 73
The Termites 192
Terry Fell 187
Terry Preston 151, 186, 192, 193,
    195, 196
Texas Playboys 21, 25, 120, 124,
    185, 198, 199
The Tex Pistols 215
Tex Ritter xiii, 19, 41, 72, 144,
    161, 166, 239
Tex's Barrel House 41, 50, 210,
    231, 244
Theresa Spanke 215
Theryl Ray Britten 156
Three Stooges 60
Thurman Billings 45
Tina Turner 61, 62
Tom Brumley 68, 70, 92, 93

Tom Collins 21, 150, 241
Tommy Collins 8, 11, 13, 36, 74,
    75, 90, 91, 96, 99, 118, 142,
    146, 148, 150, 153, 193,
    194, 213, 218, 223, 231,
    232, 236, 250, 256, 257,
    258, 265
Tommy Dorsey 25, 58
Tommy Duncan 41, 81, 185, 199
Tommy Hays 161, 179, 183, 223,
    255, 258
Tommy Roe 225
Tommy's Hilltop 236
Tommy's Place 35
Tony Villanueva 177, 257
Trout's 50, 165, 207, 215, 234,
    256, 257, 258

U

Union Avenue 50, 54, 55, 56,
    57, 58, 59, 60, 61, 62, 229,
    230, 244

V

The Ventures 82, 83, 84, 85, 212,
    245, 254
Victor Mature 184
Victor Records 7

W

Wagon Wheel 47, 64, 162
Wally Lewis 190, 191, 230

Wanda Jackson 36, 96, 142, 193
Wanda Markham 40, 256
Wartime migration 20
Waylon Jennings 96, 214
Weatherby's Furniture 131
Webb Pierce 143, 218
Weedpatch Camp 47, 227
Western Swing xiii, 15, 21, 24, 25,
    26, 67, 69, 77, 185, 198, 199,
    200, 211, 224
Western Swing Society Hall of
    Fame 211
Western Swingsters 224
Whiskeytown 178
White Elephant restaurant 129
The Who 81
Wilco 178
Wild Bill's 59
William Saroyan 127, 128, 248
Willie Cantu 92, 93
Willie Nelson 124, 145
The Wills Fiddle Band 199
W. Lee "Pappy" O'Daniel 69
Woody Guthrie 7, 21, 197, 198,
    253, 260
Woody Wayne Murray 218
Wynn Stewart 13, 42, 99, 116,
    118, 142, 157, 165, 173, 208,
    210, 214, 216, 217, 218, 223,
    254, 255, 262

Z

Zsa Zsa Gabor 196

CPSIA information can be obtained
at www.ICGtesting.com
Printed in the USA
LVOW12s1058300516

490465LV00002BC/455/P